SEXISM AND GOD-TALK

SEXISM AND GOD-TALK
Toward a Feminist Theology

ROSEMARY RADFORD RUETHER

Beacon Press   Boston

Beacon Press books are published under the auspices
of the Unitarian Universalist Association
of Congregations in North America,
25 Beacon Street, Boston, Massachusetts 02108
Published simultaneously in Canada by
Fitzhenry & Whiteside Limited, Toronto

Printed in the United States of America

(hardcover) 9   8   7   6   5   4   3   2
(paperback) 9   8   7   6   5   4   3   2

Library of Congress Cataloging in Publication Data

Ruether, Rosemary Radford.
  Sexism and God-talk.

  Includes bibliographical references and index.
  1. Woman (Christian theology)   I. Title
BT704.R83   1983   230'.088042   82-72502
ISBN 0-8070-1104-5
ISBN 0-8070-1105-3 (pbk.)

This book is dedicated to Betzie Hollants,
who has encouraged a generation
of religious feminists
in Latin America and the United States

Acknowledgments

The major part of this book was developed thanks to two endowed lectureships, the 1980 Schaff Lectures at Pittsburgh Theological Seminary and the 1982 Caldwell Lectures at Louisville Presbyterian Theological Seminary. Material on Biblical hermeneutics, on feminism and Marxism, and on criticism of Goddess feminism, as well as the poetic sermon used as postscript, was developed through the 1980 Schaff Lectures. Material on methodology, on feminism and God-language, on Christology, on ecology and eschatology, and on ministry was developed in the 1982 Caldwell Lectures. I wish to thank the Pittsburgh Theological Seminary and the Louisville Presbyterian Theological Seminary for the opportunity to test earlier drafts of this material.

Many persons have read parts of this manuscript and have offered helpful comments and corrections. I wish to thank particularly Judy Vaughan, Mary Hunt, Mary Jo Weaver, Mary Wakeman, and Janet Kalven. I also thank the Grail, which offered me space to write part of this manuscript in Grailville, Loveland, Ohio, and a community of women who read and responded to it.

I thank the students at Garrett-Evangelical Theological Seminary, McCormick Theological Seminary, and Mundelein College who participated in my course, *Sexism and God-talk,* over the years and helped me reflect on the themes of this book. Finally, I wish to thank Helen Hauldren, Linda Koops, and Tami Gearring, who typed the manuscript.

Contents

The Kenosis of the Father

A Feminist Midrash on the Gospel in Three Acts

ACT I: THE KENOSIS OF THE FATHER

"I am the Lord thy God, Thou shalt have no other gods before Me," bellowed God the Father, as He seated himself high upon His Cherubim throne and surveyed the ranks of angels doing obeisance to Him. Having expelled the quarrelsome Sons of Heaven who disputed his reign, He had finally restored order in the Heavens. Earth was a different problem. Ever since the rebellious Sons of Heaven left to rape the daughters of humankind, things had been chaotic down there. From this violence all sorts of monsters had been born.

While all about Him the ranks of the angels sang His praises unceasingly, God the Father was frustrated with His inability to have His will done on earth. He was also getting somewhat bored with having His way so completely done in Heaven. "Something is missing here," He thought. As His mind wandered, images floated to His eyes. The shapes of the daughters of humankind appeared, but he sternly suppressed them. "Ugh," He thought. "They are the cause of all Our problems. If it had not been for their seductive form, the Sons of Heaven would not have rebelled and fallen to earth. The first one, Eve, disrupted my original plans for Paradise. I had to show her what the real world means: men ruling and women obeying, bringing forth children in sorrow and living in subjugation to their husbands."

1

Another image floated before His eyes, a shining figure clothed in a dark mantle embroidered with stars. The moon crowned her head and she held fruits and flowers in her hands. "My god," he half-exclaimed, to the surprise of some of the angels who overheard Him. "The Queen of Heaven. Why does She still appear in my head? I crushed her rule a millennium ago. Can it be that somewhere, outside my omniscience and the sharp eyes of my couriers who survey all parts of my Kingdom, that she still reigns? I know all things," thought God the Father. "No reality escapes my knowledge. My decree against idolatry forbids all my subjects in Heaven and on earth from worshiping or even imagining any other idea of God but Me."

Even as these words formed in the Father's mind, the Queen of Heaven smiled and shook Her head. "No, Sabaoth, my Son. I am the Mother of gods and humans, Creatrix of all things. I am your Mother, too. Even when you deny me, I am still here. Beyond your knowledge and your decrees, there is another who is before You, who is greater than You, and who will survive the death of Your Reign in the heavens."

Sabaoth was startled by these words. He felt a sharp pang of anxiety. He had not felt such guilt since He had defeated the Queen of Heaven and deposed her daughter Eve from her power in the Garden of Paradise. He had walled off the pillars of the cosmos against the Queen so that she should never again be known or come to mind. "Could it be that my own decree against idolatry is the greatest idolatry of all?" He wondered. "The angels that sing my praises, the kings of earth that bow down before me in their temples cry that I am their only Lord and ask Me for help in their battles. Perhaps I have become more their creature than their Creator? I and the kings of earth have come to resemble each other too closely. By calling me Father, Lord, and Ruler, they claim the power to rule the earth as I rule the heavens. Beneath their feet ranks of servants bow down even as the angels bow before Me. Men teach women their place on earth, following My example. Perhaps this hierarchy of earth and heaven is a facade, a delusion, con- cealing other realities that we dare not know. The rebelliousness that I experience among my Sons, the rebelliousness that the kings of earth experience among their menservants and, even worse, their maidservants, point to this other reality. Perhaps it is She! There is another power outside Our rule that still eludes Us!"

"In former times I have known other ways of being God," God the Father reflected. "To put the mighty down from their thrones, to vindicate the oppressed and release the captives from their prisons. I must call to mind these ways of being God again, even extend them to others, to slaves, to Gentiles, perhaps even to women." A bolt of light flashed from one end of the skies to the other, rending the closed fabric of the universe and opening a crack through which poured a beam of light from beyond. Like a shooting star this light flew to earth. An echo arose from the comet like a whisper through the heavens:

> Being in the form of God, he did not count equality with God
> a thing to be prized, but emptied himself and became a servant.

At that time a young woman, betrothed to be married, was discovered to be with child. Great scandal was raised and her betrothed was about to put her aside. He was persuaded by angelic visitations that the child was a miraculous one and he consented to marry the woman, Mary, to cover the illegitimacy of the fatherless child.

ACT II: THE ICONOCLASTIC TEACHER

Scene I

A small dusty band trudged along the road toward Jerusalem. Simon bar Jonah had been a member of the Sicarii, a bandit group that struck down collaborators of the hated foreign rulers. James and John, sons of Zebedee, also had been followers of rebel groups before they attached themselves to the Rabbi from Nazareth. It was hard to explain his hold on them because, in many ways, he taught a puzzling and uncongenial message. He spoke, as the Baptist had, of the need to repent and of the nearness of the Kingdom of God. They knew what that meant. It meant that they, the true remnant of the people of Israel, must adhere strictly to the laws that had been taught by God to their ancestors. Only those who repented of all foreign ways could hope to be within the Israel of redemption when God came. The sons of Zaddok, who had withdrawn into communities in the desert, also preached these same things, but they spent their time puzzling over the ancient prophecies in their libraries. They were not ready to pick up the sword in anticipation of divine vengeance on the Kittim from beyond the seas.

Soon the heavens would open and God Himself would appear with His many hosts of angels. The Nazarenes would be ready to join with God's heavenly hosts. Together they would defeat forever the evil armies of the foreign conqueror. The Beast of Rome would be bound and thrown forever into a pit of fire. They, the loyal Sons of God, would be exalted and would become the new rulers of the earth. God's Son, the Messiah, would appear and set up thrones to judge the nations, and they would reign on his right side and on his left. All the Gentiles who had not been killed would come and lick their feet and pay tribute to the new world government that would be installed in Jerusalem. The Rabbi, Jesus, whom they followed, announced that this coming of God would happen very soon. He was, they believed, the favored instrument of God for bringing the redemption. But he often spoke in strange ways about this coming Kingdom. They were not sure what he meant by all this talk about the poor and the meek. If the Kingdom was indeed to begin in Jerusalem, then they needed to remind him that it would be they, his disciples, who would be the agents of his rule, seated on his right and on his left.

The sons of Zebedee, being bolder than the rest, went to Jesus privately and suggested that they, in particular, should be his right-hand men when he came into his Kingdom. But Jesus shook his head with that look of profound sorrow he often had when they spoke to him of their expectations. "No," he insisted, "we must have a different view of the world to come. It must not be a world where one ruler replaces another, but a world where rulers and ruled are no more. Don't you see how much your ideas of power resemble those of the Gentiles? They have rulers who lord it over them; their great men exercise authority over them. But it shall not be so among you. Whoever wishes to be great among you must be as a servant, and whoever would be first must be first in helping others. The Messiah, the One who is to come for which you look, will not come as king, but as servant of all. He will not come to be served, but to serve, and to give his life as ransom for many."

There it was again — the annoying message! No man was more daring in criticizing the authorities than Jesus. The quibbling Scribes and the wealthy nobility of the priestly classes really had their noses out of joint when he spoke. He unmasked the hypocrisy of the ruling classes and claimed that the unwashed, the poor folk of the countryside, had found God's favor. But when the disciples tried to get him to seize the times and declare himself the King Messiah to lead them in the revolt, he constantly tried to put before their eyes this other vision of the world to come, in which there would be no more rulers and ruled, no more Jew and Greek, and in which all would be brothers — and sisters! Who had ever heard of such a thing?

The women, that was the most puzzling part of his behavior. He insisted on treating them as equals. He even supported their right to be members of the fellowship of disciples gathered around him, instead of staying in the kitchen and preparing the food, like proper women of Israel. When Mary Magdalene joined the fellowship who were listening to his teaching, neglecting to help her sister Martha make dinner in the kitchen, he even justified her, saying she "had chosen the better part, which would not be taken from her."

"When has a rabbi spoken like this before?" his disciples asked among themselves. "He tells us to act like servants, but he tells women that they don't have to serve, that they can join the disciples as equals! He even suggests that the women of the poor and the unclean classes — Samaritan women, slave women, prostitutes — will come into the Kingdom of God ahead of the Scribes and the Pharisees. We enjoyed the discomfiture of the Scribes and Pharisees when he said that, but he really was going a bit far. It certainly makes sense to say that we good country folk will find God's favor against those smart city snobs. But to say that prostitutes and tax collectors will go into the Kingdom of God first! Well, there are limits to this sort of thing. We who thank God every day that we were born Jew and not Gentile, free and not slave, male and not female, know that God isn't going to change everything. There has to be some order, even in the world to come."

When the secret delegation of the sons of Zebedee became known, a wave of indignation swept through the disciples. There was jealousy and fear among them, particularly for Peter, that these two sons of thunder might have found favor with Jesus and even have persuaded him to put them first. They were relieved that Jesus had given James and John a prompt rebuke for their importunity. Only Mary Magdalene laughed out loud when she heard it, as she often did when such incidents took place. She stole a sympathetic glance toward Jesus, who was walking a bit apart in silent meditation. There was a closeness between these two that was annoying to the men, as though she understood him in some way that they did not. It seemed indecent for a rabbi to take a woman into his confidence in that way.

Scene II

Peter's heart pounded as he ran through the narrow streets

of Jerusalem. The police of the High Priest, lackeys of the Romans, were on his heels. He saw an open sewer and dived into it, crawling into a dank corner while his pursuers raced overhead. Terrible visions of the last few days were etched in his mind. He and the other fellows hadn't meant any harm when they staged that entrance into Jerusalem, with Jesus on the royal white mule and the festival crowd waving their branches and chanting the ancient greeting song to the Davidic king. They had to force Jesus' hand, make him take up his role as king. The time was ripe. He himself had said that the crisis was near, that soon God would intervene to overthrow the reign of the Evil Ones.

But when Jesus came into the hideaway on the Mount of Olives where we were preparing arms for an assault on Roman rule, he turned against it. "No," he cried. "Those who take up the sword will perish by the sword. We must not presume upon God. We must be sure that this is indeed the acceptable time and that we are indeed the ones to do God's will. If the time is truly at hand, these few arms will be superfluous. The legions of angels do not need such help from us. We look for more than just the taking of power. We look for the remaking of the earth itself: lifting the valleys, making the hills low. Only God can do this. It cannot be done with clubs and swords."

But even as he spoke, the torches of the soldiers and police were seen. There was a skirmish. Peter and some of the other disciples picked up weapons and tried to make a stand. But they were outnumbered and soon scattered and fled. They were unable to rescue Jesus. They had to leave him behind in the hands of the soldiers. After a hearing before the High Priest, they heard that he was brought before the Court of the Procurator and then dragged off to prison with several other rebels on charges of banditry and conspiracy against the government. The next day Jesus, together with several other rebel leaders, was crucified in the usual manner of Roman "justice."

The disciples were afraid to show themselves because the police and the soldiers were still hunting for them. But the women, particularly Mary of Magdala, stayed as close to the action as possible and sent them messages about what was going on. The women were among the crowd that went out to the place of the crucifixion and witnessed Jesus' death. Mary recalled that, even as he was being stretched on the cross, his eyes kept searching the heavens. He was waiting for the clouds to open and for his heavenly Father to appear with a host of angels to snatch him from the hands of his enemies and to bring about the redemption of Israel. He even cried out for Elijah. Then, just before he died, a black cloud passed over the hill, darkening the whole area. They heard Jesus call out in a loud voice, "Eli, Eli, la'ma sabach-tha'ni" (My God, my God, why have you forsaken me). Then his head slumped on his chest and all was silence.

ACT III: MARY MAGDALENE'S WITNESS

Mary had been crouched for two days near the tomb where she and the two other women had laid Jesus, with the help of Joseph of Arimathea, after the soldiers had dumped his body in the potter's field. Was this the end of their hopes? The men seemed to think so. They had all scattered at Jesus' arrest and imprisonment. Some had even started back to Galilee. But Mary knew that some new fire had been kindled in her by this man and she could not let go of it. A breeze stirred her hair. She turned around and saw a figure standing in the mist. Could it be he? The apparition spoke to her: "Mary, I am risen. I am no longer here. Do not look for me among the dead, but among the living." The figure faded away, but she saw behind it a taller and more majestic image, regal and yet somehow familiar, a woman like herself. "You, Mary," said the vision, "are now the continuing presence of Christ. Do not look backward to him, but forward. He has gone ahead into your new future. It is for you to continue the redemption of the world."

Suddenly all her confusion disappeared, and Mary felt a clear, calm center within herself. "So this is why he had to die," she thought. "He tried to teach us to give up our fantasies of power and revenge. But we could not hear him. As long as he was here among us, we wanted him to take power, to replace the kingship of the Gentiles with the kingship of Israel. But our ideas of God's rule were still based on domination and subjugation. Only by bringing these hopes to an end with his death could we be forced to give up these dreams and find a different answer within ourselves, the answer that he had been trying to teach us all along. We must make our selves and our relationships with each other anew. This is the beginning of the new world. Only when we are no longer slaves, but also no longer desire to be masters and to make our former masters into slaves, can we lay the foundation for the world to come."

Mary ran back to the room above the store where some of the disciples were hiding to tell them of her experience and the messages she had been given by Jesus and the divine woman. The men scoffed at her. "Would Jesus have appeared first to her and not to us?" they asked. "Would the Lord have preferred a woman to us men? Women by Mosaic law are not even allowed to be witnesses. Surely the Lord would not have entrusted such a message to a woman!"

Mary tried to make them understand that it was not important who gave the witness, but that he was risen and was now already in their midst. They must now embody his ongoing presence, not looking back to him in the past, but forward to the Messiah to come. Only by leaving them could he continue to be with them in this new way, teaching them not to pin their hopes on him but to build the community of the new age without rulers and without subjects. They themselves must begin to live the new life with each other.

Some of the disciples were struck by what she said. Peter had a different idea and drew their attention away from her. "Look," Peter declared, "this is what we didn't understand before. Our hopes for the coming of the messianic king have not been shattered. They have just been postponed a little while. Jesus has been snatched up to Heaven by his Father. He is reigning there on the right hand of God. Even now his heavenly Father is putting him in command of the heavenly hosts. Soon the clouds will open and he will return with the angelic army to overthrow the Romans and their lackeys, the High Priests, and put us in power.

"We, the men, must be in charge of this revelation. We must not let Mary and the other women take too much credit, just because they were present when he died and Mary was the first to see him when he rose from the dead. It will make us look ridiculous if we say that we heard this from a woman! Only men can gather a true community of Israel. Only men can represent the Messiah and his heavenly Father. We must proclaim this message in his name. There is still time for many of the Jews and even the Gentiles to listen. Jesus will become the one great name before whom every knee shall bend on earth and in heaven."

As Mary heard them talking in this way, she slipped away from the room and walked to a quiet place outside the city where she could sit with the shade of a tree shielding her from the warmth of the mid-morning sun. She knew that she had glimpsed a momentous new thing, the key to the whole mystery of the world to come that had eluded them all throughout Jesus' lifetime. Jesus had tried to make them see this, but the disciples had never understood. Perhaps even he had not seen fully the meaning of this transformation because no one he told it to had understood.

Mary glanced toward the sky. "Where was Jesus' heavenly Father when he died?" she thought. "He did not answer his cry. The heavens were silent. The angels did not appear to draw him out of many waters and set him upon the Mount of Zion to execute judgment upon his enemies and hold dominion forever, as was promised. Perhaps there are no heavenly hosts to appear in the clouds? Is the Cherubim throne empty? Perhaps it is this very idea of God as a great king, ruling over nations as His servants, that has been done away with by

Jesus' death on the cross. With Jesus' death, God, the heavenly Ruler, has left the heavens and has been poured out upon the earth with his blood. A new God is being born in our hearts to teach us to level the heavens and exalt the earth and create a new world without masters and slaves, rulers and subjects. No, not even men come first with women behind in meek servility. This is what Jesus meant when he taught us to pray for God's Kingdom to come, for God's will to be done *on earth* as it is in Heaven; to forgive each other, and not be led into temptation, but delivered from evil.

"But who will be ready to hear this message?" Mary thought. "Although Jesus had emptied the throne of God, even now Peter and some of the other disciples are busy trying to fill it again. They will fashion the Risen Jesus into a new Lord and Master to represent the heavenly Father and to rule upon the earth. Oh yes, they will be his humble servants. In his name they will rebuke the Jews and conquer the Gentiles, lording it over them as the Romans now lord over us." Mary shuddered. "Is there any way to rend this fabric, to let the light of this other world shine through? Perhaps something of this other vision will still get through the distortion. Other people, even women like myself, will glimpse something of the true vision, and they will recognize me as their sister."

Chapter 1
Feminist Theology:
Methodology, Sources, and Norms

WOMEN'S EXPERIENCE AND
HISTORICAL TRADITION

It has frequently been said that feminist theology draws on women's experience as a basic source of content as well as a criterion of truth.[1] There has been a tendency to treat this principle of "experience" as unique to feminist theology (or, perhaps, to liberation theologies) and to see it as distant from "objective" sources of truth of classical theologies. This seems to be a misunderstanding of the experimental base of all theological reflection. What have been called the objective sources of theology; Scripture and tradition, are themselves codified collective human experience.

Human experience is the starting point and the ending point of the hermeneutical circle. Codified tradition both reaches back to roots in experience and is constantly renewed or discarded through the test of experience. "Experience" includes experience of the divine, experience of oneself, and experience of the community and the world, in an interacting dialectic. Received symbols, formulas, and laws are either authenticated or not through their ability to illuminate and interpret experience. Systems of authority try to reverse this relation and make received symbols dictate what can be experienced as well as the interpretation of that which is experienced. In reality, the relation is the opposite. If a symbol does not speak authentically to experience, it becomes dead or must be altered to provide a new meaning.

The uniqueness of feminist theology lies not in its use of the criterion of experience but rather in its use of *women's* experience, which has been almost entirely shut out of theological reflection in the past. The use of women's experience in feminist theology, therefore, explodes as a critical force, exposing classical theology, including its codified traditions, as based on *male* experience rather than on universal human experience. Feminist theology makes the sociology of theological knowledge visible, no longer hidden behind mystifications of objectified divine and universal authority.[2]

The Hermeneutical Circle of Past and Present Experience

A simplified model of the Western theological tradition can illustrate this hermeneutical circle of past and present experience. We must postulate that every great religious idea begins in the revelatory experience. By *revelatory* we mean breakthrough experiences beyond ordinary fragmented consciousness that provide interpretive symbols illuminating the means of the *whole* of life. Since consciousness is ultimately individual, we postulate that revelation always starts with an individual. In earlier societies in which there was much less sense of individualism, this breakthrough experience may have been so immediately mediated through a group of interpreters to the social collective that the name of the individual is lost. Later, the creative individual stands out as Prophet, Teacher, Revealer, Savior, or Founder of the religious tradition.

However much the individual teacher is magnified, in fact, the revelatory experience becomes socially meaningful only when translated into communal consciousness. This means, first, that the revelatory experience must be collectively appropriated by a formative group, which in turn promulgates and teaches a historical community. Second, the formative group mediates what is unique in the revelatory experience through past cultural symbols and traditions. As far back as human memory stretches, and certainly within the history of Biblical traditions, no new prophetic tradition ever is interpreted in a cultural vacuum. However startling and original the vision, it must always be communicated and made meaningful through some transformation of ideas and symbols already current. The hand of the divine does not write on a cultural tabula rasa. Thus the Hebrew prophets interpreted in new ways symbols from Canaanite and Near Eastern religions. Christianity, in successive stages, appropriated a great variety of both Jewish and Hellenistic religious symbols to interpret Jesus. The uniqueness of the vision is expressed by its ability to combine and transform earlier symbolic patterns to illuminate and disclose meaning in new, unexpected ways that speak to new experiential needs as the old patterns ceased to do.

The formative community that has appropriated the revelatory experience in turn gathers a historical community around its interpretation of the vision. This process goes through various stages during which oral and written teachings are developed. At a certain point a group consisting of teacher and leaders emerges that seeks to channel and control the process, to weed out what it regards as deviant communities and interpretations, and to impose a series of criteria to determine the correct interpretive line. The group can do this by defining an authoritative body of writings that is then canonized as the correct interpretation of the original divine revelation and distinguished from other writings, which are regarded either as heretical or of secondary authority. In the process the controlling group marginalizes and suppresses other branches of the community, with their own texts and lines of interpretation. The winning group declares itself the privileged line of true (orthodox) interpretation. Thus a canon of Scripture is established.

Once a canon of Scripture is defined, one can then regard subsequent tradition as reflection upon Scripture and always corrected by Scripture as the controlling authority. In Catholi-

cism and Orthodoxy the notion of the other equally authoritative "apostolic" traditions flowing from early times and
existing alongside canonical Scripture does not quite disappear.
Creeds, liturgical customs, and oral tradition passed down
through apostolic sees also provide access to the original faith
of the "primitive community." However much the community,
both leaders and led, seek to clothe themselves in past codified
tradition that provides secure access to divinely revealed truth,
in reality the experience of the present community cannot be
ignored.

This contemporary community may consist of many different layers, from the "maximal" leaders to the "ordinary believer." Even an Athanasius or a Leo I, who claim to be merely
teaching what has always been taught, are in fact engaged in
a constant process of revision of the symbolic pattern in a way
that reflects their experience. Received ideas are tested by what
"feels right," that is, illuminates the logic of the symbolic
pattern in a way that speaks most satisfyingly to their own experience of redemption. It is true that theology can evolve into
a secondary and tertiary reflection on the logic of ideas themselves. It continues its vital development only to the extent that
such thinking remains in touch with depth experience.

The ordinary believers now have increasingly complex
formulas of faith, customs, rituals, and writings proposed to
them as the basis for appropriating the original revelatory paradigm as personal redeeming experience. These individuals, in
their local communities of faith, are always engaged in making
their own selection from the patterns of received tradition that
fit or make sense in their lives. There is always an interaction
between the patterns of faith proposed by teachers to individuals and the individuals' own appropriation of these patterns
as interpretations of experience. But these differences remain
unarticulated, held within the dominant consensus about what
the revelatory pattern "means."

A religious tradition remains vital so long as its revelatory
pattern can be reproduced generation after generation and con-

tinues to speak to individuals in the community and provide for them the redemptive meaning of individual and collective experience. Such has been the Exodus-Passover pattern for Jews and the death-resurrection paradigm of personal conversion for Christians. The circle from experience to experience, mediated through instruments of tradition, is thus completed when the contemporary community appropriates the foundational paradigm as the continuing story of its own redemption in relation to God, self, and one another.

Crises of Tradition

Religious traditions fall into crisis when the received interpretations of the redemptive paradigms contradict experience in significant ways. The crisis may be perceived at various levels of radicalness. Exegetical criticism of received theological and Scriptural traditions can bring forth new interpretations that speak to new experiences. This kind of reform goes on in minor and major ways all the time, from individuals making their own private adaptations to teachers founding new schools of interpretation. So long as this is accommodated within the community's methods of transmitting tradition, no major break occurs.

A more radical break takes place when the institutional structures that transmit tradition are perceived to have become corrupt. They are perceived not as teaching truth but as teaching falsehood dictated by their own self-interest and will to power. The revelatory paradigms, the original founder, and even the early stages of the formulation of tradition are still seen as authentic. It seems necessary to go behind later historical tradition and institutionalized authorities and "return to" the original revelation. In the literal sense of the word, there is no possibility of return to some period of the tradition that predates the intervening history. So the myth of return to origins is a way of making a more radical interpretation of the revelatory paradigm to encompass contemporary experiences, while discarding institutions and traditions that contradict meaningful, just, and truthful life. Usable interpretative patterns are taken from Scripture and early community documents to set the original tradition against its later corruption. The original revelation itself, and the foundational stages of its formulation, are not challenged but held as all the more authoritative to set them as normative against later traditions. The Reformation followed this pattern of change.[3]

A still more radical crisis of tradition occurs when the total religious heritage appears to be corrupt. This kind of radical questioning of the meaningfulness of the Christian religion began to occur in Western Europe during the Enlightenment. Marxism carried the Enlightenment critique of religion still further. Marxism teaches that all religion is an instrument the ruling class uses to justify its own power and to pacify the oppressed.[4] This makes religion not the means of redemption but the means of enslavement. The very nature of religious knowledge is seen as promoting alienation rather than integration of the human person. This kind of ideological critique throws the truth content of religion into radical ethical disrepute. Such an attack on religion is considered "true" by a growing minority of people when they perceive the dominant religious traditions as contradictory to the contemporary experience of meaning, truth, and justice.

Ideological criticism of the truthfulness of the religion may still allow for some residue of genuine insight into the original religious experiences and foundational teachers. The prophets of Jesus may be said to have had truthful insights into just and meaningful life, but this became corrupted and turned into its opposite by later teachers, even within Scripture. Discarding even the truthfulness of foundational teachers, the critic may turn to alternative sources of truth: to recent critical schools of thought against the religious traditions; to suppressed traditions condemned as heretical by the dominant tradition; or to pre-Christian patterns of thought. Modern rationalist, Marxist, and romantic criticism of religion have followed such alternatives in the last two hundred years.

Why seek alternative traditions at all? Why not just start with contemporary experience? Doesn't the very search for foundational tradition reveal a need for authority outside contemporary experience? It is true that the received patterns of authority create a strong need, even in those seeking radical change, to find an authoritative base of revealed truth "in the beginning" as well as a need to justify the new by reference to recognized authority. These needs reveal a still deeper need: to situate oneself meaningfully in history.

The effort to express contemporary experience in a cultural and historical vacuum is both self-deluding and unsatisfying. It is self-deluding because to communicate at all to oneself and others, one makes use of patterns of thought, however transformed by new experience, that have a history. It is unsatisfying because, however much one discards large historical periods of dominant traditions, one still seeks to encompass this "fallen history" within a larger context of authentic and truthful life. To look back to some original base of meaning and truth before corruption is to know that truth is more basic than falsehood and hence able, ultimately, to root out falsehood in a new future that is dawning in contemporary experience. To find glimmers of this truth in submerged and alternative traditions through history is to assure oneself that one is not mad or duped. Only by finding an alternative historical community and tradition more deeply rooted than those that have become corrupted can one feel sure that in criticizing the dominant tradition one is not just subjectively criticizing the dominant tradition but is, rather, touching a deeper bedrock of authentic Being upon which to ground the self. One cannot wield the lever of criticism without a place to stand.

The Critical Principle of Feminist Theology

The critical principle of feminist theology is the promotion of the full humanity of women. Whatever denies, diminishes, or distorts the full humanity of women is, therefore, appraised as not redemptive. Theologically speaking, whatever diminishes or denies the full humanity of women must be presumed not to reflect the divine or an authentic relation to the divine, or to reflect the authentic nature of things, or to be the message or work of an authentic redeemer or a community of redemption.

This negative principle also implies the positive principle: what does promote the full humanity of women is of the Holy, it does reflect true relation to the divine, it is the true nature of things, the authentic message of redemption and the mission of redemptive community. But the meaning of this positive principle — namely, the full humanity of women — is not fully known. It has not existed in history. What we have known is the negative principle of the denigration and marginalization of women's humanity. Still, the humanity of women, although diminished, has not been destroyed. It has constantly affirmed itself, often in only limited and subversive ways, and it has been touchstone against which we test and criticize all that diminishes us. In the process we experience our larger potential that allows us to begin to imagine a world without sexism.

This principle is hardly new. In fact, the correlation of original, authentic human nature (*imago dei*/Christ) and diminished, fallen humanity provided the basic structure of classical Christian theology. The uniqueness of feminist theology is not the critical principle, full humanity, but the fact that women claim this principle for themselves. Women name themselves as subjects of authentic and full humanity.

The use of this principle in male theology is perceived to have been corrupted by sexism. The naming of males as norms of authentic humanity has caused women to be scapegoated for sin and marginalized in both original and redeemed humanity. This distorts and contradicts the theological paradigm of *imago dei*/Christ. Defined as male humanity against or above women, as ruling-class humanity above servant classes, the *imago dei*/Christ paradigm becomes an instrument of sin rather than a disclosure of the divine and an instrument of grace.

This also implies that women cannot simply reverse the sin of sexism. Women cannot simply scapegoat males for historical evil in a way that makes themselves only innocent victims. Women cannot affirm themselves as *imago dei* and subjects of full human potential in a way that diminishes male humanity. Women, as the denigrated half of the human species, must reach for a continually expanding definition of inclusive humanity — inclusive of both genders, inclusive of all social groups and races. Any principle of religion or society that marginalizes one group of persons as less than fully human diminishes us all. In rejecting androcentrism (males as norms of humanity), women must also criticize all other forms of chauvinism: making white Westerners the norm of humanity, making Christians the norm of humanity, making privileged classes the norm of humanity. Women must also criticize humanocentrism, that is, making humans the norm and crown of creation in a way that diminishes the other beings in the community of creation. This is not a question of sameness but of recognition of value, which at the same time affirms genuine variety and particularity. It reaches for a new mode of relationship, neither a hierarchical model that diminishes the potential of the "other" nor an "equality" defined by a ruling norm drawn from the dominant group; rather a mutuality that allows us to affirm different ways of being.

IS THERE A HISTORICAL TRADITION FOR FEMINIST THEOLOGY?

First we must say that there is no final and definitive feminist theology, no final synthesis that encompasses all human experience, criticizes what is sexist, and appropriates what is usable in all historical traditions. This book, therefore, represents not *the* feminist theology but *a* feminist theology. However wide its historical sweep, back to Biblical traditions, forward toward a post-Christian world, encompassing minority as well as majority tradition, it is nevertheless an exercise in feminist theology with a particular selection of human experience. This selection is and can only be from the historical tradition, in its broadest sense, that has defined my identity. If I seek out the minority as well as the majority traditions of that community, its repressed pre-Christian side as well as its dominant tradition, I still operate within a particular historical tradition.

Many other traditions are not considered: Asian, African, Hindu, Buddhist, and so on. An Asian Buddhist or an Iranian Muslim, or even Christians from these backgrounds, would bring together a cultural synthesis different from the one I present here. This is not a "fault"; it is simply necessary recognition of historical particularity and limits. What I seek here is a working paradigm of the human situation drawn from a sufficiently large sample of experience that can eventually stimulate dialogue and lead to yet a further synthesis. Other feminist theologians must create other paradigms and make different syntheses of various cultural-religious traditions.

While particularity is affirmed, exclusivism is rejected. God is not a Christian or Jew rather than a pagan, not white rather than Asian or African. Theological reflections drawn from Judeo-Christian or even the Near-Eastern-Mediterranean-European traditions do not have a privileged relation to God, to truth, to authentic humanity over those that arise from Judaism, Islam, and Buddhism. Nor are they presumed to be the same. Exactly how a feminist theology drawn from other cultural syntheses would differ is not yet known. But we affirm at the outset the possibility of equivalence, or equal value, of different feminist theologies drawn from different cultural syntheses.

Having clarified the particularity but nonexclusivism of the historical traditions considered in this work, we can ask where within those traditions we can find usable foundations for feminism. I draw "usable tradition" from five areas of cultural tradition: (1) Scripture, both Hebrew and Christian (Old and New Testaments); (2) marginalized or "heretical" Christian traditions, such as Gnosticism, Montanism, Quakerism, Shakerism; (3) the primary theological themes of the dominant stream of classical Christian theology — Orthodox, Catholic, and Protestant; (4) non-Christian Near Eastern and Greco-Roman religion and philosphy; and (5) critical post-Christian world views such as liberalism, romanticism, and Marxism.

All of these traditions are sexist. All provide intimations of alternatives: equivalence and mutuality between men and women, between classes and races, between humanity and nature. All suggest concepts of God that would affirm such alternative relationships. Yet even these alternatives exist in forms distorted by sexism. Their potential for aiding us in imagining a new humanity can be disclosed by subjecting each to feminist critique and bringing them together in a new relationship. By allowing Canaanite religion to criticize Hebrew religion rather than only the reverse, by allowing minority Biblical and Christian traditions to criticize dominant traditions, one begins to discover lost critical principles. One senses suppressed human potential lurking beneath the dominant traditions and, in many cases, providing a lost key to the meaning of dominant traditions.

I briefly consider each area of tradition to give examples of usable principles and ideas for feminist theology and to show how even those usable principles need to be "corrected" by the feminist critical principle.

Biblical Resources for Feminism: The Prophetic Principle

There is no question that patriarchy is the social context for both the Old and the New Testament and that this social context has been incorporated into religious ideology on many levels. Nevertheless both Testaments contain resources for the critique of patriarchy and of the religious sanctification of patriarchy. We make it clear from the start that feminism must not use the critical prophetic principles in Biblical religion to apologize for or cover up patriarchal ideology. Rather, the prophetic-liberating traditions can be appropriated by feminism only as normative principles of Biblical faith which, in turn, criticize and reject patriarchal ideology. Patriarchal ideology thus loses its normative character. It is to be denounced, not cleaned up or explained away.

Feminism appropriates the prophetic principles in ways the Biblical writers for the most part do not appropriate them, namely, to criticize this unexamined patriarchal framework. Feminist theology that draws on Biblical principles is possible only if the prophetic principles, more fully understood, imply a rejection of every elevation of one social group against others as image and agent of God, every use of God to justify social domination and subjugation. Patriarchy itself must fall under the Biblical denunciations of idolatry and blasphemy, the idolizing of the male as representative of divinity. It is idolatrous to make males more "like God" than females. It is blasphemous to use the image and name of the Holy to justify patriarchal domination and law. Feminist readings of the Bible can discern a norm within Biblical faith by which the Biblical texts themselves can be criticized. To the extent to which Biblical texts reflect this normative principle, they are regarded as authoritative. On this basis many aspects of the Bible are to be frankly set aside and rejected.

This is hardly a new idea in Christianity. On the basis of an early Christian principle of ethical interiority, much of Hebrew ritual law was set aside as no longer normative, despite these texts' continued appearance in the canon of the Old Testament used by the Christian Church. Texts in both Testaments justifying slavery and hostility to religious and racial outsiders fall below most Christians' ethical sensibilities today. Thus all theologies, regardless of their claims that the Bible is totally the work of inspiration, in fact never consider all parts of the Bible equally authoritative; rather they use texts according to implicit or explicit assumptions about the normative development of Biblical faith.

Feminism, in claiming the prophetic-liberating tradition

of Biblical faith as a norm through which to criticize the Bible, does not choose an arbitrary or marginal idea in the Bible. It chooses a tradition that can be fairly claimed, on the basis of generally accepted Biblical scholarship, to be the central tradition, the tradition by which Biblical faith constantly criticizes and renews itself and its own vision. Again, what is innovative in feminist hermeneutics is not the prophetic norm but rather feminism's appropriation of this norm *for women*. Feminism claims that *women too* are among those oppressed whom God comes to vindicate and liberate. By including women in the prophetic norm, feminism sees what male prophetic thought generally had not seen: that once the prophetic norm is asserted to be central to Biblical faith, then patriarchy can no longer be maintained as authoritative.

Four themes are essential to the prophetic-liberating tradition of Biblical faith: (1) God's defense and vindication of the oppressed; (2) the critique of the dominant systems of power and their powerholders; (3) the vision of a new age to come in which the present system of injustice is overcome and God's intended reign of peace and justice is installed in history; and (4) finally, the critique of ideology, or of religion, since ideology in this context is primarily religious. Prophetic faith denounces religious ideologies and systems that function to justify and sanctify the dominant, unjust social order. These traditions are central to the Prophets and to the mission of Jesus. Hence the critical-liberating tradition is the axis around which the prophetic-messianic line of Biblical faith revolves as a foundation for Christianity. These themes can be illustrated briefly by the texts of the Prophets and the synoptic Gospels.

The denunciation of oppressive economic and political power is found in many places in the Prophets. For example,

> Woe to those who decree iniquitous decrees, and the writers who keep on writing oppression, to turn aside the needy from justice, and to rob the poor of my people of their right, that widows may be their spoil, and that they may make the fatherless their prey. (Isa. 10:1–2)

The God of Amos denounces the exploitative economic practices of the times and, because of them, declares that He will send a famine upon the land, not a famine of food but a famine "of hearing the words of the Lord" (Amos 8:11):

> Hear this, you who trample upon the needy and bring the poor of the land to an end, saying, "When will the new moon be over, that we may sell the grain? And the sabbath, that we may offer wheat for sale, that we may make the ephah small and the shekel great and deal deceitfully with false balances, that we may buy the poor for silver and the needy for a pair of sandals and sell the refuse of the wheat?" (Amos 8:4-6)

In this context God is seen not as the one who represents the powerful, but one who comes to vindicate the oppressed. God's intervention in history is to judge those who grind the faces of the poor, those who deprive the widow and the orphan.

Divine advocacy of the oppressed is also a key to Jesus' preaching in the synoptic tradition. Jesus frames the announcement of his prophetic mission in his hometown synagogue in Nazareth in the language of Isaiah 61:1-2:

> The Spirit of the Lord is upon me, because he has anointed me to preach the good news to the poor. He has sent me to proclaim release to the captives, the recovering of sight to the blind; to set at liberty those who are oppressed. (Luke 4:18-19)

Luke pointedly frames the beatitudes of Jesus both to stress their social content and to underline their judgmental side for those who are rich and powerful. Luke also transforms the traditional image of Israel as wife and servant of God. As maidservant, the New Israel or the Church represents the oppressed, who will be exalted in God's messianic revolution in history. This idea is proclaimed in Mary's Magnificat (Luke 1:48-53).

The prophetic God is seen overthrowing unjust society by turning it upside down. God's intervention not only judges the injustice of the present social order but comes to create a new social order that will truly be in keeping with the divine will. Jeremiah speaks of this era as a time when a new thing will be created on the earth: the woman will protect the man (Jer. 31:22). It will be a time when harmony and equal division of land and goods will be restored, when all will dwell under their own vines and fig trees and no one will be afraid.

The baptismal formula in Paul's letter to the Galatians extends this theme into a vision of a new social order in which all the relations of sex, race, and class of human divisiveness will be overcome in Christ. Baptism anticipates this new society in the Church in which there is neither male nor female, Jew nor Greek, slave nor free. In the Lord's Prayer Jesus speaks of the reign of God's Shalom simply as "God's will done on earth."

This means that the God-language of the prophetic tradition is destabilizing toward the existing social order and its hierarchies of power — religious, social, and economic. Its understanding of salvation is neither conformist or privatistic. Rather it is a vision of an alternative future, a new "deal" of peace and justice that will arise when the present systems of injustice have been overthrown.

In both Testaments, this prophetic critique of society also implies a critique of religion. It is an internal critique, a critique of the perversion of Biblical faith itself into a religion of cult and rote, particularly when religion is used to sanctify unjust power and to ignore God's agenda of justice. Thus Amos thunders:

> I hate, I despise your feast, and I take no delight in your solemn assemblies. . . Take away from me the noise of your songs, to the melody of your harps I will not listen. But let justice roll down like waters and righteousness like an everflowing stream. (Amos 5:21, 23–24)

Likewise Jeremiah denounces the use of the cult of the temple as a sacred canopy for things as they are:

> Do not trust in these deceptive words: this is the temple of the Lord, the temple of the Lord, the temple of the Lord. For if you truly amend your ways and your doings, if you execute

justice one with another, if you do not oppress the stranger, the fatherless or the widow, or shed innocent blood in this place, and if you do not go after other gods to your own hurt, then I will let you dwell in this place, in the land that I gave of old to your fathers forever. Behold you trust in deceptive words to no avail. Will you steal, murder, commit adultery, swear false-hood... and then come and stand before me in this house, which is called by my name and say "We are delivered" — only to go on doing all these abominations? Has this house, which is called by my name, become a den of thieves? (Jer. 7:4–11)

Jesus himself takes up this same challenge in his cleansing of the temple at the climax of his ministry.

The Hebrew prophetic critique of religion is renewed in the ministry of Jesus. The mission of the messianic Prophet is portrayed as evoking a continual confrontation with the scribal and priestly leaders and their self-serving use of religion to enforce their own sacral caste:

Woe to you, scribes and Pharisees, hypocrites! For you tithe mint and cummin, and have neglected the weightier matters of the law, justice and mercy and faith; these you ought to have done without neglecting the others. (Matt. 23:23)

Jesus' crucifixion is seen as the consequence of this confrontation with falsified religion at the right hand of oppressive political power.

The Deformation of Prophetic Themes into Ideology

It is important to see that the prophetic-liberating tradition is not and cannot be made into a static set of "ideas." Rather it is a plumb line of truth and untruth, justice and injustice that has to be constantly adapted to changing social contexts and circumstances. Simply saying the same words will not mean the same thing in a different context. When the tribes of Israel were oppressed highlanders under the wealthy city-dwelling Canaanites, the Israelites' denunciation of Canaanite religion was a discernment of the way religion operated to sacralize exploitative political and economic relations. When Israel itself seized the cities, acquired a king and a temple, and aspired to empire, these denunciations simply became ethnocentric triumphalism.

Similarly, the New Testament conflict with the dominant religious authorities of Judaism operated in the mission of Jesus and the earliest Church as a criticism of fossilized religion to call Judaism itself back to its prophetic-messianic mission. But when Christianity moved to become a separate Gentile religion and, eventually, the dominant religion of the Roman Empire, this same language was used to express both the rejection of Judaism itself as an inferior religion and the chauvinist triumphalism of the Church over the Synagogue.[5]

The meaning of the language of messianism also can change in different contexts. Much of messianic imagery was drawn originally from ancient Near Eastern kingship language. This was critically reevaluated by the Prophets, detached from its ideological justification of existing kings, and projected on an idealized future hope. The Prophets thus made messianic language a judgment on existing kings and a hope for an alternative social order. But when Christianity became an imperial religion, this kingship language was used to sacralize existing Christian monarchs as expressions of divine kingship and representatives of Christ on earth.

The meaning of servanthood language likewise changes radically in different contexts. In its use by Jesus, appropriated from the prophetic tradition, it means that God alone is father and king and we, therefore, owe no allegiance to human fathers and kings. As servants of God alone, we are freed from servitude to human hierarchies of power. When imperial Christianity again presents these human hierarchies of power as expressions of Christ's reign, however, the servanthood language is used to reinforce, in Christ's name, the servitude of subjugated people.

Key to this ideological deformation is the socioreligious group's movement from powerlessness to power. When the religious spokespersons identify themselves as members of and advocates of the poor, then the critical-prophetic language maintains its cutting edge. When the religious spokespersons see themselves primarily as stabilizing the existing social order and justifying its power structure, then prophetic language becomes deformed in the interests of the status quo. It becomes a language to sacralize dominant authorities and to preach revenge against former enemies.

One particularly important aspect of Jesus' teaching is his recognition and criticism of these deformations of messianic language. Jesus rejected kingly and chauvinistic understandings of the Messiah. He interpreted the Messiah as Suffering Servant, as one who comes to restore humanity through a ministry of service, even to the point of giving one's own life. In Matthew 20:17-18 Jesus confronts the triumphalistic concept of messianism entertained by the disciples as they journey to Jerusalem. Responding to the request of the sons of Zebedee, mediated through their mother, that they be given positions of power and domination in the Kingdom of God, Jesus replies:

> You know that the rulers of the Gentiles lord it over them, and their great men exercise authority over them. It shall not be so among you, but whosoever would be great among you must be your servant, even as the son of man came not to be served, but to serve and to give his life as ransom for many. (Matt. 20:26-28)

Jesus thus rejects not only the use of religion to sanctify dominant hierarchies but also the temptation to use prophetic language simply to justify the revenge of the oppressed. This temptation is not always avoided in Old Testament prophecy. Rather, the vision of the new age, when the oppression of Israel will be overcome, is visualized as a triumphant reversal of domination. In the Kingdom of God, Israel will be established as the center of a world empire. The peoples of the existing imperial powers — the Egyptians, Babylonians, or Romans — will come up to Jerusalem to offer tribute to the new holders of world domination.[6]

Central to Jesus' message is a radical criticism of both types of ideological deformation of religion. The first will be last and the last first. The poor will be filled with good things, the mighty put down from their thrones. The prostitutes and the tax collectors will go into the Kingdom of God ahead of the Scribes and the Pharisees. This language in the Gospels belongs to the tradition that criticizes existing power systems and places God on the side of the oppressed. But Jesus criticized the temptation to see this simply as a reversed system of domination and privilege. Rather, he pressed beyond the critique of the present order to a more radical vision, a revolutionary transformative process that will bring all to a new mode of relationship.

In God's Kingdom the corrupting principles of domination and subjugation will be overcome. People will no longer model social or religious relationships, or even relationships to God, after the sort of power that reduces others to servility. Rather they will discover a new kind of power, a power exercised through service, which empowers the disinherited and brings all to a new relationship of mutual enhancement. Jesus' image of God and Christ as Servant transforms all relations including relations to God. All power and domination relations in society are overcome by overcoming the root metaphor of relationship to God modeled on king-servant relations.

This critique of power relationships is central to Jesus' radical interpretation of the prophetic-messianic tradition. It is not surprising that when Christianity became a hierarchical and then an imperial religion, no element in the Gospels was so totally deformed to conceal and mystify its original meaning. Jesus' criticism of power and of religious models of domination is interpreted by the Church to spiritualize his understanding of the Kingdom of God. That understanding is said to be purely "spiritual"; hence it has no relevance to questions of social justice "in this world." The Church then uses this spiritual understanding of the Kingdom anti-Jewishly, to claim that Christians alone have the higher spiritual view of the Kingdom while the Jewish view is a crude nationalistic and materialistic deformation.

The Church suppresses the social justice dimension fundamental to the entire Biblical prophetic tradition of messianic hope. The continuity between the Jewish understanding of the Messiah and the Christian use of the term Christ is lost. Christianity then can claim a new Christian imperialism over not only the Jews but the rest of the world. It does so in the name of an other-worldly Christ who no longer criticizes social injustice but rather establishes the Church as God's agent to convert and conquer the world. The more radical the prophetic criticism of unjust social systems and their supporting religious ideologies, the more corrupting the ideological deformation of this vision must be to make religion the tool of the dominant social hierarchies and their religious collaborators.

The Feminist Radicalizing of the Prophetic Tradition

The renewal of the prophetic meaning of religious language from its ideological deformations is the creative dynamic of Biblical faith. This rediscovery of prophetic content, and its discerning reapplication to new social situations, is precisely what the Bible calls "The Word of God." This, in other words, is the critical principle that Biblical faith applies to itself. It is the hermeneutical principle for discerning prophetic faith within Scripture as well as for the ongoing interpretation of Scripture as critique of tradition.

Feminist theology is not asserting unprecedented ideas; rather it is rediscovering the prophetic context and content of Biblical faith itself when it defines the prophetic-liberating tradition as norm. On one level, this means that feminist theology, along with other liberation theologies, strips off the ideological mystifications that have developed in the traditions of Biblical interpretation and that have concealed the liberating content. The prophetic advocacy of the poor and the oppressed and the denunciation of unjust social hierarchies and their religious justifications leap into clear focus as one assumes a stance of social justice rather than of collaboration with unjust powers. The entire Biblical message becomes radically transformed in meaning and purpose when the full implications of the Church's social advocacy for the oppressed are grasped today. Such a reevaluation of Scripture is clearly seen in the Biblical reflection taking place in Basic Christian Communities in Latin America today.

On another level, feminism goes beyond the letter of the prophetic message to apply the prophetic-liberating principle *to women*. Feminist theology makes explicit what was overlooked in male advocacy of the poor and oppressed: that liberation must start with the oppressed of the oppressed, namely, *women* of the oppressed. This means that the critique of hierarchy must become explicitly a critique of patriarchy. All the liberating prophetic visions must be deepened and transformed to include what was not included: women.

This expansion itself implicitly recognizes that not only the dominant sociology, but also the sociology of oppressed people, has its social myopias and limitations. Oppressed people understand who is stepping on their toes and in what way, but they are often blind to the ways they step on other people's toes. This, of course, also includes women of dominant classes whose visions of liberation need to be radicalized by voices of women from oppressed classes, races, and non-Christian religions. In Old Testament prophecy, Hebrew males, identified with rural classes, saw the oppresiveness of the wealthy of the cities and the mighty of the empires. But they did not recognize the oppressiveness of their own rule over wives, daughters, and slaves. In the New Testament Paul understood the need to struggle against all traces of ethnocentric religion in the relations of Jew and Greek in the Church. But he was much less able to envision, never mind put into practice, the ideas of equality in Christ between male and female, slave and free.

This expansion of the Biblical message to include the un-included rests on the assumption that the point of reference for Biblical faith is not past texts, with their sociological limitations, but rather the liberated future. We appropriate the past not to remain in its limits, but to point to new futures. In applying the prophetic principle to the critique of sexism and the liberation of women, we deepen our understanding of social sin and its religious justifications and expand the vision of messianic expectation. By applying prophetic faith to sexism we reveal in new fullness its revolutionary meaning.

Countercultural Movements in Early Christianity and Church History

The Hebraic prophetic tradition formulated its vision of liberation in the context of socioeconomic oppression of the poor by the wealthy and of the small colonized nation by the great empires of antiquity. The writers of the New Testament recognized other areas in which social relations needed transformation. Under the impact of Jesus' deepening of prophetic criticism, the Jesus movement began to glimpse the possibility of transforming the relationships of race (ethnicity), slavery, and sexism. The baptismal formula preserved in the Pauline letter to the Galatians represents this vision, against the traditions of both Judaism and Hellenism, which celebrates the privileged status of male over female, Jew over Greek (Greek over barbarian), and free over slave. Paul saw the new age of God's Kingdom as one in which a new equality between all races and social groups is established. He anticipated this in the new relations of the baptized in the messianic community, where Jew and Greek, male and female, slaves and free would become brothers and sisters and work together in preaching and teaching.

This "countercultural" character of the Jesus movement has been constructed by the New Testament scholar Elisabeth Schüssler Fiorenza.[7] Unlike the prophetic texts of the Old Testament, however, the egalitarian vision was not preserved as the normative tradition in the New Testament. The ambiguity of

Paul toward this vision, and the patriarchalization of Christianity that occurred in the Deutero-Pauline tradition, suppressed the early vision. The post-Pauline Church all the more vehemently asserted as norms the patriarchal relations of husband over wife, master over slave. Thus the countercultural egalitarian vision must be read between the lines in the New Testament. It must be ferreted out, in fragmentary form, in contrast to the patriarchal Church which established the canonical framework for interpreting Christianity.

If this egalitarian, countercultural vision is accepted as the true norm of Christianity, then the authority of the official canonical framework is overturned. The conflict between liberating and patriarchal norms must be seen as existing in the New Testament in an even more radical way than in the Hebrew Scriptures. In the New Testament a suppressed tradition must be brought to the surface to criticize and refute the dominant hermeneutical line established by those who shaped the written canon.

In seeking an alternative, egalitarian Christianity, we are not left merely with fragments preserved under the surface of the New Testament. A host of alternative Christianities are still partly visible in the "heresies" that dominant Christianity struggled to suppress in the first centuries of the Church. It is notable that these early heresies of the first to the third centuries were regarded as erring, among other aspects, in their egalitarianism toward women. Montanism preserved the understanding of the prophetic gifts of the Spirit poured out on men and women alike. It appears that women were given not only equal prophetic authority but also equal participation in ordinary ministry in Montanism.[8]

Some forms of Gnosticism defined a concept of God/ess that combined male and female principles.[9] Woman, far from being scapegoated for sin, was given a privileged relation to the divine Sophia who mediated redemptive revelation. In the person of Mary Magdalene and other early female disciples of Christ, women's apostolic authority was defended in Gnostic

Gospels, in contrast to Petrine Christianity.[10] Women also participated in Gnostic ministry. For these "deviant" kinds of Christianity, the messianic norm of equality in Christ dictates a new relationship of men and women in the Church.[11]

The dominant Christianity never denied this equality of men and women in Christ but rather interpreted it in a spiritual and eschatological way that suppressed its relevance for the sociology of the Church. Nevertheless, fragments of the alternative vision were continually rediscovered in Christian history by women mystics, female religious communities, and popular Christian movements, some of which came to be defined as "heretical."[12] A host of such popular movements in the late Middle Ages constantly came close to rediscovering a countercultural egalitarian Christianity opposed to the patriarchal and hierarchical Church.

During the Reformation, particularly left-wing Puritans in England rediscovered intimations of an egalitarian Christianity that included women's right to preach and to act as lay governors of the Church. This egalitarianism was found, here and there, among Baptists and other left-wing dissenters in the mid-seventeenth century, the period of the English civil war.[13] The Quakers, thanks in no small part to the role of Margaret Fell, developed such egalitarian intimations into a more coherent theology and Scriptural exegesis. Quaker tracts written by Margaret Fell, by her daughters, and by George Fox affirmed the equality of men and women in the *imago dei* and in the original order of creation.[14] They wrote that the subjugation of women was not God's intent but represented the sinful distortion of human nature by sin. Israel and, still more, the messianic community of Christ restored woman to her original full personhood; but the seventeenth-century Quakers dared to assert the implications of this messianic sociology only for the Church, not for society at large.[15]

In the eighteenth and nineteenth centuries Gnostic ideas about the androgyny of God were rediscovered by mystical writers, and Utopian sects adopted them. They related the androgyny of God to the egalitarian messianic sociology that they asserted in their communities against the evil social order and the dominant Churches. The late-eighteenth- and nine-teenth-century Anglo-American Shakers represent perhaps the most interesting development of this androgynous messianic movement. The Shakers transformed all theological categories in the light of their androgynous vision. They taught that the creation of humanity, male and female, in the image of God points to the androgyny of God. Humanity images the divine, and because it was created in the dual order of male and female it cannot be redeemed by a male savior alone. The Messiah must appear in female form as well. The messianic community also must reflect this parity of male and female in its organizational structure.[16]

Further historical study would undoubtedly turn up other religious groups that preserve or rediscover hints of an egalitarian Christianity preserved under the surface of the New Testament. Feminist theology, however, cannot simply seize an alternative line of Christianity from Montanism and Gnosticism to Quakerism and Shakerism as the new orthodoxy. Several problems would arise from an effort to simply reverse the traditional norm of Christian truth to make the suppressed traditions "right" and the dominant Christianity "wrong." Much of alternative Christianity has not survived as living moments. We know its literature and ideas in only fragmentary form, preserved by hostile authorities. We can only guess at what these groups really meant by their ideas of androgynous divinity or what women's roles actually were in their movements.

Rediscovered Gnostic texts, for example, reveal the radical dualistic ontology that orthodox Christianity rejected in these movements. Where women's messianic equality was affirmed in heretical Christianity, it was generally done by asserting an eschatological order of redemption as a counterpoint to the patriarchal order of creation. Thus a paradox arises: Gnostic Christianity affirmed women's equality, but against the goodness of nature and bodily existence. Orthodox Christianity, which affirmed doctrinally (if not in its actual spirituality) the goodness of body and creation, nevertheless used its doctrine of Creation to subordinate women. Neither orthodox nor heretical Christianity brings together the wholeness of vision that feminist theology seeks. Only by correcting the defects of each with the other do we begin to glimpse another alternative Christianity.

Feminist Use of Dominant Theological Traditions

If feminism cannot seize upon marginal Christianities as unambiguously positive, it also cannot reject all of dominant Christianity as unusable for women. What is usable in the marginal and the dominant traditions? All the categories of classical theology in its major traditions — Orthodox, Catholic, and Protestant — have been distorted by androcentrism. This not only makes the male normative in a way that reduces women to invisibility, but it also distorts all the dialectical relationships of good/evil, nature/grace, body/soul, God/nature by modeling them on a polarization of male and female.

Nevertheless, corrected by feminist criticism of the androcentric hierarchicalism, these same categories of classical theology disclose entirely different possibilities. Women must reject a concept of the Fall that makes them scapegoats for the advent of evil and uses this to "punish" them through historical subordination. At the same time women cannot neglect the basic theological insight that humanity has become radically alienated from its true relationship to itself, to nature, and to God. This alienation, which is not just individual but systemic, has defined the condition of humanity in history. Not sex, but sexism — the distortion of gender (as well as other differences between human groups) into structures of unjust domination and subordination — is central to the origin and transmission of this alienated, fallen condition. Feminism, far from rejecting concepts of the Fall, can rediscover its meaning in a radically new way.

Even among feminist thinkers such as Mary Daly who regard themselves as having totally rejected the Judeo-Christian tradition for an alternative world view based solely on women's experience, the basic categories of Christian theology continue to operate in unconscious ways. One continues to find the basic paradigm of classical theology which connects an original good human nature, united to the cosmos and the divine, contrasted with an alienated, fallen, historical condition of humanity (sin, evil). Revelatory, transformative experiences (conversion) disclose the original humanity and allow one to liberate oneself from the sinful distortion of existence. This new humanity is then related to a redemptive community that gathers together and announces a prophetic, critical, or transformative mission against sinful society.

In my feminist theology I have made use of the basic paradigm of Christian systematics. This paradigmatic structure is not the only possible structure for a feminist theology, however. A feminism drawn from entirely different streams of human culture might develop, and it might have a different structure. But the Christian paradigm continues to be a powerful and formative structure. Its continuing power to provide an interpretive framework for human situations of conflict and struggle for justice is reflected by the fact that modern liberation movements, both in the West and in the Third World, continually adopt and make use of this basic pattern in secular form. For both Judeo-Christian and modern Western peoples, feminist theology is a restatement of this paradigm. As feminist theology systematically corrects the androcentrism of each category of Christianity, it is to be hoped that the alternative possibilities of the Christian pattern of theology for a liberation theology for women will come into focus.

Pagan Resources for Feminist Theology

A feminist theology that attempts to understand and transform the dominant consciousness cannot ignore the other religions rejected by Judaism in Biblical times and suppressed by dominant Christianity. It cannot ignore them because the Bible and historical Christianity shaped their identities by overt struggle against the other religions and also by covert incorporation of many aspects of the religions into their own worship and thought patterns. Some of this heritage, such as Greek philosophy, provided additional theoretical resources for patriarchal ideology.

Feminist spirituality today is reassessing pre-Christian religion. Does a pagan veneration of nature disclose a more ecological relation between humanity and nature? Do myths and cults of Goddesses provide alternative resources for women's identity? This work affirms the resources of pagan traditions for feminist theology, but in a way different from what has recently become defined as the "Goddess" or Feminist Wicca movement. It is useful to discuss briefly the differences between Goddess feminism and my use of non-Biblical religions of the ancient Near East and the Greco-Roman world in this work.

Goddess feminism reverses the judgmental dualism that sets the Judeo-Christian tradition against pagan religions. The Biblical religions are seen as solely patriarchal, existing only to affirm male superiority, while paganism is seen as providing a feminist religion based on ancient matriarchy. This view seems to me historically inaccurate and ideologically distorted. It inappropriately denies the possibility of positive resources in the Biblical tradition and overlooks the social reality of Goddess cults that made these cults vehicles of male power, but in a somewhat different way than in Hebrew society. One does not uncover the problematics or the positive resources of either the Christian or the pagan religion through this simplified dualism.[17]

Ancient paganism, like suppressed "heresies," does not exist as a living tradition. What is known of it is preserved through Judeo-Christian and Western scholarship. Modern research, to be sure, has rediscovered many unknown texts and thus gives a fuller glimpse of what these religions might have meant in their own times. But we must recognize the ideological incorporation of the "pagan" background of Judaism, Christianity, and European culture into our cultural consciousness. The memory of pagan religions has been used in two ways by Western religions and cultural traditions. One way has been to scapegoat these religions as exemplars of all that is sinful and demonic. They become the paradigms of the apostate, evil self. Goddess spirituality obviously rejects this view of paganism.

A second, equally important use of paganism in Western consciousness was developed in nineteenth-century romanticism in revolt against Christianity. In romanticism the pagan became the epitome of the repressed side of Western consciousness: nature against civilization; the intuitive and poetic against the rational; the feminine against the masculine. Goddess religion draws on this romantic tradition and bases its view of feminist spirituality on it. But it is uncritical of the romantic source of its own view of paganism and takes this view as an accurate historical account of ancient pre-Christian religions.[18]

I find two major difficulties here. First, the pattern of thought attributed to pagan religions is, in fact, not found in ancient Near Eastern religions. Instead, the ancient Near Eastern patterns of thought lack those dualistic patterns, and these nondualistic patterns may be much more helpful resources for feminist thought. By drawing uncritically on the romantic view of paganism, Goddess feminism overlooks other, perhaps more important, resources that historical paganism may have to offer. Second, this reversal of the dualism of Western consciousness by romanticism seems to be part of the problem rather than part of the solution for feminist theology. Feminist theology needs to seek a new synthesis that transcends not only patriarchal but also romantic consciousness.

This critique of Feminist Wicca has nothing to do with religious exclusivism. The appropriateness of various feminist theologies explored through a plurality of religious cultures is affirmed in this work. But once one claims to be creating any feminist theology based on particular patterns of thought and historical culture, one must account for whether the patterns of thought are liberating and whether the use of a given historical culture truthfully situates one's contemporary identity claims. Here I have some significant differences with the approach of Feminist Wicca or Goddess religion, although I also share many values with them.

In the feminist theology presented here, ancient Near Eastern religions are not judged favorably against Biblical religion. The Near Eastern religions are seen as providing autonomous and different resources that illuminate both what Biblical religion rejected and what it appropriated from them in transformed fashion. By entering into the dialectic between the Canaanite and Biblical religions from both sides, allowing Canaanite religion to speak positively to Biblical religion, as well as vice versa, we might discover new insights into the foundation of Western religions and cultural consciousness. As Mary Wakeman said, "To see patriarchy coming into existence [through ancient Near Eastern religions] is also to see it passing away."[19]

Modern Post-Christian Resources for Feminist Theology

Western consciousness in the late eighteenth to the twentieth century has developed three streams of critical culture — liberalism, romanticism, and Marxism — in opposition to the inherited religion and institutions of Christendom. Liberalism has been the ideology of bourgeois democracy. It has found its center in the defense of civic freedom and it also seeks justice socially through equality of opportunity, particularly in education and in access to professions. But it is hostile to any economic egalitarianism that touches private property. It embraces ideas of progress and believes that world conditions will gradually be ameliorated through worldwide evolutionary development of liberal institutions.

Romanticism reacts against the rationalistic scientific and technological aspects of modernity. Far from regarding these as the great instruments of human redemption, it sees technological rationality and industrialization as alienating "man" from "his" roots in nature. Whereas the Enlightenment used the word *nature* to mean the rational and even mathematical structure of reality, romanticism uses *nature* in juxtaposition to civilization. Nature is the irrational, the intuitive, the organic over against the machine culture. Romanticism celebrates what rationalists despised — the underclasses of society. Women, peasants, native peoples, and paganism embody the intuitive "soulful" types in contrast to the alienated urbanized intellectuals.

Socialism has had several traditions. Democratic socialism extends the liberal tradition into economic democracy, while anarcho-communitarian socialism has more in common with romanticism. Marxism has more in common with liberalism in its celebration of science and technology, but it becomes revolutionary rather than evolutionary because it recognizes that under the present system of class control liberal freedoms are class privileges of those who own the means of production. Liberal prosperity will not trickle down to the masses, but will lead to an even more unjust dichotomy between the "haves" and the "have-nots" as the system develops. Marxists believe there must be an overthrow and forcible reorganization of the present system of ownership in favor of the vast majority, the masses.

Marxism also continues and radicalizes the critique of religion that was begun in the Enlightenment. Religion is seen to be the ideology of the ruling classes, justifying the legitimacy and God-givenness of their power and providing a compensatory ideology of humility, submission, and deferred expectations for the lower classes. Marxism also recognizes the power of religion in its vision of a better world to come but teaches that this expectation must be dealienated. It must be taken out of its religious (alienated) mode of expression as Heaven and life after death and reinterpreted as hope for a new future on earth. Only then can the religious myth of the messianic age cease to be a tool of alienation and resignation to the present system of exploitation and become a means of energizing revolutionary struggle. Marxism secularizes the Biblical, prophetic critique of religion. It takes the place of prophetic faith as denouncer of idolatrous religion and also as bearer of the good news of a redeemed future. Contemporary dialogue between Marxism and liberation theologies takes place at this point of common interest: denouncing oppressive ideologies and announcing hope for justice on earth.

Subsequent discussions of anthropology (chapter 4) and feminist visions of social justice (chapter 9) explore further the implications of post-Christian traditions. The main lines of the feminist versions of the three post-Christian traditions are summarized here.

These critical systems of thought were developed by males and shaped by sexist assumptions. They tend either to ignore women or to place women in a male-centered set of ideas. Yet a feminist reevaluation of their critical theories has produced feminist versions of each of these movements. Liberal feminism has been the classical ideology of women's rights, in the nineteenth century and today. It seeks to extend the rights of citizenship, suffrage, ownership of property, and access to political office, education, and all avenues of employment to women. It seeks to make women "equal to men" within the public sphere.

Marxist feminism criticizes liberal feminism for its implicit bourgeois assumptions. It asserts that women cannot become equal with men simply through obtaining equal legal rights. Marxist feminism analyzes the socioeconomic structure of women's work, both in the home and in the paid labor force. The structure of female work makes women doubly exploited, as unpaid laborers in the home and low-paid laborers in the paid labor force. Marxist feminists believe that equality for women must come from a social restructuring of both class and gender hierarchy in work.

Marxist feminism also turns a critical eye on the bourgeois colonization of women as the preservers of the religious world view *vis à vis* modern secular society. The home, womanhood, and religion preserve a private island of patriarchal privilege for each male against the public realm where he competes in the depersonalized "rat race." If religion is the ideology of the ruling classes to keep the masses in their place, it is doubly so for women. Religion socializes women into the "feminine" roles of self-abnegation and submission.

Romantic feminism, on the other hand, celebrates the female qualities that liberalism ignores and that Marxism sees as a trap for women and oppressed classes. Romantic feminism uses them as expressions of a lost self, suppressed by alienated rationality. Women hold the key to this lost, better self. This concept of women as bearers of separate feminine qualities lends itself to various ideological adaptations from right to left, as we will see in greater detail in subsequent chapters. Total Womanhood uses this doctrine of complementarity to restrict women to their traditional roles and sphere. Reform feminism uses it to extend women's sphere into the world as a base for transforming the lower male world by higher feminine values. Radical feminism uses it to negate the male world and to withdraw into separatism.

In all these romantic feminisms is a sense that women have been bearers of separate values and psychological qualities that are important, and even superior, to those found in traditional masculinity. Women should not capitulate to the masculine model of personhood, but should preserve and develop their own psychic specialization.

In this work all three of these traditions — liberalism, Marxism, and romanticism — are used as important critical traditions for feminism. Women need to understand these traditions and the way feminists have often unknowingly appropriated patterns of thought from one or another. They need to become aware of the limits and characteristic defects of each viewpoint seen in isolation from the others. Why is it that liberalism becomes deformed into the ideology of bourgeois capitalism, Marxism into the ideology of bureaucratic state Communism, and romanticism into the ideology of fascism?[20] How can the feminist appropriation of these patterns of critical thought avoid such defects? Feminism seeks not simply a feminist appropriation of one or another of these traditions, but a new synthesis of all three.

CONCLUSIONS

The feminist theology proposed here is based on a historical culture that includes the pre-Christian religions suppressed by Judaism and Christianity; Biblical prophetism; Christian theology, in both its majority and minority cultures; and, finally, the critical cultures through which modern Western consciousness has reflected on this heritage. It seeks, in effect, to recapitulate from a feminist, critical perspective this journey of Western consciousness. To be sure, it would be pretentious to assume that one can really embrace the whole experience in all its aspects. There are many avenues of Christian and non-Christian culture that will not be given "equal time" in this account. What is sought here is not the inclusion of limitless possibilities, but a working paradigm of some main trends of our consciousness, both its dominant side and its underside. Thereby we can begin to glimpse both what has been lost to humanity through the subjugation of women and what new humanity might emerge through the affirmation of the full personhood of women.

An explanatory word is appropriate about the words for the divine used in this work. When speaking of the understanding of the divine of the ancient Near East, I speak of Gods and Goddesses, making clear that paired male and female concepts were used. These terms are capitalized, rejecting the traditional Western usage that left them lowercase to signal that these were false deities and not the true (Judeo-Christian) God. When speaking of the divine within the Judeo-Christian tradition, I use the term God. This is understood to be a male generic form and thus inadequate to express the vision of the divine sought in this theology. It does not imply, however, that there are not usable and authentic intimations of divinity found within traditional Jewish and Christian understandings of God.

Finally, when discussing fuller divinity to which this theology points, I use the term God/ess, a written symbol intended to combine both the masculine and feminine forms of the word for the divine while preserving the Judeo-Christian affirmation that divinity is one. This term is unpronounceable and inadequate. It is not intended as language for worship, where one might prefer a more evocative term, such as Holy One or Holy Wisdom. Rather it serves here as an analytic sign to point toward that yet unnameable understanding of the divine that would transcend patriarchal limitations and signal redemptive experience for women as well as men.

Chapter 2
Sexism and God-Language: Male and Female Images of the Divine

Few topics are as likely to arouse such passionate feelings in contemporary Christianity as the question of the exclusively male image of God. Liberals who have advanced to the point of accepting inclusive language for humans often exhibit a phobic reaction to the very possibility of speaking of God as "She." This emotional hostility has deep roots in the Judeo-Christian formation of the normative image of transcendent ego in the male God image. The underside of this transcendent male ego is the conquest of nature, imaged as the conquest and transcendence of the Mother. To probe the roots of this formation of the male God image, it is useful to reach back behind patriarchal monotheism to religions in which a Goddess was either the dominant divine image or was paired with the male image in a way that made both equivalent modes of apprehending the divine.

THE GODDESS IN THE ANCIENT NEAR EAST

From archaeological evidence one can conclude that the most ancient human image of the divine was female. From Paleolithic to Neolithic times and into the beginnings of ancient civilization, we find the widely diffused image of the Goddess without an accompanying male cult figure. E. O. James, in his classic book *The Cult of the Mother Goddess,* cites M. E. L. Mallowan's assertion that the "mother-goddess cult must indeed be one of the oldest and longest surviving religions of

47

the ancient world.''[1] A second ancient cult, found in numerous Ice Age cave paintings, focuses on the Shaman, probably male, of the hunting cult, although no representation of the divine is depicted. Thus the widely diffused images of the Goddess found throughout the ancient Mediterranean world and into India and western Europe are the only archaeological clue as to how these early peoples imaged the source and powers of life on which they depended.

Their figures typically emphasize the breasts, buttocks, and enlarged abdomen of the female; face, hands, and legs are given little attention.[2] This suggests that the Goddess is not a focus of personhood, but rather an impersonalized image of the mysterious powers of fecundity. The pregnant human female is the central metaphor for the powers of life for peoples who domesticated neither animals nor plants but were totally dependent on the spontaneous forces of the earth for gathering food. Later, when animals were domesticated, plants were sown and harvested, and humanity began to intervene in, rather than simply to depend on, the spontaneous powers of fertility, the metaphor of the Goddess continued to shape the cultural imagination. Humanity did not visualize itself as controlling these life processes so much as cooperating with them. To shape and bury in the earth images of the pregnant human female continued to be humanity's primary way of experiencing mimetic cooperation with the awesome powers of life and renewal of life.

We can speak of the root human image of the divine as the Primal Matrix, the great womb within which all things, Gods and humans, sky and earth, human and nonhuman beings, are generated. Here the divine is not abstracted into some other world beyond this earth but is the encompassing source of new life that surrounds the present world and assures its continuance. This is expressed in the ancient myth of the World Egg out of which all things arise.

The ancient apprehension of Goddess as Primal Matrix has never entirely disappeared from the human religious imagination, despite the superimposition of male monotheism. It survives in the metaphor of the divine as Ground of Being. Here the divine is not "up there" as abstracted ego, but beneath and around us as encompassing source of life and renewal of life; spirit and matter are not split hierarchically. That which is most basic, matter (mother, matrix), is also most powerfully imbued with the powers of life and spirit.

The early urban civilizations of Sumer and Babylonia continue to use the female image of the divine, but now it is paired with a male deity. Generations of old and young Gods and Goddesses express the historical memory of the emergence of urban and agricultural civilization from a prehistoric epoch. The older Gods and Goddesses represent the food-gathering era of direct dependency on spontaneous natural powers. In the new world of cities and agriculture, an emerging elite owns both the land and the labor of peasants and slaves. They order society through systems of law, irrigation, and taxation. An aristocratic and sacerdotal ruling class, both male and female, cooperate in this new system of urban and agricultural order. The image of the divine comes primarily from the characteristics of this ruling class: God or Goddess is seen in the image of sovereign power. The worshiper relates to the God or Goddess as humble subject petitioning an all-powerful Lord or Lady for favor.

Two central myths emerge in the ancient Near Eastern world that relate God and Goddess in different ways. One is the myth of the dying and rising God-king, his rescue by and marriage with the Goddess. This myth has ancient roots that go back to Sumer, if not before. Its importance is signified by its continued appearance in parallel forms: Inanna-Dumuzi in Sumeria, Ishtar-Tammuz in Babylonia, Anath-Baal in Canaan, and Isis-Osiris in Egypt. In this myth and ritual drama the ancient Near Eastern world displayed its continuing attachment to the prehistoric myth of the female as the primary divine power upon which the male as king or God depends. The king as son and consort of the Goddess represents the powers of vegetation and rain threatened yearly by searing drought. In the Babylonian and Canaanite versions he is represented as defeated by powers of death and drought and then rescued from the underworld by a powerful Goddess who conquers the dark powers and raises her son-lover from the dead.

The resurrection of the king culminates in his marriage to the Goddess, who thereby elevates her human husband to divine status and places him on the throne.[3] Renewed fertility and legitimate political power over the city-state are thereby assured. The drama ends in a paean of joy that the powers of life and just order have been secured against the threat of drought and death. The role of the Goddess was played by the leading priestess of the temple of the Goddess. The priestesses were themselves female relatives of the aristocracy and held great landed power in a theocratic system. Thus behind the coordinated power of Goddess and God-king lay the social coordination of temple and palace. The earliest power centered in the temple and only later shifted to the palace. There was at least one occurrence of a woman sovereign who reigned from the palace, and women were regularly the priestesses who exercised great power from the temple.

The second great myth that emerged from Sumer but was developed particularly in the new empire center in Babylonia was the Marduk-Tiamat story. This tells of the defeat of the old Goddess, Tiamat, and her consort and followers by the new Gods and Goddesses of the urban-agricultural world, represented by their warrior champion, Marduk, God of the city-state of Babylonia. The old Goddess comes to represent the powers of chaos, which are defeated by the new powers of order. Clear reminiscences of the old Goddess as original Matrix and Creatrix of the universe remain; Tiamat is the primal womb impregnated by Apsu, her consort, out of which emerged all beings, Gods and humans.

This primal Mother must now be conquered and her powers reorganized by new city-states. The younger deities, led by Marduk, represent the new power that subdues and orders the primal Matrix of all reality, that is, the old mother civilization of Sumer. That Tiamat is not merely a negative force to be banished by Marduk but is indeed the primary matter out of which all things emerge, the matter within which Marduk himself stands as orderer, becomes evident in the description of Tiamat's defeat:

> They swayed in single combat, locked in battle.
> The lord spread out his net to enfold her...
> He released the arrow, it tore her belly,
> It cut through her insides, splitting the heart.
> Having thus subdued her, he extinguished her life.
> He cast down her carcass to stand upon it...
> Then the lord paused to view her dead body,
> That he might divide the monster and do artful works.
> He split her like a shellfish into two parts:
> Half of her he set up and ceiled it as sky,
> pulled down the bar and posted guards.
> He bade them to allow not her waters to escape...
> He constructed stations for the great gods,
> fixing their astral likenesses as constellations.
> He determined the year by designating the zones...[4]

Having fashioned the cosmos out of the body of Tiamat, Marduk goes on to fashion the human as servant of the Gods that the Gods might be at ease. Human service to the Gods mirrors the place of the serfs on the landed estates under the aristocracy of palace and temple.

It is significant that, in the development of the mythic drama celebrated each year in the New Year festival, ancient cultures did not choose between these two stories, which imaged the Goddess in such different ways, but preferred to use both. The two stories were used as parallel myths of the defeat of the powers of drought and death and the establishment of secure order, prosperity, and fertility. The Marduk story, which might easily have been used as symbol of female defeat by patriarchy, is instead balanced by the Goddess-King story in which the ancient primacy of the Goddess is carried over and made a positive force in the renewal of life of urban-agricultural society. Here the Goddess is not merely impersonal fertility; she represents wisdom, the union of divine and human order. The threatening powers of human and natural chaos are beaten back. A world in which cosmic regularity and human design mesh in harmony is envisioned. Here the Goddess is not only Creatrix but Redemptrix, restorer and protector of cosmic harmony.

In the contemporary feminist reaction to patriarchal religion, the revival of the Goddess of antiquity as an alternative manifestation of the divine is much discussed. But both those who appropriate this idea and those who oppose it often incorrectly project modern dualisms on the ancient Goddess. The dualisms of nature/civilization, sexuality/spirituality, nurturance/dominance, immanence/transcendence, femininity/masculinity are taken for granted, and the Goddess is espoused or repudiated as representative of nature, sexuality, nurturance, immanence, and the feminine. The result is the creation of a Goddess religion that is the reverse of patriarchal religion.[5]

When we look at the images of the Goddess in her various forms in the ancient texts (2800–1200 B.C.), we discover a world whose dialectics do not fall into such dualisms. Specifically, the concept of gender complementarity is absent from the ancient myths. The Goddess and God are equivalent, not complementary, images of the divine. Psalms addressed to Ishtar do not address her as the embodiment of maternal, nurturing, and feminine characteristics, but as the expression of divine sovereignty and power in female form.[6] Sexual potency and social power are found in both the Goddess and the God. There are tensions that define ancient religion — especially between chaos and cosmos, death and life — but divine forces, male and female, are ranged on both sides of the dichotomies. Gender division is not yet the primary metaphor for imaging the dialectics of human existence. It is precisely this aspect of the religious world of the ancient Near East that provides the most striking alternative to the symbolic world generated by male monotheism.

MALE MONOTHEISM AND THE DUALIZING OF GENDER METAPHORS

Male monotheism has been so taken for granted in Judeo-Christian culture that the peculiarity of imaging God solely through one gender has not been recognized. But such an image indicates a sharp departure from all previous human consciousness. It is possible that the social origins of male monotheism lie in nomadic herding societies. These cultures lacked the female gardening role[7] and tended to image God as the Sky-Father.[8] Nomadic religions were characterized by exclusivism and an aggressive, hostile relationship to the agricultural people of the land and their religions.

Male monotheism reinforces the social hierarchy of patriarchal rule through its religious system in a way that was not the case with the paired images of God and Goddess. God is modeled after the patriarchal ruling class and is seen as addressing this class of males directly, adopting them as his "sons." They are his representatives, the responsible partners of the covenant with him. Women as wives now become symbolically repressed as the dependent servant class. Wives, along with children and servants, represent those ruled over and owned by the patriarchal class. They relate to man as he relates to God. A symbolic hierarchy is set up: God-male-female. Women no longer stand in direct relation to God; they are connected to God secondarily, through the male. This hierarchical order is evident in the structure of patriarchal law in the Old Testament, in which only the male heads of families are addressed directly. Women, children, and servants are referred to indirectly through their duties and property relations to the patriarch.[9] In the New Testament this hierarchical "order" appears as a cosmic principle:

> But I want to understand that the head of every man is Christ, the head of a woman is her husband, and the head of Christ is God...For a man ought not to cover his head, since he is the image and glory of God, but the woman is the glory of man. (1 Cor. 11:3, 7)

Male monotheism becomes the vehicle of a psychocultural revolution of the male ruling class in its relationship to surrounding reality. Whereas ancient myth had seen the Gods and Goddesses as within the matrix of one physical-spiritual reality, male monotheism begins to split reality into a dualism of transcendent Spirit (mind, ego) and inferior and dependent physical nature. Bodiless ego or spirit is seen as primary, existing before the cosmos. The physical world is "made" as an artifact by transcendent, disembodied mind or generated through some process of devolution from spirit to matter.

Both the Hebrew Genesis story and the Platonic creation story of *Timaeus* retain reminiscences of the idea of primal matter as something already existing that is ordered or shaped by the Creator God. But this now becomes the lower pole in the hierarchy of being. Thus the hierarchy of God-male-female does not merely make woman secondary in relation to God, it also gives her a negative identity in relation to the divine. Whereas the male is seen essentially as the image of the male transcendent ego or God, woman is seen as the image of the lower, material nature. Although both are seen as "mixed natures," the male identity points "above" and the female "below." Gender becomes a primary symbol for the dualism of transcendence and immanence, spirit and matter.

THE APPROPRIATION OF THE GODDESS IN JEWISH AND CHRISTIAN MONOTHEISM

In Hebrew religious development, male monotheism does not, by any means, succeed in simply supplanting the older world of Gods and Goddesses or the cult of salvation through renewal of nature-society. Rather it imposes itself on this older world, assimilating, transforming, and reversing its symbol systems. Thus, for example, the ancient myth of the Sacred Marriage lives on in Yahwism, but in a reversed form that uses this story to exert the possessive and judgmental relation of the patriarchal God over the people of agricultural society. The patriarchal

God, not the Goddess, is the dominant partner in the Sacred Marriage. The female has been reduced to the human partner as servant to God. In the prophet Hosea, the marriage symbol is taken over judgmentally as a diatribe against the "harlotry" of Israelites, who prefer Baal, the vegetation and rain God of the Canaanites, to Yahweh, the nomadic patriarch. Yahweh is depicted as the angry and threatening husband who will punish his unfaithful bride with summary divorce.

But he is also described as winning her back and making her faithful to him by drawing her out into the desert wildness. It becomes evident that one of the issues underlying this struggle between Yahweh and Baal is an uncertainty on the part of the people of the land concerning Yahweh's competence in agricultural matters. They turn to Baal because they regard him as the source of agricultural prosperity. Yahweh must thunder that he, not Baal, is the source of these benefits:

> Plead with your mother, plead — for she is not my wife and I am not her husband — that she put away her harlotry from her face, and her adultery from between her breasts, lest I strip her naked and make her as in the day that she was born, and make her like a wilderness, and set her like a parched land and slay her with thirst...
>
> Then she shall say, "I will go and return to my first husband for it was better with me then than now." And she did not know that it was I that gave her the grain, the wine and the oil, and who lavished upon her silver and gold which they used for Baal...
>
> Therefore, behold, I will allure her and bring her into the wilderness and speak tenderly to her, and there I will give her her vineyards...and there she will answer as in the days of her youth, as at the time when she came out of the land of Egypt. And in that day, says the Lord, you will call me "My Husband" and no longer will you call me "My Baal"...(Hos. 2:2–3, 7–8, 14–16)

From archaeological evidence we know that Yahweh did not replace the Goddess in the affections of many people conquered or assimilated by the Israelites. Rather, for many people, Yahweh simply replaced Baal as the husband of the Goddess. Asherah, another form of the Canaanite Goddess, continued to be worshiped alongside Yahweh in the Solomonic temple for two-thirds of its existence.[10] Ordinary graves of Israelites show Yahwist and Goddess symbols together. The upper Egyptian Jewish colony at Elephantine worshiped Yahweh as husband of the Goddess in its temple.[11] Thus, behind the apparent conquest of Yahweh over Anath-Baal lies a more complex reality. It is not insignificant that most of the polemics against Canaanite religion in the Old Testament are against Baal, not Anath or Asherah. Yahweh does not do warfare primarily against the Goddess. Rather it is Baal, her male consort, who must be replaced. The Goddess is not so much eliminated as she is absorbed and put into a new relationship with Yahweh as her Lord.

In addition to this transformation of the Sacred Marriage from a Goddess-king relation into a patriarchal God–servant wife, Yahwism appropriates female images for God at certain points. The male patriarchal image proves too limited to represent the variety of relationships to Israel that Hebrew thought wished to express. In certain texts Yahweh is described as like a mother or like a woman in travail with the birth of a child. These references occur particularly when the authors wish to describe God's unconditional love and faithfulness to the people despite their sins. They express God's compassion and forgiveness. God is seen as suffering on behalf of Israel, seeking to bring Israel to the new birth of repentance. As Phyllis Trible has pointed out, the root word for the ideas of compassion and mercy in Hebrew is *rechem,* or womb.[12] In ascribing these qualities to Yahweh, Hebrew thought suggests that God has maternal or "womblike" qualities.

The mixture of male and female imagery for God is strikingly illustrated in Isaiah:

> The Lord goes forth like a might man,
> like a man of war he stirs up his fury,

he cries out, he shouts aloud,
he shows himself mighty against his foes,

For a long time I have held my peace,
I have kept still and restrained myself,
Now I will cry out like a woman in travail,
I will gasp and pant...

These things I will do and I will not forsake them,
They shall be turned back and utterly put to shame,
who trust in graven things... (Isa. 42:13-14, 16-17)

In addition to these appropriations of womb-qualities to Yahweh, there is a second important use of female imagery for God in the Scriptural and theological tradition. In the Wisdom tradition the female image appears as a secondary persona of God, mediating the work and will of God to creation. The Book of Proverbs describes Wisdom as an offspring of God, being brought forth from God before the beginning of the earth, cooperating with God in the creation of the world, rejoicing and delighting in the work of creation. In the Wisdom of Solomon, Wisdom is the manifestation of God through whom God mediates the work of creation, providential guidance, and revelation. She is the subtle power of the presence of God, permeating and enspiriting all things:

For she is the breath of the power of God
and pure emanation of his almighty glory;
Therefore nothing defiled can enter into her,
For she is the reflection of the everlasting light,
and a spotless mirror of the activity of God
and a likeness of his goodness. (Wis. of Sol. 7:25-26)

The wise man, represented by Solomon, takes Wisdom as his bride and brings her to live with him so she can give him good counsel (8:2, 9). Behind this powerful image of Wisdom lies the Goddess who was traditionally characterized as Wisdom. But in Hebrew thought she has become a dependent attribute or expression of the transcendent male God rather than an autonomous, female manifestation of the divine.

In Christianity the idea of a second persona of God expressing God's immanence, the presence of God in creation, revelation, and redemption, was taken over to explain the divine identity of Jesus. While the passages in Hebrews, chapters 1 and 2, and elsewhere in the New Testament echo the Wisdom tradition, the word *Logos* (word) used by the Jewish philosopher Philo is preferred to *Sophia* (wisdom). The roots of the *Logos* concept in the Wisdom tradition are evident at many points. Paul says, "We are preaching a crucified Christ...who is...the Wisdom of God" (1 Cor. 1:23–24). Several of the Christological hymns substitute the word *Logos* for the word *Sophia.* Theologically, *Logos* plays the same cosmological roles as *Sophia* as ground of creation, revealer of the mind of God, and reconciler of humanity to God. But the use of the male word *Logos,* when identified with the maleness of the historical Jesus, obscures the actual fluidity of the gender symbolism by appearing to reify as male a "Son of God" who is, in turn, the image of the Father.

Reminiscences of a male-female *pleroma* (community of persons in the divine) do not vanish from Judaism, especially mystical Judaism. Although the *Sophia* image is no longer used in Rabbinic Judaism, possibly because of its use in Gnosticism, the *Shekinah* (presence) becomes the new image of God's mediating presence in female form. The *Shekinah* not only mediates God's will to Israel but also reconciles Israel with God. In Rabbinic mystical speculation on the *Galut* (exile), the *Shekinah* is seen as going into exile with Israel when God-as-Father has turned away his face in anger. The exile is an alienation or division within God, between his transcendence and his immanence, or his male and female sides. Each Shabbat celebration is a sign of the connubial embrace of God with his *Shekinah,* or bride, anticipating the final reconciliation of God with Israel (creation) in the messianic age. God becomes whole, uniting male and female side, in the time when all things become one and God is "all in all."[13]

In Christianity, all speculation on a female side of God was not cut off despite the adoption of a male *Logos* symbol. The figure of the Holy Spirit picks up many of the Hebraic traditions of the female *Sophia* and *Hokmah* (spirit). Many early Christian texts refer to the Spirit as female. This is found particularly in the Apocryphal gospels. In the Gospel of the Hebrews it is said,

> Even so did my mother, the Holy Spirit, take me by one of my hairs and carry me away onto the great mountain Thabor.[14]

In the Acts of Thomas, a baptism in the triune name is followed by a Eucharist in which the *epiclesis,* the bringing down of the Spirit on the gifts, uses female language:

> Bread of life...we name over thee the name of the mother of the ineffable mystery of the hidden dominions and powers; we name over thee the name of Jesus.[15]

The Gospel of Philip even denies that the Holy Spirit impregnated the womb of Mary on the grounds that the Spirit is female:

> Some said: "Mary conceived by the Holy Spirit." They are in error. They do not know what they are saying. When did a woman ever conceive by a woman?[16]

Such female imagery for the Spirit is found in orthodox writers as well. Clement of Alexandria and the Syriac father Aphraates use female imagery for the Spirit, as does the third-century Church order the *Didascalia.*[17] Such language seems to have survived longer in the Syriac Church.

We cannot conclude that female imagery for the Spirit is a later "deviation" of heretical Christianity. Rather, we should see an earlier Christianity, which used such female imagery, gradually being marginalized by a victorious Greco-Roman Christianity that repressed it. Gnosticism continued the imagery for God as female and greatly expanded it; but in doing so it expanded on traditions once widely shared by Christians.

In Gnostic texts, such as the Trimorphic Protenoia, the triune

God is imaged as Father-Mother and Son. The fluidity of the imagery is such that sometimes the Father is called androgynous and at other times Father, Mother, and Son are seen as emerging from a primordial womb of silence. Valentinian Gnosticism based its God-language on male-female pairs of Aeons, ending in the Aeon Sophia, who is seen as playing the role of a cosmic Eve who causes the divine pleroma to fall. She is also the means through which revelation of the higher world and reconciliation with the divine is brought about.[18]

Female imagery for the Spirit continues to ferment under the surface of Christian theology, particularly in mystical writers. Traces of it are also found in Christian iconography. In a fourteenth-century fresco in a church near Munich, the Trinity is portrayed as three figures that emerge from a common stem, with a female Spirit between the older male person of the Father and the younger male person of Christ.[19] Reformation mystical thinkers also take up themes of the female aspect of God. Such language may have been revived through contact with Jewish Kabbalah. A whole line of mystical thinkers, flowing from Jacob Boehme in the seventeenth century down into the nineteenth century, speculate on the androgynous nature of God. The eighteenth-century Shakers develop this concept in detail in new scriptures and a new vision of Christian messianism that includes a female Messiah who represents the Wisdom or Mother-aspect of God.[20]

Do these traditions of the androgyny of God and the female aspect of the Trinity resolve the problem of the exclusively male image of God? Some Christian feminists feel they do. God has both mothering or feminine as well as masculine characteristics. The feminine aspect of God is to be identified particularly with the Holy Spirit. It is doubtful, however, that we should settle for a concept of the Trinity that consists of two male and one female "persons." Such a concept of God falls easily into an androcentric or male-dominant perspective. The female side of God then becomes a subordinate principle underneath the dominant image of male divine sovereignty.

We should guard against concepts of divine androgyny that simply ratify on the divine level the patriarchal split of the masculine and the feminine. In such a concept, the feminine side of God, as a secondary or mediating principle, would act in the same subordinate and limited roles in which females are allowed to act in the patriarchal social order. The feminine can be mediator or recipient of divine power in relation to creaturely reality. She can be God's daughter, the bride of the (male) soul. But she can never represent divine transcendence in all fullness. For feminists to appropriate the "feminine" side of God within this patriarchal gender hierarchy is simply to reinforce the problem of gender stereotyping on the level of God-language. We need to go beyond the idea of a "feminine side" of God, whether to be identified with the Spirit or even with the *Sophia*-Spirit together, and question the assumption that the highest symbol of divine sovereignty still remains exclusively male.

GOD-LANGUAGE BEYOND PATRIARCHY IN THE BIBLICAL TRADITION

The Prophetic God

Although the predominantly male images and roles of God make Yahwism an agent in the sacralization of patriarchy, there are critical elements in Biblical theology that contradict this view of God. By patriarchy we mean not only the subordination of females to males, but the whole structure of Father-ruled society: aristocracy over serfs, masters over slaves, king over subjects, racial overlords over colonized people. Religions that reinforce hierarchical stratification use the Divine as the apex of this system of privilege and control. The religions of the ancient Near East link the Gods and Goddesses with the kings and queens, the priests and priestesses, the warrior and temple aristocracy of a stratified society. The Gods and Goddesses mirror this ruling class and form its heavenly counterpart. The divinities also show mercy and favor to the distressed, but in the manner of noblesse oblige.

Yahweh, as tribal God of Israel, shows many characteristics similar to those of the Near Eastern deities, as mighty king, warrior, and one who shows mercy and vindicates justice. But these characteristics are put in a new and distinct context: Yahweh is unique as the God of a tribal confederation that identifies itself as liberated slaves. The basic identity of Yahweh as God of this confederation lies in "his" historical action as the divine power that liberated these slaves from bondage and led them to a new land. This confederation is not an ethnic people, but a bonding of groups of distinct backgrounds. A core group experienced the escape from bondage in Egypt that formed the primary identity of Israel. They were joined by nomadic groups from the desert and hill peoples in Canaan in revolt against the feudal power of the city-states of the plains. Norman Gottwald reconstructs the premonarchical formation of this tribal confederation (1250–1050 B.C.). The identification of Yahweh with liberation from bondage allowed this diverse group to unite in a new egalitarian society and to revolt against the stratified feudal society of the city-states that oppressed the peasant peoples of the hills with taxes and forced labor.[21]

The Davidic monarchy represents a capitulation of Judaic leadership to the city-state model of power, but the prophets of Israel continue the tradition of protest against the hierarchical, urban, landowning society that deprives and oppresses the rural peasantry. This established at the heart of Biblical religion a motif of protest against the status quo of ruling-class privilege and the deprivation of the poor. God is seen as a critic of this society, a champion of the social victims. Salvation is envisioned as deliverance from systems of social oppression and as restoration of an egalitarian peasant society of equals, "where each have their own vine and fig tree and none need be afraid" (Mic. 4:4).

Although Yahwism dissents against class hierarchy, it issues no similar protest against gender discrimination. There are several reasons (not to be seen as "excuses") for this. First, there is always a sociology of knowledge in social ideology, even in liberation ideology. Those male prophets who were aware of oppression by rich urbanites or dominating empires were not similarly conscious of their own oppression of dependents — women and slaves — in the patriarchal family. Only the emergence of women conscious of their oppression could have applied the categories of protest to women. This did not happen in Yahwism. Second, although Hebrew religion was to shape systems of patriarchal law that emphasize gender dualism and hierarchy, in its protest against Canaanite urban society it would have known powerful females, queens, priestesses, and wealthy landowners who functioned as oppressors. It would have been difficult to recognize women as an oppressed gender group when the primary social stratification integrated some women into roles of power. Indeed, perhaps it was not until the early modern period that the perception of women as marginalized by gender became stronger than the perception of women as divided by class. Only then could a feminist movement arise that protested the subjugation of women as a group.

The New Testament contains a renewal and radicalization of prophetic consciousness, now applied to marginalized groups in a universal, nontribal context. Consequently, it is possible to recognize as liberated by God social groups overlooked in Old Testament prophecy. Class, ethnicity, and gender are now specifically singled out as the divisions overcome by redemption in Christ. In the New Testament stories, gender is recognized as an additional oppression within oppressed classes and ethnic groups.[22] Women, the doubly oppressed within marginalized groups, manifest God's iconoclastic, liberating action in making "the last first and the first last." All women are not doubly oppressed; there are also queens and wealthy women. But women's experience of oppression has begun to become visible and to be addressed by prophetic consciousness (very likely because of the participation of women in the early Christian movement).

The Liberating Sovereign

A second antipatriarchal use of God-language occurs in the Old and New Testaments when divine sovereignty and fatherhood are used to break the ties of bondage under human kings and fathers. Abraham is called into an adoptive or covenanted relation with God only by breaking his ties with his family, leaving behind the graves of his ancestors.[23] The God of Exodus establishes a relationship with the people that breaks their ties with the ruling overlords. As the people flee from the land of bondage, Pharaoh and his horsemen are drowned. God's kingship liberates Israel from human kings. The antimonarchical tradition inveighs against Israel's capitulation to the customs of the surrounding people by adopting kingship.

These Old Testament traditions are developed in Jesus' teaching. It has been often pointed out that Jesus uses a unique word for God. By adopting the word *Abba* for God, he affirms a primary relationship to God based on love and trust; *Abba* was the intimate word used by children in the family for their fathers. It is not fully conveyed by English terms such as *Daddy,* for it was also a term an adult could use of an older man to signify a combination of respect and affection.[24] But is it enough to conclude from this use of *Abba* that Jesus transforms the patriarchal concept of divine fatherhood into what might be called a maternal or nurturing concept of God as loving, trustworthy parent?

The early Jesus movement characteristically uses this concept of God as *Abba* to liberate the community from human dominance-dependence relationships based on kinship ties or master-servant relationships. In the Gospel tradition, joining the new community of Jesus creates a rupture with traditional family ties and loyalties. In order to follow Jesus one must "hate" (that is, put aside one's loyalty to) father and mother,

sisters and brothers (Luke 14:26; Matt. 10:37-38). The patriarchal family is replaced by a new community of brothers and
sisters (Matt. 12:46-50; Mark 3:31-35; Luke 8:19-21). This
new community is a community of equals, not of master and
servants, father and children. Matthew 23:1-10 states that the
relationship to God as *Abba* abolishes all father-child, master-
servant relations between people within the Jesus community:
"You are to call no man father, master or Lord." The relationship between Christians is to be one of mutual service and not
of mastery and servitude. At the end of the Gospel of John,
Jesus tells the disciples that their relationship has now become
one of equals. They now have the same *Abba* relation to God
as he does and can act out of the same principles: "No longer
do I call you servants,... but I have called you friends" (John
15:15). These traditions reverse the symbolic relation between
divine fatherhood and sovereignty and the sacralization of
patriarchy. Because God is our king, we need obey no human
kings. Because God is our parent, we are liberated from dependence on patriarchal authority.

But the language used in this tradition creates an obvious
ambivalence. It works to establish a new liberated relationship
to a new community of equals for those in revolt against established authorities. This is true not only in the formation of
Israel and in the rise of the Jesus movement; again and again
throughout Christian history this antipatriarchal use of God-
language has been rediscovered by dissenting groups. The call
to "obey God rather than men" has perhaps been the most
continuous theological basis for dissent in the Christian tradition. Throughout Christian history women discovered this
concept of direct relation to God as a way to affirm their own
authority and autonomy against patriarchal authority. God's
call to them to preach, to teach, to form a new community
where women's gifts were fully actualized overruled the
patriarchal authority that told them to remain at home as
dutiful daughters or wives.[25]

But once the new community becomes a part of the dominant

society, God as father and king can be assimilated back into the traditional patriarchal relationships and used to sacralize the authority of human lordship and patriarchy. The radical meaning of *Abba* for God is lost in translation and interpretation. Instead, a host of new ecclesiastical and imperial "holy fathers" arises, claiming the fatherhood and kingship of God as the basis of their power over others. In order to preserve the prophetic social relationships, we need to find a new language that cannot be as easily co-opted by the systems of domination.

The Proscription of Idolatry

A third Biblical tradition that is important to a feminist theology is the proscription of idolatry. Israel is to make no picture or graven image of God; no pictorial or verbal representation of God can be taken literally. By contrast, Christian sculpture and painting represents God as a powerful old man with a white beard, even crowned and robed in the insignia of human kings or the triple tiara of the Pope. The message created by such images is that God is both similar to and represented by the patriarchal leadership, the monarchs and the Pope. Such imaging of God should be judged for what it is — as idolatry, as the setting up of certain human figures as the privileged images and representations of God. To the extent that such political and ecclesiastical patriarchy incarnates unjust and oppressive relationships, such images of God become sanctions of evil.

The proscription of idolatry must also be extended to verbal pictures. When the word *Father* is taken literally to mean that God is male and not female, represented by males and not females, then this word becomes idolatrous. The Israelite tradition is circumspect about the verbal image, printing it without vowel signs. The revelation to Moses in the burning bush gives as the name of God only the enigmatic "I am what I shall be." God is person without being imaged by existing social roles. God's being is open-ended, pointing both to what is and to what can be.

Classical Christian theology teaches that all names for God are analogies. The tradition of negative or *apophatic* theology emphasizes the unlikeness between God and human words for God. That tradition corrects the tendency to take verbal images literally; God is like but also unlike any verbal analogy. Does this not mean that male words for God are not in any way superior to or more appropriate than female analogies? God is both male and female and neither male nor female. One needs inclusive language for God that draws on the images and experiences of both genders. This inclusiveness should not become more abstract. Abstractions often conceal androcentric assumptions and prevent the shattering of the male monopoly on God-language, as in "God is not male. He is Spirit." Inclusiveness can happen only by naming God/ess in female as well as male metaphors.

Equivalent Images for God as Male and Female

Are there any Biblical examples of such naming of God/ess in female as well as male metaphors that are truly equivalent images, that is, not "feminine" aspects of a male God? The synoptic Gospels offer some examples of this in the parallel parables, which seem to have been shaped in the early Christian catechetical community. They reflect the innovation of the early Christian movement of including women equally in those called to study the Torah of Jesus. Jesus justifies this practice in the Mary-Martha story, where he defends Mary's right to study in the circle of disciples around Rabbi Jesus in the words "Mary has chosen the better part which shall not be taken from her" (Luke 10:38–42).

In the parables of the mustard seed and the leaven the explosive power of the Kingdom, which God, through Jesus, is sowing in history through small signs and deeds, is compared to a farmer sowing the tiny mustard seed that produces a great tree or a woman folding the tiny bit of leaven in three measures of flour which then causes the whole to rise (Luke 13:18–21; Matt. 13:31–33). The parables of the lost sheep and the lost coin portray God seeking the sinners despised by the "righteous" of Israel. God is compared to a shepherd who leaves his ninety-nine sheep to seek the one that is lost or to a woman with ten coins who loses one and sweeps her house diligently until she finds it. Having found it, she rejoices and throws a party for her friends. This rejoicing is compared to God's rejoicing with the angels in heaven over the repentance of one sinner (Luke 15:1–10).

These metaphors for divine activity are so humble that their significance has been easily overlooked in exegesis, but we should note several important points. First, the images of male and female in these parables are equivalent. They both stand for the same things, as paired images. One is in no way inferior to the other. Second, the images are not drawn from the social roles of the mighty, but from the activities of Galilean peasants. It might be objected that the roles of the women are stereotypical and enforce the concept of woman as housekeeper. But it is interesting that the women are never described as related to or dependent on men. The small treasure of the old woman is her own. Presumably she is an independent householder. Finally, and most significantly, the parallel male and female images do not picture divine action in parental terms. The old woman seeking the lost coin and the woman leavening the flour image God not as mother or father (Creator), but as seeker of the lost and transformer of history (Redeemer).

TOWARD A FEMINIST UNDERSTANDING OF GOD/ESS

The four preceding Biblical traditions may not be adequate for a feminist reconstruction of God/ess, but they are suggestive. If all language for God/ess is analogy, if taking a particular human image literally is idolatry, then male language for the divine must lose its privileged place. If God/ess is not the creator and validator of the existing hierarchical social order, but rather the one who liberates us from it, who opens up a new community of equals, then language about God/ess drawn from kingship and hierarchical power must lose its privileged place. Images of God/ess must include female roles and experience. Images of God/ess must be drawn from the activities of peasants and working people, people at the bottom of society. Most of all, images of God/ess must be transformative, pointing us back to our authentic potential and forward to new redeemed possibilities. God/ess-language cannot validate roles of men or women in stereotypic ways that justify male dominance and female subordination. Adding an image of God/ess as loving, nurturing mother, mediating the power of the strong, sovereign father, is insufficient.

Feminists must question the overreliance of Christianity, especially modern bourgeois Christianity, on the model of God/ess as parent. Obviously any symbol of God/ess as parent should include mother as well as father. Mary Baker Eddy's inclusive term, *Mother-Father God,* already did this one hundred years ago. Mother-Father God has the virtue of concreteness, evoking both parental images rather than moving to an abstraction (Parent), which loses effective resonance. Mother and father image God/ess as creator, as the source of our being. They point back from our own historical existence to those upon whom our existence depends. Parents are a symbol of roots, the sense of being grounded in the universe in those who have gone before, who underlie our own existence.

But the parent model for the divine has negative resonance as well. It suggests a kind of permanent parent-child relationship to God. God becomes a neurotic parent who does not want us to grow up. To become autonomous and responsible for our own lives is the gravest sin against God. Patriarchal theology uses the parent image for God to prolong spiritual infantilism as virtue and to make autonomy and assertion of free will a sin. Parenting in patriarchal society also becomes the way of enculturating us to the stereotypic male and female roles. The family becomes the nucleus and model of patriarchal relations in society. To that extent parenting language for God reinforces patriarchal power rather than liberating us from it. We need to start with language for the Divine as redeemer, as liberator, as one who fosters full personhood and, in that context, speak of God/ess as creator, as source of being.

Patriarchal theologies of "hope" or liberation affirm the God of Exodus, the God who uproots us from present historical systems and puts us on the road to new possibilities. But they typically do this in negation of God/ess as Matrix, as source and ground of our being. They make the fundamental mistake of identifying the ground of creation with the foundations of existing social systems. Being, matter, and nature become the ontocratic base for the evil system of what is. Liberation is liberation out of or against nature into spirit. The identification of matter, nature, and being with mother makes such patriarchal theology hostile to women as symbols of all that "drags us down" from freedom. The hostility of males to any symbol of God/ess as female is rooted in this identification of mother with the negation of liberated spirit. God/ess as Matrix is thought of as "static" immanence. A static, devouring, death-dealing matter is imaged, with horror, as extinguishing the free flight of transcendent consciousness. The dualism of nature and transcendence, matter and spirit as female against male is basic to male theology.

Feminist theology must fundamentally reject this dualism of nature and spirit. It must reject both sides of the dualism: both the image of mother-matter-matrix as "static immanence" and as the ontological foundation of existing, oppressive social systems and also the concept of spirit and transcendence as rootless, antinatural, originating in an "other world" beyond the cosmos, ever repudiating and fleeing from nature, body, and the visible world. Feminist theology needs to affirm the God of Exodus, of liberation and new being, but as rooted in the foundations of being rather than as its antithesis. The

God/ess who is the foundation (at one and the same time) of our being and our new being embraces both the roots of the material substratum of our existence (matter) and also the endlessly new creative potential (spirit). The God/ess who is the foundation of our being–new being does not lead us back to a stifled, dependent self or uproot us in a spirit-trip outside the earth. Rather it leads us to the converted center, the harmonization of self and body, self and other, self and world. It is the *Shalom* of our being.

God/ess as once and future *Shalom* of being, however, is *not* the creator, founder, or sanctioner of patriarchal-hierarchical society. This world arises in revolt against God/ess and in alienation from nature. It erects a false system of alienated dualisms modeled on its distorted and oppressive social relationships. God/ess liberates us from this false and alienated world, not by an endless continuation of the same trajectory of alienation but as a constant breakthrough that points us to new possibilities that are, at the same time, the regrounding of ourselves in the primordial matrix, the original harmony. The liberating encounter with God/ess is always an encounter with our authentic selves resurrected from underneath the alienated self. It is not experienced against, but in and through relationships, healing our broken relations with our bodies, with other people, with nature. We have no adequate name for the true God/ess, the "I am who I shall become." Intimations of Her/His name will appear as we emerge from false naming of God/ess modeled on patriarchal alienation.

Chapter 3
Woman, Body, and Nature: Sexism and the Theology of Creation

ROOTS OF DOMINATION

In her well-known article "Is Female to Male as Nature Is to Culture?"[1] Sherry Ortner postulates a universal devaluation of women based on a cultural assumption of the hierarchy of culture (the sphere of human control) over nature (spontaneous processes that humans don't originate or control but are dependent on). Women are symbolized as "closer to nature" than men and thus fall in an intermediate position between culture as the male sphere and uncontrolled nature. This is due both to woman's physiological investment in the biological processes that reproduce the species rather than in processes that enhance her as an individual and to the ability of male collective power to extend women's physiological role into social roles confined to child nurture and domestic labor. Female physiological processes are viewed as dangerous and polluting to higher (male) culture. Her social roles are regarded as inferior to those of males, falling lower on the nature-culture hierarchy.

This is a book of theological reflections on such symbolic structures, not a book on anthropological history. So there will be no attempt to ask how this structure "happened," even if it were possible to answer that question with any completeness. But it is important to lay out several key elements in male-female relations that contribute to the devaluation of women in the analogy of devalued nature. Ultimately we have to ask why nature itself comes to be seen as devalued and inferior to the human. We cannot criticize the hierarchy of male over female without ultimately criticizing and overcoming the hierarchy of humans over nature.

One important influence on male consciousness toward women and nature must be seen in the male puberty rite that uproots the male from the female context of early socialization and forcibly identifies the pubescent male with the male community and its roles and functions. This happens in matri-lineal-matrifocal societies as well as in patriarchal societies.[2] It is inherent in the extension of the female childbearing role into early childrearing and in the segregation of the sexes into parallel communities that play complementary roles. The mother's world thus becomes the settled domestic circle of childbearing, lactation, early child nurture, the transformation of the raw into the cooked, the making of domestic implements, and so on. Female social mobility is thereby restricted. Women work in groups gathering food, hunting small animals, and transforming these products, as well as those of male hunting, into food, clothes, and artifacts for the whole society. All this is a formidable work of culture, of the human transformation of natural processes. How, then, does it come to be defined as inferior because it is "closer to nature"?

Males' ability to define woman's realm as inferior depends on the success of male hunting and warfare in becoming the link for the domestic units of society. Males then become the lawmakers, ritualists, and cultural definers of society. The male puberty rite brings male socialization out of the mother's into the father's sphere and defines the process hierarchically. In the words and rituals of the male puberty rite, the female sphere, which has heretofore been the primal matrix and encompassing world of the male child, becomes devalued and repudiated. Unlike the female, who goes through puberty as initiation back into the mother's world on an adult level, the male must become an adult through a psychocultural revolution. This accounts in part for the much more violent character of male puberty rites than of female puberty rites.

Myths of the overthrow of original matriarchy have their locus in male puberty rites. Older males tell the boys, who are being uprooted from the female into the male sphere, the fearful tales of how women once controlled the instruments of culture but were defeated by men. Men now control the symbols of cultural power (sacred flutes or holy bundles). Women must not touch them under pain of extreme retribution.[3] The young male is taught to identify with the male sphere as higher than the female sphere, the place of an earlier, lower self that he has now "transcended."

The establishment of this relationship between male and female spheres depends not only on males as definers of culture but also on the burdening of women with most of the tedious, day-to-day tasks of economic production. Males become a leisure class with relatively little to do but decorate themselves, sharpen their weapons, and prepare for the occasional great excursions of hunting and war. Confining some women to ornamental status is the luxury of a male aristocratic elite. The domination of women throughout most of human history has depended on the freeing of males for cultural control by filling women's days with most of the tasks of domestic production and reproduction.

The domination of woman's labor is essential to an understanding of the cultural metaphor of dominated nature as dominated woman. Woman's body — her reproductive processes — becomes owned by men, defined from a male point of view. Women are seen as reproducing children and producing cooked food and clothes for men. Men regard this work as beneath them and they see themselves as dominating and controlling it from above. Woman then becomes both the mediator and the symbol of the domination of "lower" material processes by "higher" cultural (male) control.

The third important structure of female inferiorization is the reduction of women to silence. The male monopoly on cultural definition makes women the object rather than the subject of that definition. Men define both male and female

spheres from the male, hierarchical point of view and restrict
or eliminate interpretations that come from the female point
of view. More highly valued cultural activities are monopolized
by men. These often have more to do with ritual and leisure
functions than with daily necessities. If women make ordinary
clothes, men may monopolize the making of festival clothes,
war bonnets, and so on. If women provide daily food, men
may monopolize festival food, barbecues, and the like. Men
occupy the sphere of freedom and confine women to the realm
of necessity. The female then comes to be seen from the male
point of view as a threatening lower "power" who seeks to
deprive him of his freedom and drag him down into the realm
of necessity. Male transcendence is defined as flight from and
warfare against the realm of the mother, the realm of body
and nature, all that limits and confines rather than being
controlled by the human (male).

THE CORRELATION OF DOMINATED
WOMAN/DOMINATED NATURE IN HEBREW
AND GREEK CULTURE

Is dominated woman/dominated nature always culturally
correlated? Sherry Ortner believes that this is a universal
cultural structure rooted in earliest human social patterns. But
she also recognizes that the cultural symbol of woman is
ambivalent and often split into opposites. Femaleness
symbolizes, on the one hand, that which is lower than male
(real humanity); it represents the devalued parts of the self and
the roles that service them. On the other hand, woman as
mother, as original source of life, primary mediator of nature
and culture, can be seen as symbol of the Divine, the encompassing powers of life and all that both supports and inspires
the human (male).

What Ortner fails to notice is that the symbol of nature is
similarly ambivalent or split. Nonhuman nature can be seen
as that which is beneath the human, the realm to be controlled,

reduced to domination, fought against as font of chaos and regression. Nature can also be seen as cosmos, as the encompassing matrix of all things, supported by or infused with divine order and harmony, within which gods and humans stand and in which they have their being.

Moreover, male culture symbolizes control over nature in ambivalent ways. The later priestly creation story of Genesis 1 may command Adam to "fill the earth and subdue it and have dominion over it," but the earlier folkloric story of Paradise (Gen. 2–3) pictures a time of dependence on a fruitful earth that gave of itself without human labor. The human effort to control and define one's own life is seen as a revolt against dependence on God, precipitated by woman and resulting in a loss of the earth as a spontaneously reproductive paradise. Work, intervention, and struggle to control nature is the curse to which man is now confined. Woman is punished for her role by being subjugated to man. Male culture compensates for the sin of intervention in nature by picturing obedience to ultimate reality as abnegation of control, as "childlike dependence" on a power that controls and defines man. (Chapter 7 discusses these ideas further.)

The correlation of femaleness with lower nature against higher order changes dramatically as we move from Babylonian to Hebrew to Greek thought. In Babylonian and Canaanite mythology both the threatening powers of chaos or primal matter and the resuscitation of the powers of life against death are symbolized by female powers (Tiamat; Ishtar-Anath). The fundamental struggle of socio-natural renewal is seen as the struggle against watery chaos to restore harmonious life-giving order (cosmos). This is a divine drama conducted on the level of Gods and kings. Ordinary humanity (male and female) are humble slaves of the Gods and Goddesses. The Divine is within, not transcendent to, the matrix of chaos-cosmos.

In Hebrew thought God has been elevated above the creation he "makes." The relation of God to creation is that of an artisan shaping an object outside himself. God sends forth his "word," which calls something into being that does not partake of his nature. Nature is no longer a womb within which Gods and humans gestate. There remain hints in the Hebrew Scriptures of the Babylonian Tiamat, the winding serpent of chaos, which God subdues in ordering the world. Unlike the later orthodox view, the God of Genesis 1 does not create "out of nothing" but conquers and orders into a cosmos the pre-existing watery chaos. But this winding serpent that God subdues and orders is symbolically neutralized; it is not explicitly female. God's spirit that subdues and orders it is transcendent to it, not its offspring. The Divine exists beyond it, symbolized as a combination of male seminal and cultural power (word-act) that shapes it from above.

In later Hebrew thought God is seen as sovereign over both cosmos and chaos. Chaos becomes an instrument of divine wrath. When humans grow rebellious, God punishes them by hurling the creation back into watery chaos at the flood, saving only a righteous remnant. The pattern is repeated in the Prophets. Human sinfulness evokes God's chastising anger, which takes the form of subjecting his people to chaos.

> For the windows of heaven are opened
> and the foundations of the earth tremble.
> The earth is utterly broken,
> the earth is rent asunder,
> the earth is violently shaken.
> The earth staggers like a drunken man,
> it sways like a hut,
> its transgression lies heavily upon it,
> and it falls, and will not rise again. (Isa. 24:18-20)

When the people repent and return to obedience to God, God will restore creation and bring it to ideal perfection in which justice and harmony reign, death is overcome, and God brings forth from the earth a feast of spontaneous abundance (Isa. 25:6-9; Joel 2:22-24; Amos 9:13). Thus the Babylonian struggle between chaos and cosmos has been transformed in

Hebrew thought into a moral, historical drama that defines the beginning and end of creation. Watery chaos is the dark background from which God rescued creation in the beginning and into which he threatens to hurl it back again as punishment for disobedience. Creation perfected into harmonious blessedness, encompassing both abundance and just distribution of the goods of creation, is the future hope toward which God points humanity as the reward of submission to him.

Women, children, and slaves are subjects of the patriarchal head of family somewhat as humanity (Israel) is wife of God, son of God, and slave of God. The human patriarch has sovereign power over them, within limits. There is not a direct correlation between women and nonhuman nature because nonhuman nature is not seen as a sphere subject directly to human (male) control. Rather it is an encompassing sphere in which God acts out wrath or reward. God's covenantal relation with humanity links the human and natural communities in one creation. Nature suffers along with humanity in the ups and downs of relationship with God.

In Greek thought a more radical dualism and alienation between male consciousness and nonhuman nature take place. Unlike Hebrew thought, Greek philosophy raises human (male) consciousness to the same transcendent status as God, outside of and above nature. Human (male) consciousness is seen as partaking of this transcendent realm of male spirit, which is the original and eternal realm of being. The visible world and bodily existence thus become objectified as an inferior realm beneath consciousness, to be subjected to its control. Primal matter is seen as recalcitrant "stuff" that resists being shaped into form through the imposition of male ideas. The mind must struggle to subdue and order this lower matter.[4]

Matter is also seen as the source of the moral devolution of mind. Mind entrapped in matter loses its "wings" and becomes subjected to moral chaos, that is, the passions. Thus the struggle to subdue and order matter ends finally not in the triumph of cosmos as final blessedness but in a flight of the mind from nature and body to a spiritual (disembodied) realm. Here it can live a blessed and congenial existence for eternity freed from the struggle against finitude, change, and death.[5]

In Greek philosophy women are symbolized as analogous to the lower realm of matter or body, to be ruled by or shunned by transcendent mind. In Aristotle's *Politics,* ruling-class Greek males are the natural exemplars of mind or reason, while women, slaves, and barbarians are the naturally servile people, represented by the body and passions, which must be ruled by the "head."[6] In *Timaeus* Plato says that when the incarnate soul loses its struggle against the passions and appetites, it is incarnated into a woman and then into "some brute which resembled him in the evil nature which he had acquired."[7] The hierarchy of spirit to physical nature as male to female is made explicit. The chain of being, God–spirits–male–female–non-human nature–matter, is at the same time the chain of command. The direction of salvation follows the trajectory of alienation of mind from its own physical support system, objectified as "body" and "matter."

THE TRAJECTORY OF ALIENATION AS SALVATION FROM NATURE

The end of the Greco-Roman world of late antiquity sees patriarchal culture exhausted in its efforts to impose its control on the recalcitrant realities of nature and society. Male consciousness turns instead to a world-fleeing spirituality as the dominant focus of energy. Late-antique culture is obsessed with the fear of mortality, of corruptibility. To be born in the flesh is already to be subject to change, which is a devolution toward decay and death. Only by extricating mind from matter by ascetic practices, aimed at severing the connections of mind and body, can one prepare for the salvific escape out of the realm of corruptibility to eternal spiritual life. All that sustains physical life — sex, eating, reproduction, even sleep — comes to be seen as sustaining the realm of "death," against which a mental realm of consciousness has been abstracted as the realm of "true life." Women, as representatives of sexual reproduction and motherhood, are the bearers of death, from which male spirit must flee to "light and life."

This flight from body and nature partly contradicts the system of social domination of women, however. Women, too, as human persons could participate in the ascetic practice of flight from body and nature. By negating their own identities as sexual beings and mothers, they might become neutral or "honorary" male spirits, equal to males in the flight to eternal life. Thus Gnosticism, the most extreme expression of cosmological dualism, sees physical nature as coming into existence through a fall. Its very nature is evil and its creators and rulers are demonic spirits. Nature ceases even to be the arena of divine sovereignty and becomes an antidivine sphere, grounded in ignorance and darkness. The true divinities and the world of life constitute a spiritual realm totally transcendent and alien to physical existence.

As symbol of the body, sexuality, and maternity, woman represents the evil lower nature. Having thrown off these roles, however, she can become male spirit "equal to the male." Moreover, the immediate source of the fall of the higher spiritual world, but also the restitution of the souls back into the spiritual world, is the divine Sophia or Wisdom, lowest being in the spiritual pleroma. Wisdom is both the death-giving mother who precipitates the world into carnal finitude and the spiritual mother who draws the fallen souls back to heaven.[8]

In orthodox Christianity the possibility of asceticism as means of spiritual equality of women was suppressed in favor of the doctrine of patriarchy as the normative order of history. Women's capacities for spiritual equality are postponed until they reach heaven and are to be earned only by the strictest subjugation to male power in Church and society. Late-medieval culture thus moves toward an increasing bifurcation of the image of woman. Spiritual femininity, symbolized by the Virgin Mary, becomes increasingly out of the reach of ordinary women. Women, even nuns, are seen primarily as sexual dangers to men, carrying in their physical beings the threat of a debased subjugation to corruptibility and death.

Particularly in clerical misogyny, woman's body is described with violent disgust as the image of decay. Her physical presence drags down the souls of men to carnal lust and thus to eternal damnation. In the writings of John Broomyard, a prominent Dominican preacher of the fourteenth century, woman is described as a painted tombstone that conceals a rotting corpse.[9] Not surprisingly, the same phobic image is also painted of nature in medieval asceticism. *Mundus,* or world, is portrayed as a haughty male demonic figure whose fine robes conceal the vermin of rotting corruption. By the thirteenth century this image of *Mundus* has been replaced on medieval cathedrals with a female figure, *Frau Welt,* or dame nature. Dame nature, from the front, has a beckoning smile and courtly attire, but from the back she is revealed to be covered with the foul, reptilian creatures of hell and the grave.[10]

Nature, to the patristic and medieval mind, lies under a curse. The fall of humanity precipitated the world into bondage. The airy realm between earth and moon is filled with demonic spirits. The devil, the prince of this realm, rules over the non-human and non-Christian world. Only through the Church, mediating grace beyond nature, nature is restored to the sovereignty of God and becomes a vehicle of grace (sacrament). But this grace, controlled by the Church and beyond the present capacities of nature, is surrounded by the demonic. To venture into realms of nature outside of Church control is to risk encounters with demons. Those who seek to probe nature's secrets do so only by making a pact with the devil.

This view is continued in Puritanism. The city set on the hill represents the elect of Zion raised to redemption through divine grace. But all around, unredeemed nature bears the face of death, sin, and the devil. To American Puritans the untamed forests of North America and the Indians that lurked in their shadows represented fallen nature inhabited by the powers of darkness.

For the late-medieval and Puritan worlds, woman, outside the control of male authority, became the embodiment of the lurking demonic power. Woman, as the cause of the fall of man and nature in the beginning, is the hidden enemy who threatens to hurl the realm of grace and salvation back into the grip of the devil. As lustful, carnal, and naturally insubordinate, woman is the likely tool of the devil in his relentless attempt to undermine God's plan of salvation. As witch, woman is the image of deceitful nature, enticing and fair without but filled with foul corruption underneath, dragging male consciousness down into the power of sin, death, and damnation. These fears of body, nature, and loss of control over the "lower orders" erupted in the fourteenth through seventeenth centuries into prolonged bouts of witch-hunting that took the lives of as many as a million people, most of them women. The old woman, her sagging breasts and wrinkled abdomen the image of the corruptible flesh of despised maternity, became the archetype of the witch as instrument of the devil.

THE MODERN RETURN TO NATURE

From the Renaissance of the sixteenth century and the scientific revolution in the seventeenth century, a revolt begins against other-worldliness and the demonization of nature. Male consciousness begins to reclaim the earth as his true home and the sphere of his control. Science exorcises the devils from nature and reclaims nature as the realm of human knowledge and use. Nature begins to be secularized; instead of the small circle of grace controlled by the Church, universal reason pervades nature, making the whole orderly, rational, and good. The rationality of the deist God, immanent in nature's laws, is analogous to human reason. Nature, therefore, is eminently knowable and controlled by "man." "Her" laws are reducible to mathematical formulas, the key to both knowledge and mastery over nature.

Scientific method abstracts "man" as knower from nature

as object of knowledge. In a new way, the male mind asserts its transcendence over nature. Nature is no longer organic body within which reason resides; it is a machine that is manufactured and run from outside by divine reason. Scientific technology raises up the dream of expanding manipulation of material nature, transforming more and more of it into artifacts of human use.[11] Soon no corner of nature, either in the depths of the psyche or in the depths of the sea, will elude human control.

Early revolutionary liberalism is wont to universalize human consciousness and to suggest that various categories of dominated people might emerge into the human realm of consciousness and of control over nature. Some consistent liberals, such as Condorcet and John Stuart Mill, even suggest that women might be emancipated into the human (male) realm. Early feminists such as Mary Wollstonecraft and the Grimké sisters base their ideas on this liberal concept of universal human consciousness and transcendence over nature.

But this universalization of the (male) human realm contradicts the socioeconomic realities of expanding technological domination of nature, purchased by increasing domination over the bodies and resources of dominated people: women and workers in industrialized countries, slaves and exploited races in the vast new lands being conquered by expanding European capitalism and colonialism. Soon the egalitarianism of early liberalism begins to be replaced by a new hierarchicalism that makes women, workers, peasants, and conquered races the image of dominated nature in contrast to the Euro-American male, the true bearer of transcendent consciousness.

The domination of nature is seen as a system of infinite expansion. The eschatological flight from the finite to the infinite has been turned on its side and converted into a doctrine of infinite progress, as both rational knowledge of and control over nature. Nature is to be impelled forward in infinite expansion of material productivity, and its limits are to be gradually conquered. Ignorance, poverty, disease, even death, will be eliminated. The kingdom of infinite blessings will be created on earth through expanding control of scientific reason over nature.

This system not only contradicts the finitude of nature but is carried out under the conditions of social domination and exploitation. In reality, the expanding prosperity of the Western elite is purchased at the expense of the impoverishment of the dominated peoples. The side effects of technology are passed along to the public in the form of pollution of soil, air, and waters. A control of disease and death that makes it impossible, at the same time, for women to control their own bodies and social roles results in rapid population expansion, especially in the colonized world. Within a brief century and a half the optimistic vision of expanding control, leading to Paradise, takes on the frightening visage of global disaster, the universal outbreak of uncontrollable pollution, famine, poverty, and warfare, which threatens the very survival of the planet.

As early as the nineteenth century, the liberal vision of expanding technological control over nature generates its own reaction in the form of romanticism. Romantics see the effort to transform more and more of nature into machine culture not as the triumph of human spirit, but as the ultimate alienation of human spirit from its own organic roots in the earth. Romantic utopians fight the efforts of capitalism to transform the preindustrial gardening and artisan cultures into industrialized agribusiness and manufacture that reduces creative work to alienated labor. They seek to restore in idealized form the communal village that would reunite family, handicrafts, and small-scale agriculture. They rediscover animistic religion, in which nonhuman nature is filled with spiritual life and one can espy dryads and nymphs in trees and brooks. To immerse oneself in nature, untamed by human hand, is to restore the soul and nurture the spirit alienated by rationality and machine culture.

Romanticism, however, is biased by its origins in alienated

white male consciousness seeking restoration of its lost ties with nature. It idealizes dominated people — women, peasants, Indians, and South Sea islanders — as bearers of unalienated nature. It thereby forbids dominated people to gain the knowledge and tools of scientific power. They are to be kept in their islands of "natural tranquility" to serve as rest and recreation places for the souls of alienated white males. The romantic project of return to nature remains aesthetic, personalistic, and escapist. Because it fails to grapple with the interconnections of social and natural domination it does not envision a real transformation of the dominant system itself into a new relationship of humans with humans, humans with nature.

TOWARD AN ECOLOGICAL-FEMINIST THEOLOGY OF NATURE

An ecological-feminist theology of nature must rethink the whole Western theological tradition of the hierarchical chain of being and chain of command. This theology must question the hierarchy of human over nonhuman nature as a relationship of ontological and moral value. It must challenge the right of the human to treat the nonhuman as private property and material wealth to be exploited. It must unmask the structures of social domination, male over female, owner over worker that mediate this domination of nonhuman nature. Finally, it must question the model of hierarchy that starts with non-material spirit (God) as the source of the chain of being and continues down to nonspiritual "matter" as the bottom of the chain of being and the most inferior, valueless, and dominated point in the chain of command.

The God/ess who is primal Matrix, the ground of being-new being, is neither stifling immanence nor rootless transcendence. Spirit and matter are not dichotomized but are the inside and outside of the same thing. When we proceed to the inward depths of consciousness or probe beneath the surface of visible things to the electromagnetic field that is the ground of atomic and molecular structure, the visible disappears. Matter itself dissolves into energy. Energy, organized in patterns and relationships, is the basis for what we experience as visible things. It becomes impossible anymore to dichotomize material and spiritual energy. Consciousness comes to be seen as the most intense and complex form of the inwardness of material energy itself as it bursts forth at that evolutionary level where matter is organized in the most complex and intensive way — the central nervous system and cortex of the human brain.

If we follow Teilhard de Chardin's interpretation of evolution, the radial energy of matter develops along the lines of increasing complexity and centralization. At certain "boiling points" of life energy, there is a critical leap to a new stage of being, from minerals to plant life, from plant life to animate life, moving through increasing stages of intelligence until the breakthrough to self-conscious intelligence.[12]

It becomes evident that one can no longer make the dichotomy between nature and history. Nature itself is historical. The universe is a great being that is born, grows, and presumably will die. Critical moments of transformation appear at stages of the universe's growth, bringing into being new possibilities. These were latent in what existed before and yet represent something new, something that could not simply be expected from the preexisting forms of being. Nature contains transcendence and freedom, as well as necessity. The change from mineral being to plant life, from plant life to animate life, and then to self-conscious intelligence is not just quantitative, but qualitative transformation. At each stage a qualitatively new dimension of life comes into being.

So far the evolutionary view of matter and radial energy in Teilhard de Chardin and others could lead simply to a new version of the chain of being. The chain of being has been laid on its side, so to speak. But this view still preserves the same presuppositions of the superiority of the "higher" over the "lower" forms and hence the domination of the "highest" form — namely, the human — over the rest solely for human self-interest. Indeed, Teilhard does not question the racist assumptions that white Western development is the privileged line of human development that has a right to control and reshape the rest of humanity.[13] This hierarchicalism of evolutionary theory has to be modified by several considerations.

We come to recognize the continuity of human consciousness with the radial energy of matter throughout the universe. Our intelligence is a special, intense form of this radial energy, but it is not without continuity with other forms; it is the self-conscious or "thinking dimension" of the radial energy of matter. We must respond to a "thou-ness" in all beings. This is not romanticism or an anthropomorphic animism that sees "dryads in trees," although there is truth in the animist view. The spirit in plants or animals is not anthropomorphic but biomorphic to its own forms of life. We respond not just as "I to it," but as "I to thou," to the spirit, the life energy that lies in every being in its own form of existence. The "brotherhood of man" needs to be widened to embrace not only women but also the whole community of life.

The more complex forms of life represent critical breakthroughs to new stages of existence that give them qualitatively more mobility and freedom for response. But they are radically dependent on all the stages of life that go before them and that continue to underlie their own existence. The plant can happily carry out its processes of photosynthesis without human beings, but we cannot exist without the photosynthesis of plants. The more complex forms of life are not the source and foundation of the less complex forms, just the opposite. An animal depends on a whole ecological community of life processes of plants, insects, other animals, water, air, and soil that underlie its existence. Still more, human beings cannot live without the whole ecological community that supports and makes possible our existence.

The privilege of intelligence, then, is not a privilege to alienate and dominate the world without concern for the welfare of all other forms of life. On the contrary, it is the responsibility to become the caretaker and cultivator of the welfare of the whole ecological community upon which our own existence depends. By what right are we the caretakers of nature when nonhuman nature takes care of its own processes very well and, in most cases, better without us? Human self-consciousness carries with it a danger that exists in no other form of creaturely life. Nonhuman creatures, to be sure, eat and are eaten by others. There is violence and bloodshed in nature, but it takes place within its own built-in balances. If one creature rapidly and drastically increases its population, it kills off its own life-support system and so dies off until it reaches a population back in balance with its ecological community.

Humans alone perpetuate their evolutionary advances primarily through cultural-social means. We don't grow our clothes on our bodies or our tools in the nails at the ends of our hands; we create these as artifacts. So we can continually change and develop them as part of our technology. More than that, we have the ability to create dysfunctional relationships with the earth, with our ecological community, and with each other and to preserve them socially. We alone can "sin." We alone can disrupt and distort the balances of nature and force the price for this distortion on less fortunate humans, as well as the nonhuman community. We cannot do this forever. Finally, the universe will create inversions, under the weight of human distortion and oppression, that will undermine the whole human life-support system. But we may be able to bring the earth down with us in our downfall. We may destroy much of the work of evolutionary development back to the most primary level of minerals and photosynthesis, and leave even this deeply poisoned against the production of life. We are the rogue elephant of nature.

Thus we have not so much the privilege of intelligence, viewed as something above and against nonhuman nature, but the responsibility and necessity to convert our intelligence to the earth. We need to learn how to use intelligence to mend the distortions we have created and how to convert intelligence into an instrument that can cultivate the harmonies and balances of the ecological community and bring these to a refinement. We can turn the desert wilderness or the jungle into the garden. But we need to do that not simply by bulldozing what is and ignoring all other needs but our own, but by understanding the integrity of the existing ecological community and learning to build our niche in that community in harmony with the rest. We do this out of a genuine recognition of our interdependence. We cannot violate the ecological community without ultimately destroying our own life-support system. The notion of dominating the universe from a position of autonomy is an illusion of alienated consciousness. We have only two real options: either to learn to use our intelligence to become *servants* of the survival and cultivation of nature or to lose our own life-support system in an increasingly poisoned earth.

This conversion of our intelligence to the earth will demand a new form of human intelligence. The dominant white Western male rationality has been based on linear, dichotomized thought patterns that divide reality into dualisms: one is good and the other bad, one superior and the other inferior, one should dominate and the other should be eliminated or suppressed. The biological base of these patterns is specialization in left-brain, rational functions in a way that suppresses the right-brain, relational sense. This one-sided brain development seems more dominant in males than in females, possibly because of later verbal development in males[14] (this issue is discussed further in chapter 4).

This biological tendency has been exaggerated by socialization into dominant and subordinate social roles. Dominant social roles exaggerate linear, dichotomized thinking and prevent the development of culture that would correct this bias by integrating the relational side. Women and other subordinate groups, moreover, have had their rational capacities suppressed through denial of education and leadership experience and so tend to be perceived as having primarily intuitive and affective patterns of thought. Thus socialization in power and powerlessness distorts integration further and creates what appears to be dichotomized personality cultures of men and women, that is, masculinity and femininity.

What we must now realize is that the patterns of rationality of left-brain specialization are, in many ways, ecologically dysfunctional. Far from this rationality being the mental counterpart of "natural law," it screens out much of reality as "irrelevant" to science and reduces scientific knowledge to a narrow spectrum fitted to dominance and control. But the systems it sets up are ecologically dysfunctional because they fail to see the larger relational patterns within which particular "facts" stand. This rationality tends toward monolithic systems of use of nature. Linear thinking, for example, directs agriculture, or even decorative planting, toward long rows of the same plant. This magnifies the plants' vulnerability to disease. Humans then compensate with chemical sprays, which in turn send a ripple effect of poisons through the whole ecological system. Nature, by contrast, diffuses and intersperses plants, so that each balances and corrects the vulnerabilities of the other. The inability to see the forest for the trees is typical of linear thinking.

Linear thinking simplifies, dichotomizes, focuses on parts, and fails to see the larger relationality and interdependence. Ecological thinking demands a different kind of rationality, one that integrates left-brain linear thought and right-brain spatial and relational thought. One has to disrupt the linear concept of order to create a different kind of order that is truly the way nature "orders," that is, balances and harmonizes, but that appears very "disorderly" to the linear, rational mind. One observes a meadow with many kinds of plants and insects balancing each other, each with their ecological niches, and then one learns to plant for human use in a way that imitates these same principles, in a more simplified and selective fashion. Converting our minds to the earth means understanding the more diffuse and relational logic of natural harmony. We learn to fit human ecology into its relation to nonhuman ecology in a way that maximizes the welfare of the whole rather than undermining and subverting (polluting) the life system.

Converting our minds to the earth cannot happen without converting our minds to each other, since the distorted and ecologically dysfunctional relationships appear necessary, yet they actually support the profits of the few against the many. There can be no ecological ethic simply as a new relation of "man" and "nature." Any ecological ethic must always take into account the structures of social domination and exploitation that mediate domination of nature and prevent concern for the welfare of the whole community in favor of the immediate advantage of the dominant class, race, and sex. An ecological ethic must always be an ethic of eco-justice that recognizes the interconnection of social domination and domination of nature.

Nonhuman nature, in this sense, is not just a "natural fact" to which we can "return" by rejecting human culture. Nature is a product not only of natural evolution but of human historical development. It partakes of the evils and distortions of human development. There is virtually no place on the planet where one can go to find "nature untouched by human hands." Even if humans have not been there before, their influence has been carried by winds, water, and soil, birds, insects, and animals who bear within their beings the poisoning effects of human rapine of the globe. Nature, in this sense, can be seen as "fallen," not that it is evil itself but in that it has been marred and distorted by human misdevelopment. The remaking of our relation with nature and with each other, then, is a historical project and struggle of re-creation.

Nature will never be the same as it would have been without human intervention. Although we need to remake the earth in a way that converts our minds to nature's logic of ecological harmony, this will necessarily be a new synthesis, a new creation in which human nature and nonhuman nature become friends in the creating of a livable and sustainable cosmos.

Chapter 4
Anthropology:
Humanity as Male and Female

Christian theological anthropology recognizes a dual structure in its understanding of humanity. This dual structure differentiates the essence from the existence of humanity. What humanity is potentially and authentically is not the same as what humanity has been historically. Historically, human nature is fallen, distorted, and sinful. Its original and authentic nature and potential have become obscured. The *imago dei,* or image of God, represents this authentic humanity united with God. It is remanifest in history as Christ to reconnect us with our original humanity. The question for feminist theology is how this theological dualism of *imago dei/*fallen Adam connects with sexual duality, or humanity as male and female.[1]

When we examine the theological tradition we see an ambiguity in the way *imago dei/*sin has been correlated with maleness and femaleness. On the one hand, deeply rooted in Christian thought is an affirmation of the equivalence of maleness and femaleness in the image of God. This has never been denied, but it has tended to become obscured by a second tendency to correlate femaleness with the lower part of human nature in a hierarchical scheme of mind over body, reason over passions. Since this lower part of the self is seen as the source of sin — the falling away of the body from its original unity with the mind and hence into sin and death — femaleness also becomes linked with the sin-prone part of the self.

This ambiguous structure of Christian anthropology expresses what today might be called a "case of projection."

Males, as the monopolizers of theological self-definition, project onto women their own rejection of their "lower selves." Women, although equivalent in the image of God, nevertheless symbolize the lower self, representing this in their physical, sexual nature. This notion that woman, in her physical, sexual nature, not only symbolizes but incarnates lower human nature and tendency to sin seldom fails to revert to the theological definition of woman's equivalence in the image of God. Woman in her essential nature is seen as having less of the higher spiritual nature and more of the lower physical nature. She is an "inferior mix" and, as such, is by nature non-normative and under subjugation.

PATRIARCHAL ANTHROPOLOGY

The patriarchal Christianity that came to dominate the Christian Church in classical orthodoxy never went so far as to completely deny women's participation in the image of God. To link woman only with the sin-prone part of the self would have been to deny her any redeemability. Christianity would have become a males-only religion to be entered by rejection of women as bearers of sin. At times, in theological definitions and, even more, in popular diatribe, Christian churchmen came perilously close to this view of woman as sin. While allowing woman baptism, patriarchal theology stressed her "greater aptness" for sin and her lesser spirituality. As an "inferior mix," woman can never as fully represent the image of God as man, who is seen as representing the rational and spiritual part of the self.

Even in the original, unfallen creation, woman would have been subordinate and under the domination of man. Normatively and ideally, the woman should have deferred to the man, who represents, in greater fullness than herself, the principle of "headship," mind or reason. He, in turn, should regard her as representing the part of himself that must be repressed and kept under control by reason to prevent a fall into sin and disorder. According to most traditional Christian theology, this would have been the case even in "paradise." Within sinful, fallen, historical conditions, however, woman's suppression must be redoubled. Proneness to sin and disorder is no longer potential but actual, and woman is particularly responsible for it. Within history, woman's subjugation is both the reflection of her inferior nature and the punishment for her responsibility for sin.

This pattern of patriarchal anthropology can be illustrated in the entire line of classical Christian theology from ancient to modern times. I mention here particularly Augustine, Aquinas, Luther, and Barth.

Augustine is the classical source of this type of patriarchal anthropology. Although elements of it are present in the New Testament and in earlier patristic theologians, Augustine expresses all aspects of it explicitly. He is, in turn, the source of this type of anthropology for the later Western Christian tradition, both Catholic and Protestant, which looks to Augustine as the font of orthodoxy. Although Augustine concedes woman's redeemability and hence her participation in the image of God, it is so overbalanced by her bodily representation of inferior, sin-prone self that he regards her as possessing the image of God only secondarily. The male alone possesses the image of God normatively. Thus in his discussion of the image of God, reflected in the Trinity, Augustine says:

> How then did the apostle tell us that man is the image of God and therefore he is forbidden to cover his head, but that the woman is not so and therefore she is commanded to cover hers? Unless forsooth according to that which I have said already, when I was treating of the nature of the human mind, that the woman, together with her own husband, is the image of God, so that the whole substance may be one image, but when she is referred to separately in her quality as a helpmeet, which regards the woman alone, then she is not the image of God, but as regards the male alone, he is the image of God as fully and completely as when the woman too is joined with him in one. (*De Trinitate* 7.7.10)

Aquinas continues the Augustinian tradition. But he makes woman's "symbolism" of the inferior side of the self literal by accepting a biological theory of woman's inferiority. Aquinas adopted the Aristotelian definition of woman as a "misbegotten male." According to Aristotelian biology, the male seed provides the "form" of the human body. Woman's reproductive role contributes only the matter that "fleshes out" this formative power of the male seed. Normatively, every male insemination would produce another male in the "image" of its father. But by some accident, this male form is sometimes subverted by the female matter and produces an inferior or defective human species, or female. This inferiority touches the entire nature of woman. She is inferior in body (weaker), inferior in mind (less capable of reason), and inferior morally (less capable of will and moral self-control).

This inferiority has been deepened by sin, according to Aquinas. But even in the original created state, woman's defective nature meant that she was by nature servile and under subjection. This creates a problem for Aquinas: why would woman have been created at all, given that God should not have created anything defective in the original plan of things? Aquinas concludes that woman, although defective and mis- begotten in her individual nature, nevertheless belongs to the overall "perfection" of nature because of her role in pro- creation. It is for this and this alone that a separate female member of the human species has been created by God; for any form of spiritual help, man is better served by a companion of the same sex than by woman.

In Aquinas' words, domination and subjugation in human relations are "twofold": In the social order that arose after sin, the ruler uses subjects for the benefit of the ruler, but even before sin there was also inequality. Males naturally excel at the higher faculty of reason; females have less rational capacity and are less capable of moral self-control. Good order requires that the naturally superior rule the naturally inferior.[2] Aquinas also believes in class hierarchy and slavery as necessary for

social order. For him these servile relations have become
necessary because of sin; but male-female hierarchy was not
just a product of sin, it was a part of the natural order created
by God.

The Reformation brought slight modifications, but no
essential change in this line of patriarchal anthropology. Luther
draws on the monastic and mystical tradition in asserting that,
in the original creation, Eve would have been equal with Adam.
Luther suggests that the original Eve cannot even be known
by reference to the present nature of woman.

> For the punishment that she is now subjected to the man was
> imposed on her after sin and because of sin, just as the other
> hardships and dangers were: travail, pain and countless other
> vexations. Therefore Eve was not like the woman of today: her
> state was far better and more excellent, and she was in no respect
> inferior to Adam, whether you count the qualities of the body
> or those of the mind.[3]

Woman, through the Fall and in punishment for the Fall,
lost her original equality and became inferior in mind and body.
She is now, within fallen history, subjected to the male as her
superior. This subjugation is not a sin against her, but her
punishment for her sin. It is the expression of divine justice.
Any revolt, or even complaint, against it by woman is a caviling
refusal to accept the judgment of God.

> This punishment too springs from original sin; and the woman
> bears it just as unwillingly as she bears those pains and
> inconveniences which have been placed upon her flesh. The rule
> remains with the husband, and the wife is compelled to obey
> him by God's command. He rules the home and the state, wages
> war, defends his possessions, tills the soil, builds, plants, etc.
> The woman, on the other hand, is like a nail driven into the
> wall. She sits at home...the wife should stay at home and look
> after the affairs of the household as one who has been deprived
> of the ability of administering those affairs that are outside and
> concern the state...In this way Eve is punished.[4]

Thus Luther's use of the doctrine of the original equality of Eve with Adam does not become a source for theological reevaluation of woman's historical subjugation. On the contrary, it simply deepens the reproach of her as one whose sinfulness lost this original equality and merited the punishment of subjugation.

The Calvinist tradition connects equivalence and subordination differently from both Luther and the earlier Catholic tradition. In Calvinism, women not only were but are equivalent with men in the image of God. In their essential nature, women have as much capacity for conscience and spiritual things as do men. The subordination of women to men is not an expression of an inferiority either in nature or in fallen history. Rather it reflects the divinely created social order by which God has ordained the rule of some and the subjugation of others: rulers over subjects, masters over servants, husbands over wives, parents over children. This hierarchical order is not a reflection of differences of human nature, but rather of differences of appointed *social office.* The man rules not because he is superior but because God has commanded him to do so. The woman obeys not because she is inferior but because that is the role God has assigned her. Social offices are necessary for good order in society.

This pattern of thought is fully explicated in the theology of Karl Barth. For Barth, this established, created order of male over female reflects the covenant of creation. God as Creator is sovereign over his Creation. The covenant of nature has not been annulled but reestablished in the covenant of grace by which Christ as head rules his people as obedient servants. Male and female, then, are necessarily ordered in a relation of those who lead and those who follow. Men and women should accept their own place in this order, the man humbly and the woman willingly. Man is not exalted thereby, nor is woman debased, but they fulfill their own place in the divinely decreed scheme of things only by accepting this proper order.[5]

The Calvinist tradition tries to turn male domination and

female subordination into a positivist, legal order of creation (the Church) and to dissociate it from notions of woman's innate inferiority or greater proneness to sin. For Calvinists, even more than for Luther, however, domination and subjugation represent the original divinely created order of things. Far from being annulled, that order is restored in fuller spiritual form in Christ. Sin, therefore, can only be a rebellion against this rightful dominance and subordination. Any effort to change this order and give woman equality with man would itself be a sinful rebellion against God's divinely enacted ordinances of creation and redemption.

EGALITARIAN ANTHROPOLOGIES

In contrast to these patriarchal anthropologies there have been, throughout the entire history of Christianity, theologies of woman's original equality with man, restored in Christ. The assertion of woman's original equality in the image of God and its restoration in Christ, however, leaves room for considerable variation in relating this equality to woman's present subjugated state in history under patriarchy. It is possible to distinguish three main typologies of egalitarian anthropology, which we call here eschatological feminism, liberal feminism, and romantic feminism.

Eschatological Feminism

Eschatological feminism is a perspective that developed parallel and even earlier than patriarchal Christianity, during the late first and second centuries. It is a way of interpreting what Elisabeth Schüssler Fiorenza has called the "egalitarian counter-cultural trend" of early Christianity. It has generally been connected with mystical ascetic sects and movements, condemned as heretical, although it has never been entirely absent from orthodox asceticism and mysticism. Remnants of it continue throughout monastic theology. It bursts forth again in Protestantism among left-wing mystical, Utopian, and millenarian sects, such as the mysticism of Jacob Boehme, the German Rappites, or the Anglo-American Shakers.

Eschatological feminism affirmed the restored equality of men and women in Christ by referring to an original transcendent anthropology that existed before the fall into the finite condition characterized by sexual dimorphism. Male and female were equal in this transcendent state. This idea takes several forms in early Christian Gnosticism. In one version original humanity was united in a spiritual androgene. Adam was both male and female, united and whole. The fall of Adam represents the splitting apart of this androgynous humanity into sexual maleness and femaleness. This also signifies the fall into mortality, finitude, and death; hence the necessity for sexual reproduction to compensate in history for the loss of immortality. Christ represents the restored androgynous Adam. He makes available to the redeemed the original lost humanity. Salvation consists of transcending our sexual, bodily nature through ascetic practices and recovering our spiritual, androgynous nature. This also signifies the escape from mortal into immortal existence. Celibacy typically is seen as the key expression of redeemed humanity that has left the world and is preparing for Heaven.

Gnosticism can easily fall into an androcentric androgyny that correlates the male part of the original androgynous humanity with spirituality and the female with carnality. In orthodox male monasticism this androcentric androgyny would then reinforce the sort of patriarchal anthropology we have discussed. But Gnosticism also suggests that there is a spiritual femaleness as well as a carnal femaleness. God is both male and female. Holy Wisdom, the female persona of God, mediates the fall into bodiliness and also the escape from creation into redeemed spiritual life. In the words of Shaker theology, "We have a Mother as well as a Father in Heaven." Redeemed humanity as male and female represents the reuniting of the self, in both its spiritual masculinity and its spiritual femininity, against the splitting into sexual maleness and sexual femaleness.

Gnosticism affirms the equality of woman with man in redeemed humanity by declaring that woman too can rise above her carnal femaleness and regain her spiritual androgyny. Unlike patriarchal orthodoxy, for Gnosticism the order of the Church should follow the order of redemption. The order of creation is the expression of fallen, sinful humanity. Men and women, equally redeemed by Christ, should be equal in the leadership of the Church. But this male and female leadership is restricted to a spiritual elite of celibate Christians who have been "fully converted" and who have adopted the angelic lifestyle of Heaven rather than the fallen sexual lifestyle of historical humanity.

Eschatological feminism implicitly agrees that the subordination of women in society is unchangeable within history. Sexuality, the division into gender, splits spiritual humanity and brings about the subordination of woman to man. Whether divinely mandated or the result of sin, patriarchy is of the nature of historical existence. Original equality restored in Christ, therefore, cannot change this historical condition, it can only free one to escape from it into a transcendent sphere.

Eschatological feminism insists on equality in the Church, for the Church belongs not to the world but to the transcendent sphere of redemption. But eschatological feminism has no message of equality of women in the world. As long as women remain in sexual and procreational relationships, they are necessarily subjugated to patriarchal domination. The message of equality in Christ does not invite women to change the world but to leave it, to adopt the redeemed lifestyle and enter the spiritual community that is preparing for the end of the world and transcendent life in Heaven.

This pattern of eschatological feminism is rediscovered and developed in the late-eighteenth- and nineteenth-century Anglo-American sect of the Shakers, for whom spiritual androgyny not only refers to the original equality of male and female in the image of God but also to the androgyny of God as Father and Mother. Christ, the restored spiritual humanity, must appear as both male and female. The Shakers, the United Society of Believers in Christ's Second Appearing, are led by equal orders of celibate men and women. They do not seek to change the larger social order but to invite the redeemed to leave the lower order of generation and move to the higher order of regeneration, "where there is neither marrying nor giving in marriage."

Two centuries earlier, Quaker theology affirmed as the true Christian message the original equality of men and women in creation and its restoration in Christ. Quakers saw this only as mandating women's equality in the Church, including women's right to preach and to govern. But in the world, including in the marriages of believers, the male was still to rule. Thus Quakerism also implicitly accepted the duality of orders of creation and redemption. Patriarchy was regarded as appropriate for the order of society. Equality could be affirmed only for the eschatological order anticipated in the Church.[6] Quakerism, however, did not accept celibacy and so partially broke with the eschatological pattern and anticipated elements of the liberal pattern.

Liberal Feminism

Liberal feminism has roots in both Biblical and scholastic anthropology, but it represents a radical remodeling of the patriarchal component of these traditions under the impact of the eighteenth-century Enlightenment. Liberalism rejects the classical tradition that identified nature or the order of creation with patriarchy. Instead it identifies nature or order of creation with the original unfallen *imago dei* and affirms the equivalence of all human beings in this original creation. All human beings, male and female, share a common human nature, characterized by reason and moral conscience. Liberalism takes a minimalist rather than an exalted view of the human nature that all human beings share equally. It is not a question of whether all people are geniuses or saints. Rather, the common possession of reason and moral conscience means simply that, as the eighteenth-century French philosopher Condorcet puts it, "that men are beings with sensibility, capable of acquiring moral ideas and of reasoning on these ideas." From this possession of a common human nature flows equal rights in society, according to Condorcet: "So women, having these same qualities, have necessarily equal rights. Either no individual of the human race has genuine rights or else all have the same; and he who votes against the right of another, whatever the religion, color or sex of that other, has henceforth abjured his own."[7]

Liberalism secularizes the doctrine of the *imago dei*. The equivalence of male and female refers to the actual capacities of men and women as finite, historical persons. Whence then comes patriarchy and the distortion of equality into domination and subjugation? Liberalism interprets this not as a fall into bodily, finite existence but as a fall into injustice. Historical injustice has distorted the original equivalence of all human beings and has created instead hierarchical societies of privilege and deprivation, domination and exploitation. The common rights of all persons to property and to participation in the government have been distorted into inherited privileges of the few based on false concepts of innate superiority. The rest of humanity — lower classes, nonwhite races, and women — have been deprived of their human rights and reduced to subjugation.

The process of redemption also is secularized. It no longer represents an escape from history and ordinary human potential into a transcendent sphere. Rather, it points to a new historical future to be achieved through social reform or revolution that overthrows the unjust order of privilege and exploitation. The equivalent human nature of all persons, while suppressed in this unjust history, is still available as a norm to guide the new reformed society. Equality of women is not a "reform against nature" but a reform mandated by nature itself.

By placing original equality within the natural world, liberalism also sees the restoration of equality as a reform or revolution to be carried out within history. It is to be directed toward all social institutions that subjugate women, toward the creation of a social order in which women are able to enjoy equality of rights and equality of opportunity to exercise those rights in all spheres of life, not only in the home but in the public world as well. The Marxist feminist tradition builds on the liberal tradition. It recognizes that inequality is not simply a legal structure but also an economic system of discrimination against women. Social reform-revolution must open the economic as well as the political order to women equally with men.

For Christian liberals such as Sarah and Angelina Grimké, who appropriated liberal feminism into the theological doctrine of the *imago dei,* the institutional Church must be reformed as well. The Church must reform its patriarchal structures to include women's right to full participation in all leadership roles. But the reform of the Church is not set apart as transcendent to world history; rather it is an instance of social reform. The Church as bearer of redeemed humanity ought especially to represent this equality of men and women in its institutional life. But it does so as a paradigm of what all social institutions should become, not as a representative of an eschatological humanity outside of and beyond history. (Liberal feminism is discussed further in chapters 8 and 9.)

Romantic Feminism

In contrast to liberal feminism, romantic feminism stresses the differences between male and female as representative of complementary opposites: femininity and masculinity. In contrast to patriarchal anthropology, romantic feminism takes its definition of femaleness not from carnality and sin but from spiritual femininity, that is, intuitive spirituality, altruism, emotional sensitivity, and moral (sexual) purity. These ideas of spiritual femininity are particularly developed in Mariology.

But Mariology, in classical Catholicism, is set against historical women as representatives of carnal femaleness. Mary was the spiritual lady in whose service one rejected real (carnal) females. In Protestantism and bourgeois Catholicism, Mariological femininity is partly secularized to characterize the ideal nature of women, especially middle-class wives or "good Christian women."

Romanticism comes close to reversing the traditional patriarchal correlation of *imago dei* and fallen humanity with spiritual maleness and carnal femaleness. Instead it is the female who represents, in a purer and less ambiguous way, the original goodness of humanity as *imago dei*. This does not mean that men do not also possess this good human nature originally. But because they have to enter the sphere of power, competition, and sin, the good human nature becomes obscured in men. Men, as makers of history, take on the nature of historical humanity characterized by force and domination. Women, as those forbidden to enter the sphere of force and domination, retain more of the original purity and goodness of human nature. Women, shielded from history, are *less fallen* than men. They are more capable of altruistic, loving, self-giving life, less prone to the sins of egoism that are a sinful but necessary part of historical existence.

This romantic notion of femininity as more altruistic, less egoistic, and less prone to sin lends itself to a bewildering spectrum of different social platforms and programs in modern Western societies. The variety of these social platforms makes it difficult to recognize the common presuppositions of romantic anthropology that underlie them all. I will briefly characterize three typical expressions of romantic anthropology, covering the spectrum from conservative to radical: conservative romanticism, reformist romanticism, and radical romanticism.

Conservative Romanticism

Conservative romanticism correlates the sphere of altruism, purity, and love with the home and the realm of pride, egoism, and sin with the public sphere of politics, war, and work. Woman, although ideally the exponent of a higher, more loving humanity, possesses this good nature only in a fragile and vulnerable way. She can preserve her goodness only by the strictest segregation in the home, by eschewing all participation in the realm of public power. If woman leaves the home to take up a traditional male occupation, she will straightway lose this good femininity and become a she-male, a monstrous virago, or will become debased to carnal femaleness, fallen woman.

Man, on the other hand, is able to bear the sterner require-ments of ambiguous historical existence; his nature is more fitted to egoism and power. Yet he also wants to cultivate in his private life the gentler capacities of human nature. Woman's role is to uplift man. But she can do so only by cultivating her life in the home as the haven of altruistic, spiritual, and nurturing humanity. The male, then, will be able to retreat to the home to ease the strain of historical struggle and to be brought back in touch with a more loving humanity.

Loving and altruistic human life is, by nature, incompatible with historical existence. It cannot be carried into the world directly, for the world is characterized by egoistic power struggles. But the male, who moves back and forth between this fallen sphere (work) and the sphere of higher goodness (home) can be morally purified and uplifted by the female. He can then carry this higher goodness back into the world to express it, at least partially, under the ambiguous conditions of history. Conservative romanticism thus opposes equal rights of women in the public sphere in the name of the higher and purer goodness of woman as homemaker.

Reformist Romanticism

Reformist romanticism agrees with conservative romanticism in the belief in woman's purer and less ambiguous nature and its correlation with her role as nurturer of husband and children in the home. Unlike conservative romanticism, it takes more literally the view of the good nature of woman as innate rather than as something woman might lose if she enters the sphere of power. Reformist romanticism shares with liberalism the belief that the higher nature of humanity can be a basis for reform of social institutions rather than just a call to escape from them into a separate and more spiritual sphere. For reformist feminism, the bourgeois ideal of the family is seen as a launching pad for a mission into the world to uplift and transform it to the higher standards of goodness, peace, and loving service of womanhood and the home.

Woman's mission to uplift not just men but male institutions to the higher standards of the home was expressed in the most wide-ranging programs of social reform during the era of the Social Gospel in late-nineteenth-century America. Leaders like Frances Willard of the Women's Christian Temperance Union were particularly effective in converting the language of conservative romanticism into the program of reformist-romantic feminism. Women as educators of children must become founders of schools, particularly for infants and small children. As mothers, women have a natural interest in orphanages to provide homes for the homeless. As the keepers of cleanliness, they should extend themselves in all sorts of campaigns against dirt and disorder in society, ranging from physical dirt to political corruption. "A new broom sweeps clean" was the domestic image of this crusade of political reform that would "clean up city hall and throw out the dirty politicians." Moral reform, such as the redemption of prostitutes and the penalization of the men who patronize or profit from them, is a natural task of good women as keepers of chastity.

In its most visionary moments, reformist-romantic feminism glimpses the contours of a new society characterized not only by honesty, purity, and cleanliness but, above all, by peace. The nature of woman is incompatible with war. Not only have women historically been noncombatants, but the nature of woman is particularly related to all that brings peace and love rather than egoism, strife, and violence. Thus a new era of world peace, the abolition of strife, and the dawning of the reign of peace on earth represent the millennial vision of reformist-romantic feminism at its highest.

Unlike conservative romanticism, however, reformists don't think women can accomplish this vision by staying at home and uplifting men on a private level. Women must enter the world and use their higher instincts to change its social structures and relationships. To do this, they must have *power.* They need the vote and the right to education and political office. They need to be able to enter the world and all its roles in order to transform them through their higher feminine nature. This is where reformist-romantic feminism falls into jeopardy. Only by the most strenuous belief in the innate superiority of women can they believe that women can carry the superior goodness of the home into the world without succumbing to the ambiguous nature (egoism and force) of the world.

Radical Romanticism

Radical romanticism despairs of reforming ambiguous and evil male institutions. By implication it also is more pessimistic about the possibilities of converting male nature to female goodness. Rather, it repudiates male culture (including patriarchal religion) and withdraws into the female sphere as a separatist enclave of female values. It seeks to convert this female sphere from a dependent appendage to the male world of politics, war, and work into a self-sufficient utopian community. Here the higher female qualities of love, relatedness, and mutuality can reign unimpeded by ambiguous male institutions.

It is not clear in radical feminism whether men can be redeemed. For some radical feminists, men as persons can be separated from fallen male institutions and can be converted into the higher female sphere individually. For others, male proneness to egoism, pride, and domination is innate, so deeply a part of the socialization of all males as to be inseparable from their natures. Women should despair not only of male culture but of men as persons and should create a world of women without men. Separatist feminist utopianism dreams of an alternative world where women have learned to reproduce without men, to produce only female children, and to give their love only to women.[8] This utopian world of good femaleness must be walled off against the evil male world of genocide, rape, and war.

TOWARD A FEMINIST ANTHROPOLOGY BEYOND LIBERALISM AND ROMANTICISM

Contemporary feminism inherits the traditions of both liberal and romantic feminism. It becomes divided and confused over the opposite values and directions espoused by each viewpoint. Both liberalism and romanticism are inadequate and yet both testify to important truths that I wish to affirm. A more adequate feminist anthropology would be one that finds a creative synthesis between the two. Liberal feminism too readily identifies normative human nature with those capacities for reason and rule identified with men and with the public sphere. It claims that women, while appearing to have lesser capacities for these attributes, actually possess them equally; they have simply been denied the educational cultivation of them and the opportunity to exercise them. Opening up equal education and equal political rights to women will correct this and allow women's suppressed capacities for reason and rule to appear in their actual equivalence to men's.

There is important truth to this. Women, through the opening of equal education and political rights, have indeed demonstrated their ability to exercise the "same" capacities as men. But liberalism does not entirely recognize the more complex forms of women's psychological and economic marginalization that result in only token integration of women into "equal" roles in the public sphere. Liberalism assumes the traditional male sphere as normative and believes it is wrong to deny people access to it on the basis of gender. But once women are allowed to enter the public sphere, liberalism offers no critique of the modes of functioning within it.

Romanticism, in contrast, recognizes the moral ambiguity of the roles traditionally associated with masculinity. It idealizes the home, the private sphere of interpersonal relations, and places of "unspoiled nature" outside of urbanization and industrialization as havens of a more integrated humanity. It idealizes women precisely in their segregation from this ambiguous world. It tends to overlook the ambiguity and violence present in the sphere of private relationships, both the violation of women to keep them there and the way in which unexpressed angers and frustrations from the work world can be unleashed in the home. Altruism and service, while compensating women for acquiescence to relations of domination, also become a means of passive aggression masquerading as "helping others."

Romanticism is not entirely wrong in believing there are clues to a better humanity in the virtues relegated to women and the home in bourgeois society. But these virtues exist in deformed and deforming ways within the institutionalization of "woman's sphere." Moreover, the capacities traditionally associated with men and with public life also contain some important human virtues that women should not be forbidden to cultivate.

Thus neither masculinity traditionally defined nor femininity traditionally defined discloses an innately good human nature, and neither is simply an expression of evil. Both represent different types of alienation of humanity from its original potential. Socially, both home and work represent realms of corruption. If women will not be automatically redeemed by being incorporated into male political power and business in its present form, men will not automatically be redeemed by learning to nurture infants and keep house.

Androgyny has been used in recent feminist thought to express the human nature that all persons share. *Androgyny* refers to the possession by both males and females of both halves of the psychic capacities that have been traditionally separated as masculinity and femininity. The word *androgyny* is misleading, however, because it suggests that males and females possess both "masculine" and "feminine" sides to their psychic capacity. The term thus continues to perpetuate the ideas that certain psychic attributes are to be labeled masculine and others are to be labeled feminine and that humans, by integrating these "masculine" and "feminine" sides of themselves, become "androgynous."

There is no valid biological basis for labeling certain psychic capacities, such as reason, "masculine" and others, such as intuition, "feminine." To put it bluntly, there is no biological connection between male gonads and the capacity to reason. Likewise, there is no biological connection between female sexual organs and the capacity to be intuitive, caring, or nurturing. Thus the labeling of these capacities as masculine and feminine simply perpetuates gender role stereotypes and imports gender complementarity into each person's identity in a confusing way. Moreover, the idea of androgyny still preserves the idea of complementarity in complex form, since it suggests that males should integrate their androgynous identity around a "masculine" core of psychic capacities and females should integrate their androgyny around a "feminine" core.[9] We need to affirm not the confusing concept of androgyny but rather that all humans possess a full and equivalent human nature and personhood, *as male and female.*

Maleness and femaleness exist as reproductive role specialization. There is no necessary (biological) connection between reproductive complementarity and either psychological or social role differentiation. These are the work of culture and socialization, not of "nature." Recent research on the bicameral brain has shown that the right brain specializes in intuitive, musical, relational, and spatial capacities and the left brain in linguistic and mathematical thinking. But this is, in no way, a basis for differentiating males and females as masculine and feminine, since obviously males and females possess both sides of the brain.

We referred in chapter 3 to recent evidence that women mature earlier and create a more integrated relationship between right- and left-brain capacities. Males mature later and tend to have greater left- and right-brain specialization.[10] Added to this are cultural factors that identify maleness, particularly in Western societies, with left-brain characteristics. Male culture forces on males further specialization in left-brain capacities, repressing the development and integration of right-brain characteristics. Females, in turn, have been prevented from developing their left-brain characteristics.

This research discloses *not* a biological basis for differentiation of males and females into different psychic profiles but rather the capacity of both sexes for psychic wholeness. It also suggests that women have a tendency toward greater integration and males toward a more dualistic perception of these characteristics. Thus brain research discloses a possible biological basis of men's cultural tendency to identify their ego with left-brain characteristics and to see right-brain characteristics as the "repressed" part of themselves, which they in turn project upon and identify with women. Androgyny, then, is basically a male and not a female problem. Females do not need to adopt this concept to express their quest for psychic wholeness.

Women should not identify themselves with those repressed parts of the male psyche that males have projected upon them as "feminine." Nor should they adopt the male, one-sided psychic profile that identifies the ego with linear, rational types of thinking. Rather they need to appropriate and deepen the integration of the whole self — relational with rational modes of thought — that is already theirs. This may mean that they need to extend the development of those capacities for rational thought that have been culturally denied them. They need to do this not in a dualistic way but in a way that integrates these rational capacities with relational modes of thought. In this sense women are right when they instinctively feel they have a specifically female way of developing their persons that is different from men's. But the understanding of this has been confused by its identification with the male-defined "feminine."

The extension and deepening of psychic integration lead women necessarily toward a critique not just of male psychic dualism but also of male sociological dualism. Psychic integration demands a social revolution. This means not just the integration of women into roles in the public sphere, defined by rational action, and the integration of males into domestic roles of caring and nurturing. These are indeed important beginnings, but the crossing of the psychic-social boundaries of the male dualistic world leads women on to a further vision, a transformation of the relationship between the spheres of psychic capacities and social roles.

Women, building upon psychic integration, seek a new sociological integration that overcomes the schizophrenia of mind and of society. Women want to integrate the public and the private, the political and the domestic spheres in a new relationship that allows the thinking-relational self to operate throughout human life as one integrated self, rather than fragmenting the psyche across a series of different social roles. Women want to tear down the walls that separate the self and society into "male" and "female" spheres. This demands not just a new integrated self but a new integrated social order.[11]

Thus the recovery of holistic psychic capacities and egalitarian access to social roles point us toward that lost full human potential that we may call "redeemed humanity." Redeemed humanity, reconnected with the *imago dei,* means not only recovering aspects of our full psychic potential that have been repressed by cultural gender stereotypes, it also means transforming the way these capacities have been made to function socially. We need to recover our capacity for relationality, for hearing, receiving, and being with and for others, but in a way that is no longer a tool of manipulation or of self-abnegation.

We need to develop our capacities for rationality, but in a way that makes reason no longer a tool of competitive relations with others. Recovering our full psychic potential beyond gender stereotypes thus opens up an ongoing vision of transformed, redeemed, or converted persons and society, no longer alienated from self, from others, from the body, from the cosmos, from the Divine.

In traditional Christian theology, Christ is the model for this redeemed humanity that we have lost through sin and recover through redemption. But Christ as symbol is problematic for feminist theology. The Christological symbols have been used to enforce male dominance, and even if we go back behind masculinist Christology to the praxis of the historical Jesus of the synoptic Gospels, it is questionable whether there is a single model of redeemed humanity fully revealed in the past. This does not mean that feminist theology may not be able to affirm the person of Jesus of Nazareth as a positive model of redemptive humanity. But this model must be seen as partial and fragmentary, disclosing from the perspective of one person, circumscribed in time, culture, and gender, something of the fullness we seek. We need other clues and models as well, models drawn from women's experience, from many times and cultures.

The fullness of redeemed humanity, as image of God, is something only partially disclosed under the conditions of history. We seek it as a future self and world, still not fully achieved, still not fully revealed. But we also discover it as our true self and world, the foundation and ground of our being. When we experience glimpses of it, we recognize not an alien self but our own authentic self. We experience such glimpses through encounters with other persons whose own authenticity discloses the meaning of such personhood. By holding the memory of such persons in our hearts and minds, we are able to recognize authenticity in ourselves and others.

The life and death of Jesus of Nazareth is one such memory, one such paradigm.[12] It is no less paradigmatic when we recognize that it is partial and needs to be joined by other models, other memories, particularly those that disclose the journey to redemptive personhood from women's experience. Thus the question of anthropology leads us, theologically, to the problem of Christology. Has Christology, in fact, been a model of redemptive personhood for women, or has it become a tool for enforcing female subjugation in patriarchal society? What are the possibilities, and limits, of discovering an alternative, usable Christology, a paradigm of redemptive personhood, for women in the praxis of the historical Jesus?

Chapter 5
Christology:
Can a Male Savior Save Women?

HISTORICAL BACKGROUND

The Christology that became enshrined as orthodoxy at the Council of Chalcedon is the product of a very complex development. It is not the result of a consistent evolution out of the Hebraic understanding of the Messiah, but it represents a repudiation of key elements of Jewish messianic hope and their replacement by ideas that Judaism continues to reject as idolatrous. Nor is it a faithful rendering of the messianic announcement of Jesus of Nazareth and his views of the coming Reign of God. There are, of course, historical origins of Christology in Jesus' messianic proclamation, and behind Jesus' self-understanding lies a long history of Jewish messianic hope. But Christian Christology changed the original framework and meaning of these ideas, although it continued to declare dogmatically the identity between its formula and the "true meaning" of the Biblical points of reference. It is beyond the scope of this chapter to trace the transformations that led from one to the other, but some historical background will be useful before discussing the different typologies of Christology that developed in the Christian tradition.

Ancient Near Eastern Roots

Classical Christology brings together two ideas: that of a messianic king of a new age of redemption and that of divine wisdom which grounds and discloses the cosmos and unites the human with the divine. It is significant that both ideas, in their remote, pre-Hebraic origins, feature a central female divine actor. The patriarchalization of these themes takes place by a repression, first in Judaism and then in Christianity, of the female symbol.

Canaanite and ancient Near Eastern thought is centered in the story of annual world renewal in which the dying and rising vegetation king is resurrected through the power of the Goddess. Likewise the figure of divine wisdom is represented in the various cultures of the Eastern Mediterranean as the Goddess. So powerful was this tradition that when the Hebrews adopted, in Hellenistic form, the idea of divine wisdom, they too depicted it as a female figure who disclosed the wisdom of God and was the divine instrument in creation and revelation.

The figure of divine wisdom in Proverbs 8 and in the Wisdom of Solomon is theologically identical to what the New Testament describes as the *Logos,* or "Son" of God. Because Christianity chooses the male symbol for this idea, however, the unwarranted idea develops that there is a necessary ontological connection between the maleness of Jesus' historical person and the maleness of *Logos* as the male offspring and disclosure of a male God. The female figure of divine wisdom is displaced from the orthodox Trinity, although Gnostic forms of Christianity continue to conjure this figure and to see her as the origin of the creation, fall, and redemption of spiritual humanity.

Messiah and Reign of God in Hebraic Thought

In Hebraic prophetic thought the ancient Near Eastern theme of the annual renewal of the world and its rescue from chaos and death undergoes a transformation. Like their neighbors, the Hebrews continue to hope for the coming of a Great Year in which the blessings of bountiful harvests and harmony with nature will be united with security, peace, and justice in human relations. The moral and social component of this hope is not unique to the Hebrews but is also typical of Near Eastern thought. Although these hopes continue to be rooted in the New Year festival, the Hebrews break this hope loose from its connections with the agricultural cycle. Instead they interpret this drama as a moral and historical one. The devastation of people and land in the grip of the forces of drought and death is no longer seen as a dying and rising God-king but as the land and people itself in relation to a sovereign God who directs history.

The devastation of the people and the land is interpreted as divine punishment for transgressions of the commands of God, especially the command to be faithful to "Him" and to shun the other Gods of the land. The future hope of bountiful harvests, peace, and justice is held out as a reward for turning away from apostasy. The Hebrews thus develop a way of interpreting their own historical vicissitudes as judgment and punishment by God. Yet they hold open a vision of a Good Age to come when they have rectified their errors and God will fulfill the promises of the covenant.

The idea of the Messiah is a special feature of this general hope for a coming Reign of God or Great Year of the Lord. It develops in relation to the adoption of the Canaanite practice of kingship and temple in Jerusalem and so is uniquely linked with the memory of Davidic kingship. The word *Messiah,* or "God's anointed," in fact, occurs most often in the Hebrew Bible simply as a reference to the reigning Davidic king. In the Davidic kingship ideology the king is both the elect of God (Son of God) and the paradigmatic representative of the people of Israel before God (Son of Man). Through the king's righteousness and special relation to God, the favor of God and the felicity of the people is assured. The king is the instrument of the people's salvation.

But actual kings seldom fulfill these expectations, so the hope becomes displaced to the future in the form of a coming king, a child who will be the promised instrument of redemption. After the exile, when the reigning Davidic kingship is lost, this hope can be fastened on the expectation of a restored Davidic monarchy. God will restore a Son of David to Israel. He will deliver the people from bondage under their enemies in battle and restore Israel as an autonomous power whose reign will be established from sea to sea and from the river to the ends of the earth (that is, throughout the Middle East).[1]

The development of the concept of the Reign of God is partially independent of these notions of the Messiah. Not all forms of Judaism are attached to the ideology of Davidic kingship. Some strands of Jewish thought continue to think of a coming time of peace and justice under a direct Reign of God without reference to a Davidic king as instrument. The Davidic King-Messiah is basically a conquering warrior who liberates the people from their enemies and then reigns over a new kingdom. He fulfills the dream of a righteous king through whom God grants complete favor to Israel. He is in no way an incarnation of the Divine or a redeemer, in the Christian sense of one who forgives sins through redemptive self-sacrifice. He is expected to win, not to suffer and die. Needless to say, in the Hebraic framework the Messiah can only be imaged as a male.

Jesus' Radicalizing of the Hope for the Reign of God

Jesus' messianic proclamation centers on his interpretation of the tradition of a coming Reign of God. He does not evoke the hope for the Davidic Messiah, doubtless because of his Galilean origins where this Judean tradition was not cultivated. Furthermore, he exhibits a sharp negativity toward any efforts to equate his expectation with that of a coming king; he absents himself from crowds who seek to proclaim him king. The Davidic tradition is woven into the Jesus story in Christian exegesis, first by the interpretation of his advent into Jerusalem in the imagery of the advent of the conquering Davidic Messiah of Zechariah and second by the story of his Davidic genealogy and birth in Bethlehem. But these are later developments probably contrary to Jesus' original perspective.

Later in this chapter we return to a more detailed analysis of the picture of Jesus in the synoptic Gospels in relation to women. But here it suffices to note that Jesus seems to express a radicalized view of the concept of a coming Reign of God as a time of the vindication of the poor and the oppressed. The poor and the oppressed are not seen in nationalist terms as Israel, but rather as marginalized groups and classes within the Jewish world of his day. Although Jesus is aware of the oppressive Roman powers as the ultimate context of oppression, he focuses instead on the Jewish ruling classes — the local rulers, landlords, and religious authorities. He directs his criticism particularly at the religious authorities. It is they who have excluded, through their law- and class-based religion, the "little ones" from hope of redemption. The religiously and socially marginalized are praised as able to hear and respond to the word of the prophet, whereas the reigning authorities remain encapsulated in their systems of power and are unable to hear what God is saying to them.

Jesus' vision of the Kingdom is neither nationalistic nor other-worldly. The coming Reign of God is expected to happen on earth, as the Lord's Prayer makes evident (God's Kingdom come, God's will be done on earth). It is a time when structures of domination and subjugation have been overcome, when the basic human needs are met (daily bread), when all dwell in harmony with God and each other (not led into temptation but delivered from evil). Although it will certainly be a great revolution in human affairs, it will come about as a divine response to human repentance. It is the people of Israel specifically who must repent the systems of fossilized religious righteousness and class oppression that have distorted the vision of God's mercy and promises.

Jesus repudiates the nationalist-revenge mythology of much of the messianic tradition. The messianic age will not be a time when Israel will defeat its enemies and be installed in possession of a great Near Eastern empire through which it will rule its former masters. Rather it will be a time when all structures of ruler and ruled are overcome. In line with this interpretation of the Reign of God, Jesus resymbolizes the messianic prophet (and, by implication, God) not as king but as servant. The messianic person and those who follow him must not seek a new situation in which they will dominate others, but they must become servants of all. By adapting the word *servant* (slave) in this way Jesus drastically reverses the social references of divine redemptive activity, identifying redemption with the lowest persons in society (slaves) rather than the highest (kings).

Jesus does not mean that he and his followers are to be like servants or slaves as society understands the "good slave," that is, as one who unquestioningly subjects himself or herself to the existing social order of bondage. Jesus uses the term *servant* for himself and his disciples in a prophetic-religious sense, presupposing a special relation to God. By becoming servant of God, one becomes freed of all bondage to human masters. Only then, as a liberated person, can one truly become "servant of all," giving one's life to liberate others rather than to exercise power and rule over them.[2]

Implicit in the early Jesus movement is a challenge to religious authority embodied in past revelation and institutionalized in the hands of a privileged group of interpreters. Jesus declares that God has not just spoken in the past but is speaking *now*. Prophecy is not canonized in past texts; the Spirit of God speaks today. Those of low or marginal status (Jesus and his disciples) speak not simply as interpreters of past traditions but as the direct word of God (with authority, not as the Scribes and Pharisees speak). Jesus frees religious experience from the fossilization of past traditions (which doesn't mean he rejects those traditions) and makes it accessible in the present. And Jesus does not think of himself as the "last word of God," but points beyond himself to "One who will come."

Thus Jesus restores the sense of God's prophetic and redemptive activity taking place in the present-future, through people's present experiences and the new possibilities disclosed through those experiences. To encapsulate Jesus himself as God's "last word" and "once-for-all" disclosure of God, located in a remote past and institutionalized in a cast of Christian teachers, is to repudiate the spirit of Jesus and to recapitulate the position against which he himself protests.

THE PATRIARCHALIZATION OF CHRISTOLOGY

The transformation of Christian reflection on Jesus into orthodox Christology takes place over the five centuries during which the Christian Church itself is transformed from a marginal sect within the messianic renewal movements of first-century Judaism into the new imperial religion of a Christian Roman Empire. Christology, the Christian proclamation of Jesus as Savior, as distinct from Jesus' own proclamation of repentance in anticipation of "One who is to come," begins with the shock of the Crucifixion. This is a denouement for which the disciples are not fully prepared, imbued as they are with messianic traditions of divine victory. At first they drift away discouraged, but they later reassemble under collective experiences of Jesus' Resurrection.

The Resurrection experience enables the disciples to repudiate the possibility that the Crucifixion signaled the failure of Jesus' mission or his rejection by God. Rather, this mission is to be reinterpreted in terms of a redemptive suffering servant who atones for the sin of Israel and who, in turn, is transmuted to the heavens from which he will return as conquering Messiah. Jesus is rescued by God from death and given ongoing life in the present and future. In the present he lives on in the prophetic Spirit which the early Christian community experiences as alive in their midst, as a power of both ecstatic utterances and gifts of forgiveness and healing. This prophetic Spirit is understood to be the Risen Lord alive in their midst or, according to the Johannine tradition, a Spirit which Jesus "sent" to replace himself once he himself had gone "to the Father."

This spirit-filled community understands itself apocalyptically as living in the final moments of fallen human history, anticipating an intervention of God soon to come in which the evil powers and principalities of the world around them will be overthrown. They themselves will "rise" to join a new heaven and earth that God will establish on a renewed earth. The identification of Jesus with the messianic person who will descend as agent of this world transformation (the One who is to come) enables these early Christians to give the title Messiah (Christ) to Jesus.

This first synthesis of charismatic and apocalyptic Christology proves unstable, however, although elements of it remain and indeed continue to be rediscovered in popular Christian movements up to the present. Moveover, a conflict gradually arises between the original charismatic order of Christian leadership and a developing institutional order (prophets and martyrs versus bishops). The sayings of Jesus in the Gospels are basically the work of Christian prophets. They were not originally preserved by a process of historical memory in which the prophets wrote down what they remembered Jesus to have said. This does not mean that they preserve nothing similar to what the historical Jesus actually said. Rather, it means that what is preserved is the "spirit," the iconoclastic and prophetic vision of Jesus. The Christian prophets (male and female) speak out of this "spirit" of Jesus to utter sayings that represent Jesus' teachings not in the past but in the present, as a power alive in their midst.[3]

Soon, however, a developing institutional ministry (bishops) felt the need to cut off this ongoing speaking in the name of Christ. The fall of Jerusalem in 70 A.D. and the cutting off of the Christian Church from the original Mother Church in Jerusalem may have been a catalyst. Sayings and teachings of Jesus are gathered together in writing and cast in the form of biographical dramas. These now become the definitive texts of the sayings of the Lord. Those who continue to speak in the name of Christ become heretics (Montanists). Revelation is said to be closed and located in the past in a historical Christ and a past apostolic community. The ongoing power of the Spirit sent by Christ to the community is no longer to "blow where it will" but is institutionalized in the authority of bishops. They received the original "deposit of faith" from the apostles and they pass it down unaltered in their official teaching traditions. Both the interpretation of the words of Christ and the power of reconciliation with God is to be wrested from the hands of charismatics, prophets, and martyrs and placed in the hands of the episcopacy, which takes over the claims of apostolic authority.[4]

Early Catholic Christianity in the Gospel of Luke manifests the de-eschatologizing of Christology. The Church no longer sees itself as existing in a narrow margin on the edge of final world transformation between the snatching up of the crucified Jesus to the right hand of God and Jesus' imminent return as conquering Christ. It no longer lives in the time of the "messianic birth pangs," as is the case in Matthew, Mark, or the book of Revelation. Rather Christ has become the center of history between two eras of salvation history, the time of Israel and the time of the Church.[5] Christ becomes a timeless revelation of divine perfection located in a past paradigmatic moment. This disclosure of timeless perfection is closed. The Risen Lord does not live on in ecstatic utterances of Christian prophets or prophetesses; rather he ascended into heaven after forty days. Access to Christ is now through the official line of apostolic teaching. Only males can occupy the apostolic teaching office and thus represent Christ. Women are to keep silent.

The third and decisive step in the patriarchalization of Christology takes place in the fourth century with the establishment of the Christian Church as the imperial religion of a Christian Roman Empire. A Christianity installed in political power over the "world" can now reintegrate the Messiah symbol with its ancient roots in kingship ideology. The thousand-year reign of Christ can now be identified with Christendom. The Christian emperor, with the Christian Patriarch on his right hand, now represents the establishment of Christ's reign upon the earth. The emperor's enemies, both within and without the empire, vanquished by his might, represent the binding of the demonic hosts, according to Eusebius of Caesarea, eulogist of the emperor Constantine.[6]

In the imperial Christology of Eusebius, messianism is reintegrated into a kingship ideology that provides the "sacred canopy" over the existing political and social hierarchy. Likewise the Christological doctrine of Christ as *Logos* or ground of the created world is identified with the foundation of the existing social system. Christ as *Logos* or *Nous* (mind) of God discloses the divine mind and provides the plan and government of the established social cosmos. All is integrated into one vast hierarchy of being.[7] Just as the *Logos* of God governs the cosmos, so the Christian Roman Emperor, together with the Christian Church, governs the political universe; masters govern slaves and men govern women. Women, slaves, and barbarians (as well as religious minorities, Jews, pagans, and heretics) are the *a-logoi,* the "mindless" ones, who are to be governed and defined by the representatives of divine *Logos.* Christ has become the Pantocrator (All-Ruler) of a new world order. Christology becomes the apex of a system of control over all those who in one way or another are "other" than this new Christian order.

Women, of course, are still regarded as humble members of the Christian body, but their inability to represent Christ is sealed by the definition of Christ as founder and cosmic governor of the existing social hierarchy and as the male disclosure of a male God whose normative representative can only be male. With the adoption of Aristotelian biology in medieval scholasticism, this antiwoman use of Christology is argued not only on the plane of symbol but on the plane of biology.

The male alone is the normative or generic sex of the human species; only the male represents the fullness of human nature, whereas woman is defective physically, morally, and mentally. It follows that the incarnation of the *Logos* of God into a male is not a historical accident but an ontological necessity. Just as Christ has to be incarnated in a male, so only can the male represent Christ.[8]

This kind of male-dominant Christology has emerged in recent years as the keystone of the conservative reaction against women's ordination. In Roman Catholic, Anglican, and Orthodox writings against women's ordination a constellation of arguments emerges that interrelates maleness, Christology, and priesthood.[9] For these writers it is no longer a matter of the order of creation. They wish to insulate their argument against women's ordination from any changing patterns of secular social relations. Rather, women's inability to represent Christ in the priesthood becomes an unchangeable "mystery" that lies on a sacramental and metaphysical plane.

Christ as head and bridegroom of the Church must necessarily be male, and hence his representative, the priest, must also be male. Only males can be bridegrooms (although these writers find no difficulty in the idea that males in the laity are, symbolically, "brides" in this scheme). Behind this argument of the necessary maleness of Christ lies the theological assumption of the maleness of God. The human male can represent both the divine (male) and also the creaturely sides of this hierarchy. Women can represent only the creaturely (female) side, never the divine (male) side. The Vatican declaration in 1976 against women's ordination sums up this Christological masculinism with the statement that "there must be a physical resemblance between the priest and Christ."[10] The possession of male genitalia becomes the essential prerequisite for representing Christ, who is the disclosure of the male God.

ALTERNATIVE CHRISTOLOGIES

Although masculinist Christologies became the dominant tradition, Christianity has never lacked minority and alternative perspectives. Two somewhat different lines of tradition run parallel in Christian history: "androgynous Christologies" and "spirit Christologies." Androgynous Christologies see Christ as the representative of the new humanity that unifies male and female. The root of these Christologies lies in the basic Christian affirmation that Christ redeems the whole of human nature, male and female. These traditions take their cue particularly from the early baptismal formula quoted in Paul that there is neither "male nor female, for we are all one in Christ" (Gal. 3:28).

The androgynous Christologies are found particularly in the mystical tradition. They see the split between maleness and femaleness overcome on a spiritual plane in the redeemed humanity. A second, somewhat different emphasis is found in "spirit Christologies." The distinction between the two emerges in the following discussion.

Androgynous Christologies

Behind the androgynous Christologies, as well as androgynous anthropologies, often lurks the myth of an original androgyne. In this myth Adam originally contained both male and female. The splitting of the female from the male side of Adam signals the downfall of humanity and the advent of sex and sin. Christ, the new androgynous Adam, enables the redeemed to transcend the split of male and female and regain their spiritual humanity. These ideas are suggested in many of the Gnostic Gospels. The Second Epistle of Clement (12:2) says:

> For the Lord himself being asked by someone when his Kingdom would come, said: When the two shall be one, and the outside as the inside, the male with the female, neither male nor female.

Women are seen as equal participants in this spiritual humanity, but only by transcending their identities as sexual persons and mothers. In the Gospel of the Egyptians Jesus declares, "I have come to destroy the works of the female," that is, sexual desire and procreation (9:63), while the Gospel of Thomas vindicates the inclusion of women in the redemptive community by having Jesus say, "Lo, I shall lead her and make her male, so that she too may become a living spirit resembling you males, for every woman who makes herself male will enter the kingdom of heaven" (Logion 114). Similar ideas were revived in early modern mystics such as Jacob Boehme and Emanuel Swedenborg. Boehme particularly influenced many mystical Utopian sects, such as the German Rappites, who emigrated to America in the nineteenth century. Notions of an androgynous divinity, an original androgynous humanity, and the restoration of spiritual androgyny in the redeemed are frequently found in these movements.

The Christ figure reinforces the androcentric bias of these concepts of androgyny. Christ represents the male as the normative human person. Femaleness represents the lower instinctual and bodily side of "man," which was originally unified in a spiritual whole. The separation of the female out of the side of Adam represents the disintegration of this original whole, the revolt of the lower against the higher side of "man." The very existence of woman as a separate gender represents the fall of "man." Femaleness is still correlated with the lower side of human nature, which is to be abolished in Heaven.

A somewhat different tradition develops in medieval Jesus mysticism, expressed particularly by Julian of Norwich. Here Jesus is proclaimed both mother and father. Like a mother he feeds us with his own body. He nurtures us with milk, like newborn babes. The ambience of these images of the mothering Jesus is found especially in eucharistic piety.[11] Since both the human and the divine persons of Jesus are established in Catholic thought as male, however, Jesus as a male person is given "mothering" attributes. In Christ the male gains a model of androgyny, of personhood that is both commanding and nurturing. The female mystic gains the satisfaction of relation to a tender and mothering person, but she herself does not gain a comparable androgyny. The Church does not allow her to represent the "masculine" authority of Christ as priest or public teacher.

Nineteenth-century romanticism comes close to reversing these value symbols of masculinity and femininity. With the secularization of society and the privatization of religion, Christianity becomes identified with the shrinking sphere of middle-class femininity. Woman comes to be identified with the spiritual, pious, and altruistic impulses, whose purity can be preserved only by the strictest segregation from the public world of male materialism and power. Many writers come close to identifying woman as the more naturally "Christlike" type. A sweet fragile femininity also comes to characterize the pietistic images of Jesus. But this feminization of Christ, while it makes woman closer to the spiritual pole, still does not liberate her for public influence in society or in the Church.

Horace Bushnell, in his treatise "Women's Suffrage: The Reform Against Nature" (1869),[12] argues that the male nature represents the law, whereas the female nature represents the Gospel. The Gospel is the higher revelation of grace, forgiveness, and altruistic love. Women have a natural affinity for these higher spiritual characteristics. But the Gospel is impractical and incapable of providing the principle of leadership in public society. It is here that males, as representatives of law, must still rule in the public sphere of Church and society. Thus, by a peculiar reversal of classical Christian anthropological reasoning, Bushnell argues that women's Christlike nature makes them unfit for ordained ministry. Femininity and Christlikeness are both defined into a private realm of altruistic otherworldliness which, while appropriate for redemption, is inappropriate for the exercise of public power, even in the Church.

Reformist feminists draw different conclusions from the thesis of woman's more Christlike nature. For them this suggests a messianic meaning to the emergence of woman. If woman represents the higher human qualities of peace, purity, and reconciliation, then these are too good to keep at home. They are just what the world needs now to redeem it from the various evils that corrupt society. The home and woman's higher feminine nature become the launching pad for a crusade into society to elevate it to the female standards of goodness.

All of these concepts of androgyny, whether they identify woman with the lower material nature and hence with finitude and sin, or whether they identify her with the higher spiritual qualities of altruistic love, never succeed in allowing woman to represent full human potential. The very concept of androgyny presupposes a psychic dualism that identifies maleness with one-half of human capacities and femaleness with the other. As long as Christ is still presumed to be, normatively, a male person, androgynous Christologies will carry an androcentric bias. Men gain their "feminine" side, but women contribute to the whole by specializing in the representation of the "feminine," which means exclusion from the exercise of the roles of power and leadership associated with masculinity.

Spirit Christologies

The *locus classicus* for spirit Christology is early Christian prophetism rather than early Christian Gnosticism and mysticism. The foundational text of Christian prophetism, Acts 2:18, describes the prophetic Spirit as poured out on the "man-servants" and the "maidservants." The power of the Spirit is identified with the continuing presence of the Risen Lord. The oracles of prophets and prophetesses are the ongoing revelation of a Christ who continues to speak directly in the assemblies of Christians.

Not only may women be vehicles and spokespersons of this

Risen Christ, but they can also be encountered as exemplars of Christ. This is found both in the literature of the new prophetism, Montanism, and in martyr literature (which often has affinities with Montanism). Thus, for example, in the *Acts of the Martyrs of Lyons and Vienne,* the martyr Blandina, during her agony, is described as an *alter Christus:*

> Now Blandina, suspended on a stake, was exposed as food to wild beasts which were let loose against her. Even to look on her, as she hung cross-wise in earnest prayer, wrought great eagerness in those who were contending, for in their conflict they beheld with their outward eyes *in the form of their sister the One who was crucified for them*...[Emphasis mine][13]

Among the Montanist oracles of the Christian prophetesses Maximilla and Priscilla, we find not only statements that in hearing Priscilla they hear Christ, but also visions in which Christ appears in the form of a woman:

> Christ came to me in the likeness of a woman, clad in a bright robe, and planted wisdom in me and revealed that this place is holy and that here Jerusalem comes down from Heaven (Priscilla).[14]

This kind of spirit Christology does not separate out a past perfect historical Christ from the ongoing Spirit. Rather it sees Christ as a power that continues to be revealed in persons, both male and female, in the present. Christ is located in a new humanity that discloses the future potential of redeemed life. The reality of Christ is not completed in the past but continues to be disclosed in the present.

As the institutionalized Church succeeded in suppressing this early identification of the Risen Christ and the ongoing power of the Spirit, spirit Christologies came to be expressed in revolts against the Christian establishment, in the name of a "third" era of revelation through the Spirit. Hints of this concept of the Third Age of the Spirit are already suggested in Montanism. A full-blown revolt against the limitations of a past historical

Christ, institutionalized in the clerical Church as the final era of salvation history, takes shape from the twelfth century on in medieval Catholicism.

The followers of Joachim of Fiore believed that the Second Age of the Son, represented by the clerical Church, would soon be superseded by a Third Age of the Spirit, which would bring redemption to perfection.[15] Revelation through the "Son" is seen as imperfect or incomplete. It has become a hindrance to the emergence of new dimensions of human hope. The reestablishment of a hope for redemption located in future history creates a revolt against the encapsulation of Christ in the past. A new stage of revelation and redemption, even a new dimension of divine power and meaning, are yet to be disclosed. The Spirit becomes the principle of revolt against a past perfect Christology.

Few Joachites saw the vindication of the female as part of their agenda of the Third Age. One such group gathered around Prous Boneta, the founder of a Provençal Beguine sect in the early fourteenth century. They believed Boneta was the incarnation of the Holy Spirit, the New Eve who would bring final salvation to all humanity. Another Joachite group in Milan declared their leader, Guglielma (c. 1271), the incarnate Spirit. As the second person of the Trinity has appeared as a male, so the new dispensation of the Spirit will appear as a female. All authority has departed from the corrupt hierarchy. A new Church, built on the foundations of the Spirit, will bring forth four new spiritual Gospels and women will be spiritual leaders.[16]

Such movements, eccentric as they may appear owing to their extreme marginalization and repression in medieval Catholicism, are significant because they represent a much more radical dissatisfaction with the masculinist Christ and clerical Church. They do not simply add a "feminine" or "mothering" element to what is still a male-centered symbol. They dare to dream of a new dispensation of the Divine in which women will represent new, not yet imagined dimensions of human possibility and divine disclosure.

The Joachite revolt against institutionalized Christology spawned two lines of offspring in the post-Reformation. One line was an obscure group of sects that continued to rediscover visions of a new dispensation of God over against established Christianity. Some of these sects asserted that the new dispensation would supersede the old precisely by its disclosure through, or representation by, the female. The most important such movement was the Anglo-American Shakers, which first developed in late-eighteenth-century England.

The Shakers based their belief in a dual Christ, male and female, on their doctrine of the androgyny of God. God is both Father and Mother, and humanity as male and female is made in the image of the androgynous God. Redemption, having taken place so far only in the "male line," is therefore incomplete. The female side of God, Holy Wisdom, has not yet been disclosed. The Shakers followed aspects of the androgynous mystical tradition in their division of God and humanity into male and female sides.[17] The masculine Christ was inadequate because he could not disclose this feminine side of God. But the Shakers go beyond the androgynous tradition in rejecting the possibility that this revelation of the undisclosed "feminine" can be satisfied by adding "feminine" qualities to the male symbol of Christ. This new and final stage of redemption must be disclosed through a female. A male Christ alone cannot disclose the fullness of human possibility and divine nature as male and female.

The belief that there must be a new stage of redemption in female form was not limited to the Shakers, but enjoyed widespread currency in the nineteenth century. It is found in such diverse forms as French utopian socialists, the St. Simonians, and the New England Transcendentalists.[18] It is constantly hinted at in Mary Baker Eddy, founder of the Church of Christ, Scientist, who declared that since the highest meaning of God is love, the "feminine" nature is closer to God than the masculine. Although Eddy stopped short of allowing her followers to call her a new Christ, she hints that she is a new "Mary" who brings forth the new divine child of divine science.[19] Her movement signals a new and higher stage of messianic disclosure.

Mainstream reformist feminists, such as Frances Willard, were too theologically conservative to suggest that their female reform movements represented a new disclosure of Christ superseding the Christ of the New Testament. But there is a messianic enthusiasm about their descriptions of their movements that partakes of the same heady atmosphere.[20] They do not hesitate to suggest that the emancipation of woman represents the fulfillment of the prophecy of Joel in which the pouring forth of the prophetic spirit upon women will usher in the final era of world salvation.

A second line of offspring of Joachite prophecy is found in Enlightenment and post-Enlightenment radicalism. The adoption of the secular-religious dualism obscures the fundamentally messianic roots of these movements. Enlightenment thinkers declare, in a secular version of Joachite prophecy, that a new Age of Light (reason) is being disclosed that will supersede and liberate humanity from the superstitious clericalism of the Christian Church. The Christian era as a whole now becomes a past and evil "dark age" of humanity. The dawning new age of reason will emancipate humanity from the dead hand of clerical power into a new world of limitless possibilities. Modern movements — liberalism, socialism, fascism — thus make their appearance by declaring themselves the embodiment of an emancipatory "third age" superseding the Christian era. Radical feminism, which announces the "return of the Goddess" with woman as her representative, continues a line of modern revolts against the Christian world in the name of a new disclosure of unfulfilled human possibilities.[21]

A FEMINIST CHRISTOLOGY?

Our exploration of Christology has led to an impasse. A Christology that identified the maleness of the historical Jesus with normative humanity and with the maleness of the divine *Logos* must move in an increasingly misogynist direction that not only excludes woman as representative of Christ in ministry but makes her a second-class citizen in both creation and redemption. Androgynous Christologies try to affirm the female side in the vision of a Christ that is "neither male nor female." But the identification of this androgynous Christ with the male Jesus continues to give an androcentric bias to the vision of redemptive humanity. Woman can represent only the "feminine" side of a male-centered symbol the fullness of which is disclosed only in a male person.

Spirit Christologies begin by affirming that the risen Christ continues to be disclosed through spirit-possessed persons who may be male or female. But the splitting of the past revelation of Christ as the historical Jesus from the ongoing Spirit leads eventually to a revolt against a Christ encapsulated in the past. Institutionalized revelation becomes inadequate to the disclosure of new possibilities, specifically female possibilities. Where does this leave the quest for a feminist Christology? Must we not say that the very limitations of Christ as a male person must lead women to the conclusion that he cannot represent redemptive personhood for them? That they must emancipate themselves from Jesus as redeemer and seek a new redemptive disclosure of God and of human possibility in female form?

A starting point for this inquiry must be a reencounter with the Jesus of the synoptic Gospels, not the accumulated doctrine about him but his message and praxis. Once the mythology about Jesus as Messiah or divine *Logos,* with its traditional masculine imagery, is stripped off, the Jesus of the synoptic Gospels can be recognized as a figure remarkably compatible with feminism. This is not to say, in an anachronistic sense, that "Jesus was a feminist," but rather that the criticism of religious and social hierarchy characteristic of the early portrait of Jesus is remarkably parallel to feminist criticism.

Fundamentally, Jesus renews the prophetic vision whereby

the Word of God does not validate the existing social and
religious hierarchy but speaks on behalf of the marginalized
and despised groups of society. Jesus proclaims an iconoclastic
reversal of the system of religious status: The last shall be first
and the first last. The leaders of the religious establishment
are blind guides and hypocrites. The outcasts of society —
prostitutes, publicans, Samaritans — are able to hear the
message of the prophet. This reversal of social order doesn't
just turn hierarchy upside down, it aims at a new reality in
which hierarchy and dominance are overcome as principles of
social relations.

Jesus revises God-language by using the familiar *Abba* for
God. He speaks of the Messiah as servant rather than king
to visualize new relations between the divine and the human.
Relation to God no longer becomes a model for dominant-
subordinate relations between social groups, leaders, and the
led. Rather, relation to God means we are to call no man
"Father, Teacher or Master" (Matt. 23:1-12). Relation to God
liberates us from hierarchical relations and makes us all
brothers-sisters of each other. Those who would be leaders
must become servants of all.

Women play an important role in this Gospel vision of the
vindication of the lowly in God's new order. It is the women
of the oppressed and marginalized groups who are often
pictured as the representatives of the lowly. The dialogue at
the well takes place with a Samaritan woman. A Syro-
Phoenician woman is the prophetic seeker who forces Jesus
to concede redemption of the Gentiles. Among the poor it is
the widows who are the most destitute. Among the ritually
unclean, it is the woman with the flow of blood who extorts
healing for herself contrary to the law. Among the morally
outcast, it is the prostitutes who are the furthest from righteousness. The role played by women of marginalized groups
is an intrinsic part of the iconoclastic, messianic vision. It means
that the women are the oppressed of the oppressed. They are
the bottom of the present social hierarchy and hence are seen,

in a special way, as the last who will be first in the Kingdom of God.

This role is quite different from doctrines of romantic complementarity. The Gospels do not operate with a dualism of masculine and feminine. The widow, the prostitute, and the Samaritan woman are not representatives of the "feminine," but rather they represent those who have no honor in the present system of religious righteousness. As women they are the doubly despised within these groups. They carry the double burden of low class and low gender status. The protest of the Gospels is directed at the concrete sociological realities in which maleness and femaleness are elements, along with class, ethnicity, religious office, and law, that define the network of social status.

Jesus as liberator calls for a renunciation, a dissolution, of the web of status relationships by which societies have defined privilege and deprivation. He protests against the identification of this system with the favor or disfavor of God. His ability to speak as liberator does not reside in his maleness but in the fact that he has renounced this system of domination and seeks to embody in his person the new humanity of service and mutual empowerment. He speaks to and is responded to by low-caste women because they represent the bottom of this status network and have the least stake in its perpetuation.

Theologically speaking, then, we might say that the maleness of Jesus has no ultimate significance. It has social symbolic significance in the framework of societies of patriarchal privilege. In this sense Jesus as the Christ, the representative of liberated humanity and the liberating Word of God, manifests the *kenosis of patriarchy,* the announcement of the new humanity through a lifestyle that discards hierarchical caste privilege and speaks on behalf of the lowly. In a similar way, the femaleness of the social and religiously outcast who respond to him has social symbolic significance as a witness against the same idolatrous system of patriarchal privilege. This system is unmasked and shown to have no connection with favor with

God. Jesus, the homeless Jewish prophet, and the marginalized women and men who respond to him represent the overthrow of the present world system and the sign of a dawning new age in which God's will is done on earth.

But this relation of redeeming Christ and redeemed women should not be made into ultimate theological gender symbols. Christ is not necessarily male, nor is the redeemed community only women, but a new humanity, female and male. We need to think in terms of a dynamic, rather than a static, relationship between redeemer and redeemed. The redeemer is one who has been redeemed, just as Jesus himself accepted the baptism of John. Those who have been liberated can, in turn, become paradigmatic, liberating persons for others.

Christ, as redemptive person and Word of God, is not to be encapsulated "once-for-all" in the historical Jesus. The Christian community continues Christ's identity. As vine and branches Christic personhood continues in our sisters and brothers. In the language of early Christian prophetism, we can encounter Christ *in the form of our sister*. Christ, the liberated humanity, is not confined to a static perfection of one person two thousand years ago. Rather, redemptive humanity goes ahead of us, calling us to yet incompleted dimensions of human liberation.

Chapter 6
Mariology as Symbolic Ecclesiology: Repression or Liberation?

THE PATRIARCHAL FEMININE AS
MATER ECCLESIA, PSYCHE, AND VIRGIN MARY

In chapter 2 we saw how the appropriation of ultimate divine sovereignty as a male symbol allowed the female to appear only as the receptive and/or mediating principle of the male sovereignty. In the orthodox Christian Trinity, even this possibility of an intermediate feminine persona in God was eliminated. The feminine, then, can appear in Christian theology only as an expression of the creature, not as an aspect of God. The feminine represents either the original creation, the good material shaped by the hand of God, or the new creature, the eschatological community reborn from the Passion of Christ. As such, the good feminine is a spiritual principle of passive receptivity to the regenerating powers of God.

Bridal Israel and the Church as Virgin Mother

The most important theological symbol of the feminine in the Christian tradition is that of the Church, the redeemed community as "Bride of Christ" and "Mother of Christians." This symbol is rooted in the Old Testament motif of Israel as God's wife. As we have seen, this was developed in a negative or judgmental way in Hosea and other prophets. In the Song of Songs, a maverick piece in the Old Testament, a different possibility appears. The Song of Songs probably has its roots

139

in Canaanite psalms of the love between Anath and Baal.[1] The
Canaanite conception of this divine love made the lovers equals.
It is not a patriarchal relationship in which Baal is the active
partner and Anath the passive one. Rather, there is mutual
seeking and attraction.

The Song of Songs transposes this tradition of divine love
into a Hebrew idiom that represents the love of a maiden and
the king, with the mutuality and equality of the lovers retained.
The Song speaks sometimes from the male point of view
seeking his beloved and sometimes from the female side.[2] The
lovers speak of each other as sister and brother, and the
language is sensual and erotic.

Modern exegetes have spoken of this poem as only a
"human" love song having no analogy to divine love. They
regard the allegorizing of it as inappropriate.[3] But this is a false
distinction. In antiquity, divine love was the prototype of
human love. One sang of the love of God and Goddess at
human marriages and of the birth pangs of the Mother Goddess
at human birthings to stimulate and provide the patterns for
these human activities. Perhaps what is jarring for Christian
exegetes is precisely the complete mutuality and equality of
the lovers. If this is an analogy of divine-human love, it fundamentally disrupts the hierarchical pattern of divine-human
and male-female relations.

Nevertheless, the Song entered the Hebrew canon only by
being accepted as an allegory of the love relationship between
Yahweh and Israel. In the first century, Rabbi Akibah won
its acceptance into the Hebrew canon by arguing that the
allegory was its true meaning.[4] The Rabbis strictly forbade it
to be sung in taverns and on secular occasions. The Christian
Church, in turn, took up the piece as a symbol of the mystical
love between Christ and his Church or between Christ and the
soul. The eroticism of the song was sublimated, and a hierarchical presupposition of dominant divine maleness and submissive human femaleness was imposed on its interpretation.

In the New Testament, the hierarchical pattern of divine male over human female as an analogy for patriarchal marriage is not only continued but exaggerated. This is particularly evident in the post-Pauline letter to the Ephesians (chapter 5). Here the headship of Christ over the Church is the model for the proper relationship of paternalistic husband and submissive wife in Christian marriage. By making the husband analogous to Christ in relation to his wife, the author even suggests that a wife should consider her husband representative of Christ or God! Her husband is her Lord, as Christ is Lord of the Church. She is his body, as the Church is the body of Christ.

This analogy of Christ to Church as husband to wife is all the more bizarre by being transposed into an eschatological idiom. The Church as body of Christ is the eschatological Church, redeemed by Christ's redemptive acts. She has become perfect and spotless, as the eschatological bride of Christ who is without sin. To make this relationship of Christ and the Church a model of human marriage is odd and contrived. It suggests that the husband should be looked at as redeemer of his wife. She, in turn, should become spotless, perfect, and without sin (virginal?) through submission to his redemptive authority.

As a model of human marriage, this relationship is so unrealistic as to suggest that the author (probably not Paul) is somewhat confused. He takes a symbol of the eschatological union of Christ and the Church, which is actually antithetical to human marriage and sexuality, and tries to impose it inappropriately on human marriage in order to counteract the tendencies of the early Church to dissolve marriage into eschatological equality between celibate women and men. The author is caught midway between the Pauline eschatological vision of the Church and the reactionary direction of the household codes, which try to return the Christian Church to the models of historical patriarchy. The result is a contradiction that, nevertheless, for two thousand years has been preached to Christian couples as though it were a possible model of real marriage. This has been done by a selective interpretation that

makes the text primarily a model of benevolent paternalism
and female submission.

In the Church Fathers, the symbol of the Church as eschatological bride of Christ is continued, but here its antithesis
to real marriage and sexuality becomes clear. In the *Symposium*
of Methodius (d. A.D. 311) ten Christian virgins discourse on
Christian virginity, culminating in a hymn to Christ as bridegroom of the Church. The virgins sing that they have spurned
mortal marriage and worldly wealth so that they could come
to Christ in immaculate robes and enter into his blessed bridal
chamber.

The marriage of Christ with the Church mingles the motifs
of the New Adam–New Eve with the eschatological bridegroom
and bride. The Church is born from Christ's side in his passion
on the cross. But she is also inseminated by this passion and
brings forth redeemed, virginal offspring who have transcended
sin and death. Christ is both her mother, as the New Adam,
and her husband!

> ...the Church has been formed from His [Christ's] flesh and
> bones. For it was for her sake that the Word left His heavenly
> Father and came down to earth in order to cling to His Spouse
> and slept in the ecstasy of His Passion. Voluntarily did He die
> for her sake "that He might present her to Himself a glorious
> Church and without blemish, cleansing her by the laver [Eph.
> 5:26] for the reception of that blessed spiritual seed which He
> sows and plants by secret inspiration in the depths of the soul,
> and like a woman the Church conceives of this seed and forms
> it until the day she bears and nurtures it as virtue.
>
> So too the word "increase and multiply" is duly fulfilled as
> the Church grows day by day in size and beauty and numbers,
> thanks to the intimate union between her and the Word, coming
> down to us even now and continuing His ecstasy in the memorial
> of His Passion. For otherwise the Church could not conceive
> and bring forth the faithful "by the laver of regeneration" unless
> Christ is emptied Himself for them too for their conception of
> Him, as I have said, in the recapitulation of His Passion, and
> came down from Heaven to die again and clung to His Spouse

the Church, allowing to be removed from His side a power by which all may grow strong who have been built upon Him, who have been born of the laver and receive of His flesh and bone, that is, of his holiness and glory. (*Symposium,* Logos 3. 8)

The nuptials of the Church with Christ are set in contrast to and annul the human nuptials that procreate moral offspring through sexual intercourse. A new and higher spiritual intercourse, a spiritual conception and birthing in the womb of baptism, overcomes the carnal gestation and birth of human mothers from which we all receive sin and death. Rebirth in Christ reverses the death-dealing powers of human birth, bringing life everlasting. Unlike human sexuality, which "degrades" the woman's body by depriving it of its virginity, the spiritual intercourse and conception of Christian rebirth restores virginity. The Church as bride of Christ brings forth virginally, and her offspring are virgins who spurn the mortal embraces that bring death in favor of the divine embraces with Christ that bestow eternal life.

Patristic theologians frequently discourse on the negative status of real marriage in the new dispensation of Christ. It is still allowed, but it is no longer mandated in the Christian era. It brings forth only the paltry thirtyfold yield of virtue, in contrast to widowhood, which brings forth sixtyfold, and virginity, which yields a hundredfold.[5] St. Jerome even opines that the only good thing about marriage is that it produces Christian virgins who can then aspire to that higher life that had been lost by their ignominious mothers.[6]

The early Christian symbol of the Church as eschatological bride of Christ and mother of Christians is developed in a framework that is clearly antisexual and antimaternal. The concept of eschatology itself is shaped by negation of the sexual and maternal roles of real women. The female roles have been both sublimated and taken over into male "spiritual" power. Male headship power controls the higher conception, gestation, birth, and suckling and relates this to a transcendent sphere that negates the "carnal" maternity of women. It then becomes possible to symbolize the female life-giving role as the source of "death," while expropriating the symbols of conception, birth, and nurture to males.

Male eschatology is built on negation of the mother. Rejection of sexuality and procreation is not merely a function of prudery. Or, rather, antisexual asceticism is itself based on the fantasy that, by escaping the female realm of sexuality and procreation, one can also free oneself from finitude and mortality. The escape from sex and birth is ultimately an attempt to escape from death for which women as Eve and mother are made responsible. Male eschatology combines male womb envy with womb negation.

The eschatological Church has escaped the limitations of historical existence and is already anticipating the Reign of Christ. The doctrine of the Assumption of Mary symbolizes the Church triumphant, ascended to Heaven and seated at the right hand of Christ. Christ receives Mary (the Church) as his bride and crowns her as Queen of Heaven. From above, she reigns at his side over all. To her, too, every knee shall bend in Heaven and on earth. The assimilation of Christ into the Constantinian cosmic Pantocrator equates this eschatological Reign with the present reign of Christian hierarchical authorities. The Church triumphant, reigning as Queen of Heaven from the right hand of the throne of Christ, also claims to reign over the kings and emperors of earth. She is the mediatrix of all graces, funneled from Christ through her "neck," to the body of Christians on earth. Mariology becomes a tool of ecclesiastical triumphalism.

Celibate males are the primary powerholders of the Church. They represent the "male feminine" in the hands of antipro-creative males. Female virgins are marginalized as humble servants of this male celibate control over the "spiritual feminine." After all, they are still female and potentially sexual. Married couples become a lower caste in the Church. Within the "laity" women are at the bottom of the ladder. They are lower than slaves (whose subjugation is merely historical and not cosmological) and tend toward the demonic. So it is not contradictory, but understandable, that a male celibate culture that exalted the symbol of the "spiritual feminine," as Mary and Mater Ecclesia, almost to the status of the divine vilified and demonized the sexual and maternal roles of real women.

The Nuptials of the Soul

The imagery of the mystical union of Christ and the soul is dependent on the Christ-Church relationship. It transposes this relationship from the corporate, sacramental level to the personal, mystical level. Only within the Church as bridegroom of Christ, font of grace and matrix of spiritual rebirth, is it possible for the soul to be united with Christ, the divine *Logos*. This concept of the soul or psyche as a female (passive-receptive) awaiting divine insemination is not confined to Christian sources. Christian mystics draw on the Platonic allegorization of the Eros-Psyche myth.[7] Already in the Hellenistic Jewish philosopher Philo this concept of the feminine soul in relation to the fecundating power of the divine *Logos* is present.

Philo primarily uses the female as the symbol of the lower realm of the passions and the body. This is the world of sense perception that deforms the higher understanding of noetic reality. It is the cause of deceit and the source of all sin and evil. Women symbolize the vices. The soul, when it becomes animated by the divine Word, turns away from this "womanish" sphere and becomes virginal and male. Thus Philo says:

> The union of human beings, that is made for the procreation of children, turns virgins into women. But when God begins to consort with the soul, He makes what before was a woman into a virgin again, for He takes away the degenerate and emasculate passions which made it womanish and plants instead the native growth of unpolluted virtues. Thus He will not talk with Sarah till she has ceased from all that is after the manner of women and is ranked once more as a pure virgin. (*De Cherubim* 50)

For Philo the soul, as reason, is seen as the dominant and male principle in relation to the body and its passions. But in relation to God the soul can be regarded as passive and feminine. Although the negative use of the female as symbol of the carnal is primary, Philo does have a secondary use of the feminine, as the passive receptivity of the soul to divine power. Here the matriarchs symbolize the spiritual or virginal feminine, but only when they have quit sexual relations and procreation and become chaste.[8]

It is Origen, the Alexandrian Christian philosopher whose allegorical method of exegesis closely follows the tradition of Philo, who establishes the Song of Songs as the key text for the mystical union of the soul with the divine *Logos*. Origen also acknowledges the ecclesiological meaning of the text as the "wedding song" of Christ with the Church, which culminates and fulfills the incomplete union of God with Israel. But this exegesis moves primarily toward the mystical sense of the poem. In interpreting the text "The King hath brought me into his chamber," Origen says:

> But since the reference is either to the Church who comes to Christ or to the soul that cleaves to the Word of God, how should we understand Christ's chamber and the storehouse of the Word of God into which He brings the Church or the soul thus cleaving to Him — you can take it either way — except as Christ's own secret and mysterious mind? Of this Paul also said: "We have the mind of Christ, that we may know the things that are given us from God." These things are those that eye "hath not seen, nor ear heard, neither hath it entered into the heart of man, what things God hath prepared for them that love Him." So, when Christ leads the soul to understand His mind, she is said to be brought into the King's chamber, "in which are hid the treasures of His wisdom and knowledge." [Col. 2:3] (bk. 1, sec. 5)

Origen strictly cautions the readers of the Song of Songs against interpreting its language on a physical, sexual level. Only those who have purified themselves from sex and "carnal thoughts" should read it. The seemingly sensual language is only to be taken allegorically, as symbols of inward and spiritual relations to God.[9] This same admonition is repeated by the subsequent Christian commentators on the poem.[10]

Despite these admonitions against carnal thoughts, the use of the Song of Songs as the text for mystical ascent and union with God allows Christian mysticism to draw upon and sublimate erotic energies. This plays an obvious role in a celibate culture. The celibate male can turn his affection to the person of the Virgin Mary as his "lady," in order to repress (or relegate to a lower level) real sexuality with women. Spiritual eroticism is to be directed to the higher, spiritual feminine that elevated and transformed the soul, rather than to the debasing, carnal female.

Similarly, women can be urged to spurn all thoughts of marriage by sublimating their affections in an interior relation to Christ. Jerome in his letter on virginity to the teenager, Eustochium, daughter of Paula, urges her to shut herself up in her bedchamber and become absorbed in thoughts of her love relationship with Christ as the antidote to sexual temptation:

> Ever let the privacy of your chamber guard you; ever let the Bridegroom sport with you within. Do you pray? You speak to the Bridegroom. Do you read? He speaks to you. When sleep overtakes you He will come behind and put His hand through the hole of the door and your heart shall be moved for Him; and you will awake and rise up and say: "I am sick for love." Then He will say, "A garden enclosed is my sister, my spouse; a spring shut up, a fountain sealed." [Cant. 4:12] (Ep. 22. 25)

The root of mystical powers in erotic energies is not some "dirty secret" of which we should be ashamed. On the contrary, it manifests the truth of the human being as a psycho-physical unity, not a dualism of body and spirit. The problem with this mystical tradition is not the interconnection of mystical and erotic ecstasy, but its deformation into dualism and the shaping of it by a patriarchal imagination that makes the erotic relationship a sadomasochistic one of male assault and female submission. The creative dialectic of thinking and feeling, idea and intuition, is turned into a one-sided relationship. Mystics have often broken the bounds of this patriarchal imagination (and the Song of Songs, with its imagery of mutuality, was particularly apt as a text that allowed them to do that). But the official pattern of dominance and submission stifles the full dialectic of creative energies. The impregnation of the soul by transcendent mind becomes a one-way process. We are not allowed to experience a more mutual relationship in which the soul impregnates the mind and makes it fertile.

The mystical tradition of the connubial embraces of Christ and the Church, Christ and the soul, built on the imagery of the Song of Songs, does not disappear with Protestantism and the rejection of celibate spirituality. The tradition continues in seventeenth-century Puritan sermons and tracts. Cotton Mather, in his tract *A Glorious Espousal: A Brief Essay to Illustrate and Prosecute the Marriage, Wherein Our Great Savior Offers to Espouse Himself to the Children of Men,*[11] repeats the same theme. Here the espousal of the Soul with Christ is its predestined election, and the consummation of the union is the experience of redeeming grace. The drama of the love poem can now be interpreted as the unfolding of the soul's conviction of its sin, recognition of its election, and its various stages of experience of grace and regeneration. The Christian who experiences these overtures of Christ will reply, "Lord, I am thine, save me." In Mather's words:

> In this act of Resignation there must and will be nothing less than thy very All included. Resign thy Spirit unto Him and say, O my Savior, I desire that all the faculties of my soul may be filled with thee, and used for thee. Resign thy Body unto Him.[12]

Christ will consummate the union, saying to the soul that he would

bring thee into my Father's house and the King bring thee into
His chamber, and then fill thee with Joy unspeakable and full
of glory, from wonderous endless, inconceivable demonstrations
of my Love unto thee...[13]

In Mather, as in the patristic and medieval traditions, this
femininity of the soul in relation to Christ applies to men and
women alike. The male too must learn to break his will and
become passive and "feminine" under the sovereign power
of God. This hierarchical pattern is more closely assimilated
into the human social hierarchy of male over female in Puritanism than it was in celibate mysticism because the message
is now preached within the ordinary context of the parish
church and married couples, not as esoteric mysticism for a
celibate elite.

The femininity of the soul to Christ was the apex of a whole
system of masculine rule and feminine submission that included
the submission of the laity to the clergy, servants to masters,
and, of course, wives to husbands. Men too learned how to
cultivate their "femininity" in relation to hierarchical authority
— God, ministers, governors, masters — above them. But that
did not alter in the least that in relation to those under them
they played "God" as masculine authority. Women too had
some authority, delegated by their husbands, over children and
servants. But the metaphor reinforced the female's primary
role and identity as the passive, submissive partner in authority
relationships. Most of all, women must never assume authority
in relation to their husbands or to the public authorities of
Church and state. To do so was not merely crime but heresy,
Such women were in rebellion against God's revealed man-
dates for creation and redemption.[14]

Mariology and the Spiritual Feminine

The Mariological tradition functions in patriarchal theology
primarily to reflect and express the ideology of the patriarchal
feminine. The Virgin Mary becomes the theological personifi-

cation of Psyche and Mother Church as Virginal Bride and Mother of Christians. She is the font of grace and, ultimately, the resurrected body and glorified Church ascended to Heaven and reigning at the side of Christ. The linking of Mary, Jesus' mother, with this theology of the Church is begun in Luke's infancy narrative, the primary source of Mariology in the New Testament. Here Mary becomes the "first believer" whose assent to God's will makes her the means of God's messianic redemption. Second-century Mariology develops this into the theme of the New Eve. Mary is the obedient female who reverses the disobedience of the First Eve and thus makes possible the advent of the New Adam, Christ.[15]

The theme of the virgin birth of Christ is found in the infancy narratives of Luke and Matthew. Originally this idea expressed the sense of Christ's advent as totally dependent on divine initiative, not the product of the "works of man." But the virgin birth was not seen by Matthew as precluding sexual relations between Mary and Joseph after Jesus' birth (Matt. 1:25). The Evangelists all report the tradition that Jesus had blood brothers and sisters (presumably children of Mary, since she is always linked with them).[16] Soon the theology of the virginal Church began to make these earlier traditions unacceptable for many Christians however. If Mary is the spotless Church of eschatological regeneration, then her virginity represents a decisive break with carnal sexuality and reproduction. Her virginity must have remained intact through the birth and she remained virgin thereafter. The perpetual virginity of Mary is the correlate of Mary as the representative of the eschatological community.[17]

The doctrines of the Assumption and the Immaculate Conception represent further formulations of the logic of this theology. If Mary is the sinless matrix of the sinless Christ who transcends carnal reproduction, then she herself must have been preserved from the "taint" of carnal reproduction. Although she was not reproduced virginally, God must have effected a miracle at the moment of her conception to prevent the consequences of sexual reproduction — original sin and mortality — from ever being actualized in her. From this it follows that she could not have really died. If she is not subject to the penalty of sex and death, she could only have "slept" in the grave briefly and then been taken up to Heaven, body and soul, by Christ.[18]

Mary's Assumption thus anticipates the resurrected body of Christians, the glorious body of the Church, whereby the redeemed creation itself will recover its original union with the immortal soul and so will become no longer corruptible. Then the Church, the redeemed, cosmic body of society and creation, will lose its present "subjection to decay" and become the glorious spiritual body of the eschatological New Creation. In the words of the modern Mariologist Otto Semmelroth in his book *Mary, the Archetype of the Church:*

> The material world's completed redeemed state must also shine forth in Mary as Archetype of the Church. . . the redeemed state of the physical cosmos at the end of time shines forth in her body. In her body she co-enacted subjectively Christ's death. In her, as Archetype, her body shows the Church's fully redeemed body. Her body lights the way for the body of the Church and shows that the transfiguration dwells like a seed within her corporality.[19]

At the same time, both Mary's Immaculate Conception and her prefiguring of the redeemed state of corporal creation reach back to the lost alternative before the Fall. Then pure nature, as it came forth from the hand of God, was totally under the power of the Spirit, and so was without evil and was not subject to death. Mary represents the original, good matrix of nature before its alienation from the Spirit. She preserves that original nature that God blessed and called "very good" in the beginning. She exemplifies the primordial potential for good of created existence undeformed by sin.

In this theology of the male feminine, we sense the hidden and repressed power of femaleness and nature as they exist both beneath and beyond the present male dualisms of matter and spirit. Precisely for this reason we cannot accept this theology on male terms. We must question the male theology of female "disobedience" and sexuality as the cause of sin, and mortality as the consequence of sin. This very effort to sunder us from our mortal bodies and to scapegoat women as cause of mortality and sin is the real sin. This sin has alienated us from that fruitful unity of mind and body that we have lost and that we seek in our redemptive quest.

LIBERATION MARIOLOGY: THE CHURCH AS HUMANITY REDEEMED FROM SEXISM

Is there any basis for an alternative Mariology, one that is not the expression of the male feminine which scapegoats female sexuality for sin and death? Is there a Mariology — a doctrine of the Church as symbolically female — that would allow us to name sexism itself as sin and point toward the liberation of women and men from the dualisms of carnal femaleness and spiritual femininity?

At least a beginning of this theology of the Church can be made by taking another look at the theology of Luke. The key text for the Lucan identification of Mary with the Church, the New Israel, is the Magnificat (Luke 1:46–55). This text echoes the Hymn of Hannah, the mother of Samuel. Hannah's favor with God, which issues in the "elect child," is seen as God's redemptive favor upon Israel. Hannah's redemption by God from the shame of barrenness is used as an image of God's revolutionary power in history. God reverses the present order of power and powerlessness; he breaks the power of the mighty and gives strength to the feeble:

> For the Lord is a God of knowledge and by Him actions are weighed.
> The bows of the mighty are broken, but the feeble grid on strength.
> Those who were full have hired themselves out for bread,

but those who were hungry have ceased to hunger...
He raised up the poor from the dust; he lifts the needy from
   the ash heap...(1 Sam 2:2-5, 8)

Luke reiterates this theme. God's grace upon Mary, the
divine favor by which she will bear the messianic child, is seen
as an expression of a revolutionary transformation of an unjust
social order. God has defeated the oppressors:

He has shown the strength of His arm,
He has scattered the proud in the imagination of their hearts,
He has put down the mighty from their thrones and exalted those
   of low degree;
He has filled the hungry with good things,
and the rich he has sent empty away.
He has helped his servant Israel in the remembrance of His
   mercy. (Luke 1:51-54)

Luke's analogy between pregnancy and liberation differs in
important ways from that found in 1 Samuel. Hannah's
liberation resides in her "redemption" from the shame of
barrenness. As an older woman with no (male) children, she
is without respect or dignity as a wife. She is ridiculed by her
husband's concubine, who is fertile. Mary, on the other hand,
is a girl not yet married. Her pregnancy does not follow from
the proper role of women. Indeed, it puts her under danger
as someone who has been making her own choices about her
body and sexuality without regard for her future husband. She
may be accused of being a prostitute or a "loose woman" and
"put away." In Luke, the decision to have the redemptive child
is between her and God. Joseph is not consulted (in Matthew,
however, the deal is agreed upon in proper patriarchal fashion
between Joseph and God, without consulting Mary).[20]
   Luke goes out of his way to stress that Mary's motherhood
is a free choice. When the angel arrives, Mary does not consult
Joseph, but makes her own decision. Luke sees this free choice
as an expression of her faith. This is the key to the new redemptive community of Jesus, as distinct from the old kind

of family relationships. In a text that is found in all three synoptic Gospels, the voluntary community based on mutual choice is seen as the true family of Jesus, as contrasted with the old, unbelieving family:

> And he [Jesus] replied, "Who are my mother and my brothers?" And looking around on those who say about him, he said, "Here are my mother and my brothers! Whoever does the will of God is my brother and my sister and my mother." (Mark 3:34–35)[21]

Mary's birth-giving can become a symbol of the Church, the new believing community, because it expresses a free act of faith. Another Lucan text dispels the Marian piety that would honor Mary primarily by hymning the miracle of her "holy womb." A woman in the crowd voices the conventional wisdom that would praise the mother of such a grace-filled child:

> "Blessed is the womb that bore you and the paps that gave thee suck." But he [Jesus] replied, "Rather, blessed are those who hear the word of God and keep it." (Luke 11:27–28)

In contrast to the patriarchal theories of divine grace, exemplified in Augustine and Calvin, Lucan Mariology suggests a real co-creatorship between God and humanity, or, in this case, woman. The free act of faith is possible only when we can recognize the genuine unity between response to God and our own liberation. Faith ceases to be heteronomous submission to external authorities and becomes a free act.

Only through that free human responsiveness to God is God enabled to become the transformer of history. Without such faith, no miracles can happen. When such faith is absent, Christ can do nothing. This is the radical dependence of God on humanity, the other side of our dependence on God, which patriarchal theology has generally denied. Mary's faith makes possible God's entrance into history.

What does God enter history to do, through Mary's faith?

According to Luke, God enters history in the person of Christ to effect a liberating revolution in human relationships. Mary is exalted because, through her, God will work this revolution in history. Or, to be more accurate, she herself is both subject and object of this liberating action. She makes it possible through her act of faith, but the liberating action of God in history liberates her. She herself embodies and personifies the oppressed and subjugated people who are being liberated and exalted through God's redemptive power. She is the humiliated ones who have been lifted up, the hungry ones who have been filled with good things.

Luke's liberation language is explicitly economic and political. The mighty are put down from their thrones; the rich are sent away empty. This theme grates unpleasantly on the ears of most affluent Christians. Since many North American Christians regard themselves as near, if not exactly on, the thrones of the mighty and as moderately "filled with good things," they are offended by the idea of salvation as God's judgmental choice. They prefer to jump immediately to the idea that God loves the rich and the poor alike. This assumes that God loves the rich and the poor, oppressors and oppressed, in the same way, accepting them "as they are." The unstated bias is that God also leaves them the way they are, as oppressed and oppressors, poor and rich; salvation has nothing to do with changing this relationship. Such thinking does not entertain the possibility that God's redemptive love might be experienced differently by poor and rich, oppressed and oppressors, battered women and macho men.

In contrast to this separation of salvation from real social transformation, Luke suggests that God's redemption is experienced differently by rich and poor. The poor and oppressed experience themselves being restored to their humanity, entering a new age in which the rod of oppression is broken. Those who are privileged in the present age initially experience God's liberation as wrath, as the breaking of their systems of privilege and the shattering of their ideologies of righteousness. Only after they accept the judgment of God on their state of unjust privilege is it possible for them to join the liberated poor in the new age of God's peace and justice. Thus, Luke does not minimize the socioeconomic dimension of redemption, as does Matthew with his spiritualization of the Beatitudes; in fact, he emphasizes it by adding the negative judgmental side of God's redemption as judgment on the rich:

> Blessed are the poor, for yours is the Kingdom of God.
> Blessed are you who hunger now for you shall be satisfied.
> But woe on you who are rich, for you have received your consolation.
> Woe to you who are full now, for you shall hunger...(Luke 6:20–25)

Social iconoclasm plays a key role in Luke's understanding of God's redemptive work. Luke stresses stories of divine favor and forgiveness on classes of people who are despised by the wealthy, powerful, and traditionally religious. Jesus eats with sinners and gives favor to publicans. The good Samaritan and the rich man and Lazarus also make the point that those reviled by society express true faith and find favor with God.

Among Luke's stories of social iconoclasm, a large number, as we saw in chapter 5, deal with the vindication of women. Poor women and despised women, widows, unclean women, prostitutes, Samaritans, and Syro-Phoenicians are those in whom the messianic prophet finds the faith that is absent among the "righteous of Israel." The story of the widow's mite, the forgiveness of the prostitute who has faith, the healing of the woman with a flow of blood, the defense of Mary's right to discipleship are among the Lucan stories that lift up the typology of women as people of faith.

Luke's sensitivity to women as members of the poor and the despised, whose faith is vindicated by the messianic prophet, adds an additional dimension to the identification of Mary as liberated Israel in the Magnificat. As a woman, specifically a woman from among the poorer classes of a colonized people under the mighty empire of Rome, she represents the oppressed community that is to be lifted up and filled with good things in the messianic revolution. Mary as Church represents God's "preferential option for the poor," to use the language of Latin-American liberation theology.

It is important to identify correctly the way God's preferential option for the poor defines the primary nature of the Church. It is not that the Church, as representative of the rich, advocates the poor, in the manner of charity and noblesse oblige. Rather it is God, first of all, who opts for the poor, precisely because the rich have opted against them. This is why the poor are poor. God opts for the poor to overthrow unjust relationships. This makes the poor the preferential locus for understanding who and where the Church actually is. The Church is, first of all, the poor and oppressed, whom God is vindicating. The nonpoor and the privileged can join the Church only by joining God in this preferential option for the poor, by identifying themselves with the cause of the oppressed. This is very different from the monopolization of the Church by the social establishment, who then take it upon themselves to patronize the poor and keep them dependent in the process.

If we take seriously the female personification of the Church within this perspective, then we must take the analysis of oppression and liberation a step further. If women of the oppressed classes and social groups represent the poorest of the poor, the most despised of society, then such women can become the models of faith and their liberation becomes the special locus of the believing and liberated community. We need to move beyond the typology of Christ and the Church as dominant male and submissive female. Rather, what we see here is an ongoing process of *kenosis* and transformation. God's power no longer remains in Heaven where it can be used as a model of the "thrones of the mighty." In the iconoclastic and messianic prophet, it has been emptied out into the human situation of suffering and hope.

The response of faith to this presence of the liberating Gospel calls the oppressed out of servitude and brings them into their inheritance as people of God and heirs of the new age. If poor women of despised classes represent this ingathering community, it is because they particularly have little stake in the present systems of oppression and so are most attuned to the message. It is women especially who represent the Church by calling others out of bondage into freedom. The despised woman as poorest of the poor has symbolic priority in the Church. As such, she also represents the hosts of other oppressed groups in need of God's favor. In Matthew's words, "The prostitutes and the tax collector will go into the Kingdom of God first, ahead of you [the chief priests and elders]" (Matt. 21:31).

Chapter 7
The Consciousness of Evil:
The Journeys of Conversion

Traditional Christian theology has separated the topics of evil and conversion. Evil is described as a primordial "event" whereby the ambiguities of human existence, such as obedience and free will, were turned to the wrong choice. Humanity became alienated from its authentic self, unable to rectify itself and in need of a divine redemption that was now beyond its own capacities. Redemption and hence the possibility of conversion are then presumed to have become available to humanity, as Christians, only after the redemptive work of Christ. This construct is a symbolic one, mythologized as separate historical "events."

Consciousness of evil, in fact, originates in the process of conversion itself. To locate and identify certain realities as "evil" means to already have taken the fundamental existential turn of disaffiliating oneself from them. The way in which one situates the ideal or good potential self over against evil, then, generates a certain description of the etiology of evil. One constructs stories of "how evil began," whether it is Eve's "tempting" of Adam through the serpent or the crushing of matriarchy by patriarchy. This does not mean that evil has no objective historical reality. It simply means that we can't lose sight of the fact that the center of the drama is the human person situating itself in opposition to perceived falsifications of its own being in the name of a transcendent possibility of a good self.

The perception of evil against the good self has shifted

159

dramatically in human history and, with it, the understandings of the nature and etiology of evil. Feminism represents a fundamental shift in the valuations of good and evil. It makes a fundamental judgment upon some aspects of past descriptions of the nature and etiology of evil as themselves ratifications of evil.

Christian theology has spoken of evil, in the sense of sin, as a specifically human capacity. There may be evil in non-human nature, such as misfortunes and catastrophes, but only humans can "sin." Sin implies a perversion or corruption of human nature, that is, of one's good or authentic potential self. This capacity to sin is seen as based on the distinctively human characteristic of freedom. Humans stand out against their environment and are able to imagine alternatives to what is. They are able to generate, mentally and culturally, ideals and projects of what might be, as something better than what is, and they can use this ideal to judge and change the existing situation. Human beings, then, stand in the existential dialectic between the "is" and the "ought." The two are interdependent. One can project "oughts" only in the context of what is. "What is" is, in turn, a construct shaped by one's perception of an alternative, better option. One cannot, for example, describe the present situation as patriarchy or capitalism until one has developed an alternative, feminism or socialism. These alternatives are understood as redemptive alternatives, that is, expressions of the good potential for authenticity in the light of which the present situation is recognized and judged as "evil" or "corrupt."

Some feminists feel that the good-evil dichotomy is not one that feminists should accept. It is the underlying "error" of patriarchal thinking that the dialectics of human existence — male/female, body/consciousness, human/nonhuman nature — are turned into good-evil dualisms. Moreover, these dualisms of the polarities of human existence scapegoat the "evil" side as "female." Sexism is the underlying social foundation of the good-evil ideology.

It would seem, however, that feminism presumes a radical concept of "sin." It claims that a most basic expression of human community, the I-Thou relation as the relationship of men and women, has been distorted throughout all known history into an oppressive relationship that has victimized one-half of the human race and turned the other half into tyrants. The primary alienation and distortion of human relationality is reflected in all dimensions of alienation: from one's self as body, from the other as different from oneself, from nonhuman nature, and from God/ess. Feminism continues, in a new form, the basic Christian perception that sin, as perversion of good potential into evil, is not simply individual but refers to a fallen state of humanity, historically. Feminism's own claim to stand in judgment on patriarchy as evil means it cannot avoid the question of the capacity of humanity for sin.

The difficulty in analyzing the validity of the concept of good and evil is in the distortion of this dichotomy into a ratification of evil itself. If, as we have said, it is generic to human nature to stand out against its environment and to imagine alternative images of the authentic and good self, then the very concept of evil and good is generated as the extreme polarities of this perception of an inadequate present over better possibilities. Human capacity to imagine and create is rooted in this ability to project alternatives.

The human also stands out against its environment in other ways, by separating the human from the nonhuman and "our kind" of humans from others. The self-other dichotomy in its earliest forms was understood collectively rather than individualistically. The tribal group, as the collective self, was a primary basis for human boundary-drawing of the self against the "other": nonhuman nature and other human groups with whom no common humanity was recognized. The confusion of the self-other with the good-evil duality seems to have occurred very early in the history of human consciousness.

The males of tribal groups particularly became the centers of their own definition of the collective self against the other as female, as other tribes, and as nonhuman nature. We know that many tribes do not even have an inclusive word for *human*. Their word for their own tribe functions as an equivalent of the word *human,* reducing groups outside to nonhuman.[1] Similarly, the word for human in many languages is identical with the word for male, reducing women to a subsidiary status.[2]

The authentic, good self is identified with the favored center who dominates the cultural interpretation of humanness, and others are described in negative categories by contrast. This negative perception of the other is then reinforced when the favored group is able to gain power over the others, either to annihilate them or reduce them to servile status. The two elements are intertwined: The perception of the other as inferior, less capable of the good self, rationalizes exploitation of them. But the two need to be distinguished. The perception of the other as evil is not just the ideological superstructure of exploitative relations, as Marxists would have it. It already is found in situations where groups coexist, each thinking of the other as inferior. But when one conquers the other, the ideology of superiority of the dominant group stifles and suppresses the corresponding sense of self of the other and becomes the dominant ideology for rationalizing the other group's inferiority.

The suppressed group may continue to think of itself as superior, in a covert way. But it also, to some extent, internalizes the dominant ideology, which shapes its own socialization, and so becomes filled with fear and ambiguity about its own humanity. Thus, we must see two interconnected but distinguishable aspects to the ideology of the "other" as of lesser value: projection and exploitation. Projection externalizes the sense of inadequacy and negativity from the dominant group, making the other the cultural "carrier" of these rejected qualities. The dominant group can then rationalize exploitation as the right to reduce the other to a servile condition, abuse, and even kill them on the ground of their lesser value.

The element of projection leads to irrationalities that exceed merely the self-interest of the dominant group. Genocidal campaigns, witch-hunts, and pogroms go beyond self-interest of the powerful into a fantasy realm in which the dominant group imagines that by purging society of the "other" it can, in some sense, eradicate "evil."

Feminists, in rejecting this kind of naming of evil, are at the same time suggesting that evil does exist, precisely in this false naming, projection, and exploitation. This very process of false naming and exploitation constitutes the fundamental distortion and corruption of human relationality. Evil comes about precisely by the distortion of the self-other relationship into the good-evil, superior-inferior dualism. The good potential of human nature then is to be sought primarily in conversion to relationality. This means a *metanoia,* or "change of mind," in which the dialectics of human existence are converted from opposites into mutual interdependence. One receives back the gift of community, which has always been there but was denied by polarization: the community of person with person, individually and collectively, across differences of gender, tribe, and culture. One receives back community with nonhuman nature, which has always been there, supporting our reality. Community with God/ess exists precisely in and through this renewed community of creation.

A recent article by P. Masani tries to understand the origin of sin by using the Marxist distinction between egoistic self and the collective "species" self that is grounded in community. Sin is seen as the false separation of the self as ego from collective relations and a self-exaltation against the community in a prideful and exploitative way.[3] But this explanation of sin is too simple. It is drawn both from a male perspective and from the perspective of modern individualism. Egoistic individualism is a relatively late development of consciousness that in modern times has been available to no more than a tiny educated and aristocratic elite. We have suggested here an earlier construct of group egoism that sets itself against alien groups: women, other races, nature, and so on. This group egoism is both antagonistic to others and yet is passive in its adoption of group models of identity for the self. This, in turn, forces even greater passivity and lack of selfhood on women and other oppressed people who are socialized to acquiesce in the relationships set by the dominant male group ego.

Sin, therefore, has to be seen both in the capacity to set up prideful, antagonistic relations to others and in the passivity of men and women who acquiesce to the group ego. This passivity has been primary for women, but the hostility of the male group ego toward inferiors is also based on the insecurity of lacking a grounded self. One's "superiority" is based on a passive identification with the group ego, so one is always afraid that if one appears different, the male group ego will repudiate you as a member of that group. Men are kept in line with the ego model of masculinity by constant threats that their fellow males will repudiate them as "effeminate." One cannot just idealize collective group ego as salvation but must seek a new synthesis in which the dichotomy between egoistic individualism and passive acquiescence in group roles is transcended in the self that is grounded in community as a free and individuated self.

This conversion, or *metanoia,* from group egoism and passivity to the self grounded in community does not imply that we simply discover "paradise" at hand and the tension between good and evil vanishes as a cultural mistake. Rather, we must reckon with the fact that distorted relationships, translated into power tools of exploitation, have built up a powerful counterreality, a reality that perpetuates itself, both through socioeconomic and political structures and through ideology that shapes education and socialization at every level. Conversion to community then becomes an alternative upon which we base ourselves in order to wage a cultural and social struggle against this counterreality. One seeks to dismantle the institutional structures and refute the ideologies that incarnate alienation and to shape a new vision, culture, and society that would incarnate the grounded self in community.

GOOD AND EVIL AS MALE AND FEMALE

Among the primary distortions of the self-other relationship has been the distortion of humanity as male and female into a dualism of superiority and inferiority. This is fundamentally a male ideology and has served two purposes: the support for male identity as normative humanity and the justification of servile roles for women. However much women may be socialized into these myths of female inferiority and evil and are induced to collaborate with them, women are neither their originators nor their primary perpetuators. This point needs to be emphasized because male ideologists are continually inventing rationalizations that suggest that women contributed to the invention of these ideas and practices and that they are beneficial to women as well as to men. There is a great need for men, precisely because they live in intimate relations with women, to avoid the question of collective guilt and responsibility for sexism.

This does not mean that women are historical innocents. They have benefited from other historical oppressions along race and class lines. They also have collaborated with sexism in lateral violence toward themselves and other women. We simply assert here the obvious: sexism is gender privilege of males over females. It is males *primarily* who have originated this form of oppression, benefited from it, and perpetuated it, legally and ideologically.

Myths of female evil are found in the early strata of human culture. One early locus, as suggested earlier in this book, may have been the male puberty rites in which the male was uprooted from the mother's world and initiated into the father's. Tales were told of evil mother-rule "once upon a time." The conquering of women by men was celebrated both as the etiology of present male status and as a mandate to maintain that status against women.

In Western European culture two primary myths have scapegoated women as the primordial cause of evil. The Greek story of Pandora in Hesiod's *Work and Days* is a myth of the etiology of evil that starts with Zeus' own desire to keep the arts of civilization from humanity. But Prometheus steals fire from the gods and so suffers terrible punishment for having favored "mankind." Zeus needs to punish "mankind" for these benefits, so he fashions a female, Pandora, endowed with all female graces but filled within with "falsehood, treacherous thoughts and a thievish nature." He sends her as a gift to humanity, together with a box full of troubles.

Before the coming of Pandora, humanity lived in a paradisal state, "free and secure from trouble, and free from wearisome labour, safe from painful diseases that bring mankind to destruction." Pandora lifts the lid from the box and unleashes all manner of evil and troubles upon mankind, leaving only "hope" lingering under the lid. For Hesiod, Pandora stands for woman herself as a bane upon males, without whom they would live a happy and blessed existence.[4]

The Hebrew myth of Eve has had much greater cultural impact than that of Pandora, since Christian theology has understood it to be divine revelation and hence has taken this rather odd folktale with consummate theological seriousness. It is perhaps not insignificant to note that Hebrew thought itself, in the Scriptures and early Rabbinic writings, did not take this story very seriously. Although it appears as one creation story in the early Genesis material, it is never referred to at any other place in Hebrew Scripture as the basis of the etiology of evil. For Judaism, the primary myth of evil lies in the story of God's election of Israel and its subsequent apostasy from God by seeking idols. It is this drama of good and evil, and not the Eve story, that shapes Hebrew thought.

When, in intertestamental apocalyptic thought (180 B.C.-A.D. 95), concepts of the female genesis of evil became prevalent, the myth used to express this was not the Eve story, but the Watcher story of Genesis 6:1-4. In this story the sons of God (angels or Watchers) mate with the daughters of humanity and produce giants (interpreted later as demons).

Women's beautiful hair and adornments, which seduced the angels and brought forth the demonic powers, are described as the origin of the evil influences that surround and seduce humanity into evil.[5] The Gospels likewise ignore the Eve story as the basis of the origin of evil. They share the late Jewish world view in which human decision making, for good or evil, is surrounded by powerful demonic influences that tip the balance to the negative side. But the etiology of the demonic powers is not spelled out.

Hence, it is Pauline theology, with its dualism of Old and New Adam, that lays the basis for a new theological seriousness toward the story of Adam's fall. In the post-Pauline epistle 1 Timothy, Eve's secondary position in creation and primacy in sin are used to justify the resubjugation of women in the Christian Church.[6] Pauline theology raises the problem of sin to a dimension unknown in Judaism. While Judaism recognizes an element of collective historical evil as cosmic powers that pull humans to bad choices, it presumes that human freedom to choose good over evil remains fundamentally intact.

Pauline theology, as it came to be interpreted by Augustine and his successors, saw the Adamic fall as obliterating human freedom to choose good. Humans become alienated from their own good human potential, which must be given back to them as a gift through the Crucifixion of Christ. Thus, the scapegoating of Eve as the cause of the fall of Adam makes all women, as her daughters, guilty for the radical impotence of "man" in the face of evil, which is paid for only by the death of Christ! In the words of the Latin Church Father Tertullian:

> *You* are the Devil's gateway. *You* are the unsealer of that forbidden tree. *You* are the first deserter of the divine law. *You* are she who persuaded him whom the Devil was not valiant enough to attack. *You* destroyed so easily God's image man. On account of *your* desert, that is death, even the Son of God had to die. (*de Cult Fem* 1. 1)

This does not mean that Judaism does not have ways of mythologizing women's inferiority and potential for subverting male definitions of good humanity. In folk Judaism, these are expressed by the Lilith story, the story of Adam's first wife, who refused to submit to him and fled into the desert, there becoming a source of all kinds of evils and dangers to family life. Eve becomes the second submissive wife, taken from Adam's side, whom God gives Adam to replace the rebellious Lilith.[7] But this story is not taken by Judaism as "high" theological teaching. It is Christianity that has particularly elevated the story of Eve's responsibility for the fall of Adam to a position of ultimate theological seriousness.

In the stories of Pandora, the Watchers, Lilith, and Eve, the female is seen as the enemy of harmony, good order, and felicity in human affairs. These myths reveal a tremendous male fear of women's suppressed power, which, having been once unleashed, overthrew original paradisal conditions and introduced disease, mortality, hard work, and frustrating struggle for survival in place of what was ease and happiness in the midst of spontaneous plenty.

If this "original paradise" is recognized to be a mythologizing of early infancy, in which the mother provides the time of ease and plenty from her own body, then such male myths actually scapegoat women as mothers for the loss of the paradise which *she* had once provided but which is lost to the male, wrenched from childhood into the adult (male) world of harsh struggle. It is not accidental that figures such as Eve, Lilith, and Pandora, transformed into myths of the female origins of evil, are also ancient Mother-Goddesses. The Mother-Goddess who provided paradise is transformed, in male puberty rites, into the evil female who deprived the male of paradise.

Male mythology not only makes woman responsible for the advent of evil in the world, but it also translates female evil into an ontological principle. The female comes to represent the qualities of materiality, irrationality, carnality, and finitude, which debase the "manly" spirit and drag it down into sin and death. An example of this is Philo's interpretation of the creation of Eve in his commentary on Genesis, an account that had great influence on the Church Fathers' exegesis of this text. According to Philo, "man" was first created as a spiritual idea, an image of the divine *Logos*. Material humanity, by contrast, is a compound of mortal bodiliness and immortal soul, the image of the divine *Logos*. Before the creation of Eve, the material or bodily component of Adam was under the control of his spiritual self, and so the propensities of the body to mortality and sin were held in check. The creation of Eve, however, represents the separation of Adam's mortal, bodily lower half and his soul. With Eve's creation, Adam becomes seduced to his lower self through sexual desire, which "is the beginning of iniquities and transgressions, and it is owing to this that men have exchanged their previously immortal and happy existence for one which is mortal and full of misfortune."[8] In Philo's account, not only Eve's disobedience after her creation but her mere existence represents the "fall" of "man" away from the higher male spiritual principle and his entrapment in the lower, female material principle.

Stories like the myth of Eve also enforce the continued repression and subjugation of woman, as "punishment" for her primordial "sin" in causing the fall of "man" and the loss of paradise. Because women are in fact not inferior, but full human persons of equivalent capacities upon whom all males, as children, were once dependent, the task of suppressing women into dependence on males is a never-ending struggle. It is not a "coup" accomplished once upon a time in some mysterious victory of patriarchy at the dawn of history. It must be reiterated generation after generation, by repeating the myths of woman's original sin to the young, both male and female, and by reinforcing laws and structures that marginalize women from power roles in society. Even then the task is not accomplished. Wives show an alarming lack of submission, an irrepressible tendency to assert shreds of autonomy and resistance. The whole range of coercive techniques, from brute force to contempt and ridicule to artful blandishments, is necessary to keep her in her "place." Religion is relied upon as both the foundation and the daily aid in this project.

New myths and methods of terrorizing women into keeping their place are invented to suppress or eliminate those women who have somehow escaped becoming sufficiently docile to their own servitude. In modern times, Freudian and other forms of patriarchal psychotherapy have become primary tools for this second-level enforcement of women's subjugation. In late-medieval and early modern Europe, witchcraft persecution provided a central tool for terrorizing insufficiently subservient women. In the inquisitors' writings of the late-medieval period, the myth of the female as less capable of intellectual and moral self-control, and hence as more prone to the demonic, was made explicit. In the *Malleus Maleficarum,* the handbook of the persecution of witches written by two Dominican inquisitors in 1486, witchcraft is explicitly linked to women's inferior "nature":

> As for the first question, why a greater number of witches is found in the fragile feminine sex than among men, is indeed a fact that it were idle to contradict...Since women are feebler both in mind and body, it is not surprising that they should come under the spell of witchcraft. For as regards intellect, or the understanding of spiritual things, they seem to be of a different nature from men...But the natural reason is that she is more carnal than a man, as is clear from her many carnal abominations. And it should be noted that there was a defect in the formation of the first woman, since she was formed from a bent rib, that is, a rib of the breast which is bent as it were in a contrary direction to a man. And since through this defect she is an imperfect animal, she always deceives...And all this is indicated by the etymology of the word, for *Femina* comes from *Fe* and *Minus,* since she is ever weaker to hold and preserve the faith. Therefore a wicked woman is by her nature quicker to waver in her faith and consequently quicker to adjure the faith, which is the root of witchcraft.[9]

The dynamics of witchcraft persecution, as a means of terrorizing older and insufficiently docile women, are illustrated in the trials that took place in Puritan Massachusetts between 1647 and 1700. Puritanism, or separatist Congregationalism, had been a dissenting religion in England. Women who joined this movement were unusually courageous and independent and were encouraged to be so by Puritan divines against the wishes of Anglican authorities. Puritanism also had a strict doctrine of woman's place in marriage, as submissive helpmeet to the male. This and this alone was woman's vocation and reason for existence.

Once this movement was transplanted to New England, the contradiction between its theory of woman's place and the presence of a large number of outspoken and independent women became evident. The heresy trials against Anne Hutchinson and other women who became critics of the clergy as well as the witchcraft persecutions functioned either to cow or to eliminate these "improper" women and to reinforce the normative standard of women's behavior and place in Puritan society.

Carol Karlsen has demonstrated the role of the persecutions in a detailed demographic and cultural study of the women accused of witchcraft.[10] She has shown that the primary group of persons accused were women. Although men were also accused, they were almost always relatives, usually husbands of accused women, and the accusations against men were seldom taken very seriously. Moreover, the primary group vulnerable to such accusations was older women between forty and sixty, or women past childbearing age. When younger women or female children were accused, it was generally because they were daughters or granddaughters of so-called witches. The older women, moreover, were the ones most likely to be executed.

Further, the primary group of women at risk in Puritan society were generally women who were widows or single and who had some reputation as healers or midwives (a common role of all women, but some had special gifts). They were women who often had come into some inheritance of land, either because they had no brothers or because parents or husbands had chosen to bequeath to them more than the usual amount of property. They were also women with a reputation for lack of docility to male neighbors and the clergy.

Thus, the group of women most at risk of persecution were women who, in one of several ways, fell outside the normative role of the "goodwife": they were personally and economically independent and they were no longer fulfilling the roles of wife and mother, but managing their own affairs independently. If the witchcraft accusations did not actually result in their execution, they generally left such women in penury, dependent on begging from town funds or relatives for support. If such a woman fled the area, she would also forfeit her property. Thus, the witchcraft accusations, which went on continuously for more than fifty years after the Puritans became established in the colonies, served to crush a particular class of women who were dangerous to the normative definition of woman in society.

Since male Puritans were married rather than celibate, as the Dominican inquisitors were, and thus had a stake in securing the cooperation of women in their own subjugation, they could not characterize the nature of all women as evil. Rather, they set forth a definition of the "good woman" as submissive helpmeet as the primary way of allowing women to achieve virtue and salvation. But the underside of this ideology of the "goodwife" was the witch, the "bad woman," who failed to fit into her assigned status as helpmeet, but threatened to run her own affairs and speak her own mind. The ruthless crushing of this group of women in the second half of the seventeenth century served as an ominous "lesson" to other Puritan women to keep to their places in the established order. By 1700, the persecutions gradually ended, not only because Enlightenment rationality made the myths of witches less acceptable but perhaps because they were no longer necessary. The clergy and male authorities had won.

Women in Puritan Massachusetts had "learned their lesson," at least for a time.

SEXISM AND ORIGINAL SIN

The recognition of sexism as wrong, evil, and sinful brings about the total collapse of the myths of female evil. The recognition that the social structures of marginalization of women are unjust creates a fundamental *metanoia,* or turning around, from the perception of woman as "other" to the recognition of woman as equivalent human person. This *metanoia* necessarily starts within woman herself, who in turn demands a recognition of woman's personhood from men as well.

Once a breach in the wall of sexist ideology and depersonalization of woman is made, the entire ideological and social superstructure built up over thousands of years of sexism and justification of sexism is open to question. Every aspect of male privilege loses its authority as natural and divine right and is reevaluated as sin and evil. This is deeply frightening to males. Consequently, they have been quick to slam the door on the slightest beginnings of such questioning and to mount counterrevolutionary campaigns of resubjugation of women whenever feminist movements have begun. But it is also frightening to women. They have to question all the ways they have traded a diminished humanity for dependent forms of security.

More than that, women have to suspect that the entire symbolic universe that surrounds them, which has socialized them to their roles, is deeply tainted by hostility to their humanity. This touches on all their most intimate relations, to mother and father, ministers and teachers, husband, male and female children. An entire social and symbolic universe crumbles within and outside them. They recognize in the familiar the deeply alien. The very grammar they have been taught to use to express themselves, the symbols they use to praise God and locate themselves in relation to God become bitter-tasting in their mouths as they come to recognize these words and symbols as tools of a vast and ancient system of negation of their own humanity. Few women have the courage to advance more than a few steps on this journey of recognition of sexism as evil, so vast and convoluted are the layers of enchantment, delusion, and seduction.

Sexism as sin centers on distorted relationality. The objectification of woman as bearer of repressed and negative parts of the male psyche involves the distortion of the being of both males and females. Men fail to integrate into their own identity those repressed capacities which they project onto women. Women, in turn, are denied those capacities for autonomous selfhood, decision making, and critical intelligence monopolized by males. This distortion of relationality into masculine-feminine complementarity, far from representing ideal relationship as male ideology would have it, in fact destroys authentic I-Thou relationship between men and women.

There can be no I-Thou relationship where there is no authentic self that is allowed to stand over against and respond to another. What is called "relationship" is really an interdependence of masks and roles that is fundamentally pathological. Each side of the gender dualism depends on the other for what it lacks in itself. The man regresses to childhood dependence in those areas in which he depends on the woman to serve him. The woman is helpless in the public realm to which she is denied access and for which she lacks the skills of survival.

Her dependence is much more serious because the two realms are not at all comparable in power. Without access to public power and skills, woman cannot survive alone, whereas man's control of power and resources means that woman's services are more readily replaceable. Yet the basic humanity of both is fundamentally truncated. Because each lacks an individuated self, there is no genuine person-to-person communication between them. He reduces her to the body that services his domestic and sexual needs but with whom he does not communicate. She experiences the slow soul-starvation of communication denial.

The reduction of woman to the body-object of male use is enforced by a vast network of control, ranging from the most subtle to the most brutal. Direct physical assault is certainly the ultimate weapon that males assume they hold in reserve over women. Although the battered wife now comes to be regarded as a special "social problem," in fact there are few women, even today, who have not experienced at least one or two beatings from husbands or boyfriends. Historically, this weapon of control over women has been taken for granted as a male prerogative, defended in civil and ecclesiastical law.[11]

Male power over women means a denial of women's right to control their own bodies. Denial of reproductive decision making is fundamental to this control. The male who "owns" a woman is assumed to have total sexual access to her. She must not reject his advances or make decisions about the effects of his "seed" upon her body and her life. The woman not under a particular male's control and protection, in turn, is regarded as available for rape. The rape of women is fundamentally an expression of hostility and contempt for women, rather than an expression of "uncontrollable sexual desire."[12] This is shown particularly by the way it is often accompanied by violence and mutilation. In tribal societies, men gang-rape women who are found alone, unprotected by a male and out of their place and role in women's sphere of activities.[13] In war, gang-rape of conquered women also is a way in which males send messages to other males. The impotence of the conquered male is manifest in his inability to protect "his women" from rape by other males.[14]

Control over woman's body involves objectifying woman's body and viewing it as a commodity. This involves various mutilations; woman's body is twisted and distorted to make it an object of display and conspicuous consumption. The mutilated genitals, bound feet, or corseted waists of female "fashions" have been among the most violent expressions of this objectification. Female fashions even today have some of the same effects of commoditization. Mascara, eyeliner, and eye shadow transform woman's eyes from a means of sight into an object to be seen. Paris and New York dress fashions, with their pale, emaciated models dressed in contorted garments, express nothing so much as a culture of male fashion designers who express their hostility to women by sadistic tyranny over their body image.

It might be objected that humans, male and female, are creatures of display; feathers, body tattoos, powdered wigs, and high heels have been worn by men as well as women. One has to look carefully at the messages of dress and display, however. The feathers and robes of males display their power and authority in ceremonial situations. Men who are found in foppish dress, such as the eighteenth-century aristocrat or the ghetto pimp, are precisely males reduced to parasitic leisure classes.

Women's dress has been continually designed to enforce passivity, to make woman's body an object to be displayed rather than a means of her own self-actualization. It is not surprising that the most extreme styles for women — the tight corsets, the high heels, the elaborate headdresses — have been reserved primarily for the upper classes, that is, for those women whom men do not need as laborers but can afford to make into objects of display. The peasant Chinese woman and the Negress in the plantation fields were not so favored with these signs of "femininity," since their bodies were needed for physical labor. Thus, despite the avalanche of ridicule that greeted their efforts, nineteenth-century feminist reformers were not off the mark when they insisted that dress reform was fundamental to women's emancipation.[15] One might say that the measure of women's liberation in any culture is at least partly indicated by whether or not they wear shoes that allow them to walk freely!

The denial of sexual and physical integrity, the commoditization of women's body, is only part of the story. Essentially, sexism means that women are tied to a series of menial labor roles that men do not want to do but wish to have an intimate servant class do for them. The human is born physically immature and has a long period of dependence crucial to its unique developmental capacities. The male has not wanted to have primary responsibility for the physical needs of children until they reach a near-adult developmental level. Then he might take over the male adolescent to make him into a "man." But to care for infants has always been a task that men wish to relegate to women.

Nothing is more frequently rationalized as "natural" than this role of women with infants and small children. Yet it should be evident that once a child is born and is no longer suckling, it is no more physically attached to woman's body than to man's. If the development of a sense of grounding demands body contact with the mother, the need for body contact with the father could be argued even more, precisely because that is less a physiological given. If a woman spends fifteen months gestating and suckling a child, one should argue that men need to compensate with a proportionate amount of time in close body contact with infants and small children.[16] The tying of woman's physiological role to disproportionate care for the child throughout infancy and childhood is neither a biological nor a psychological given, but a cultural means of forcing upon women a job that men have both idealized and, at the same time, have shunned as dirty, tedious, and beneath their dignity.

One can say much the same for the enforcement on women of the tedious and rote roles of domestic labor: the cooking, the housecleaning, the washing of garments, the repetitive servicing of daily needs. Sexism means that women are the servant class for these tasks. Even in affluent households where "servants" do these tasks, it is basically females who supervise such tasks done by other, yet more subjugated females.

In industrial society, women enter the paid labor force, but they are mostly confined to a sex-segregated labor ghetto in which they do work that is an extension of women's work in the home. Seldom, and only after great struggles, do a few women manage to occupy prestigious jobs in male professions. Even here, they are present in token numbers. Work segregation is still the fundamental pattern of society. Women's work universally is regarded as of low status and prestige, poorly paid, with little security, generally of a rote and menial character. The sexist structuring of society means the elimination of women from those activities that allow for and express the enhancement and development of the self, its artistic, intellectual, and leadership capacities. These roles are monopolized by a small male elite.

Sexism creates a vast pollution of the channels of human communication. The biasing not only of language and symbols, verbal and visual, but the organization of space, the nonverbal language of dress and body signals, keeps all this intact, as both law and custom, so that neither male nor female is capable of imagining, much less acting upon, an alternative. Culturally, sexism defines the whole system of reality, from "matter" to "God." One cannot challenge sexism without the dethronement of the cultural universe as an authentic and good model of life.

If sexism is both violence and violation to women's bodily integrity, humanity, and capacity for full selfhood, sexism is also the distortion of male humanity. Although males have sought to monopolize the most valued human tasks, to keep for themselves both the highest culture and the leisure that allows the pursuit of culture and creativity, they have not thereby succeeded in actualizing a humanity that we should generally want to emulate. Both in its brutality and in its intellectual abstractionism, sexism distorts male humanity and thereby distorts the whole human enterprise. If the distortion of female humanity is a tragedy of victimization at many points, the distortion of male humanity is an endemic disease that both humanity and the planet itself may not long survive without dramatic conversion. The distortion of males in macho-masculine culture permits both a ravaging of relationships and an insensitivity to this ravaging.

Daniel Maguire defines the evil of macho-masculinity as (1) violence, (2) hierarchical and anticommunitarian bias, (3) abstractionism, (4) consequentialism, and (5) misogyny.[17] Male humanity is distorted into a fundamental proneness to translate all relationships into aggressive, assaultive modes of behavior. Whether it is women, land, or ideas, the normal male mode of relationship is one of conquer or be conquered, dominate or be dominated. The "other" is obliterated or reduced to an object of control. What vanishes in this is the other person with whom one can relate, each becoming a center of mutual enrichment for the other.

The other male sins listed by Maguire are outgrowths of the first. Hierarchicalism sees all relationships in a one-up, one-down fashion. One is either controller or controlled, master or servant. Abstractionism means that one turns reality into theoretical fantasies that do not need to be checked and corrected by relation to real persons. One abstracts oneself, other persons, social groups, nature, and God into linear concepts and goals that can be pursued without notice of the actual consequences to human persons, including oneself. To burn the body of the heretic in order to save "his soul" and to burn the Vietnam village in order to "save it" for democracy are expressions of abstractionism. The ability to do violence to others is built, psychologically, on this ability to abstract oneself from real contact and shared feeling with existing human reality.

Consequentialism flows from abstractionism. It means putting theoretical goals above the actual effects created by the means used to reach the goals. Profits pursued at the expense of the impoverishment of an increasing sector of the human race, even in industrialized countries, is one such expression. Stockpiling nuclear weapons for ultimate security, weapons that can annihilate the whole human race and reduce the planet to lifeless rubble many times over, is the ultimate virulent expression of the cult of "end" pursued without recognition of the effect of the means and processes chosen.

These patterns of thought are built on and contribute to misogyny, a hatred of women, that both projects onto women the negative side of the alienated self and in the process cuts off male humanity from the humanization that comes from contact with real relations and processes of life. In this sense, female existence, although victimized, is less dehumanized.

This cataloging of the sins of sexism suggests to some a disproportionate stigmatization of males as responsible for evil and a consequent exculpation of women. Sin becomes something that males alone have done. Women have only been victims. Voices are raised demanding a recognition that we are "all sinners equally," as though spreading sin around equally is a matter of "fairness." We need to be very clear on this point. Recognizing sexism as sin has nothing to do with any notion that males are "by nature" evil or that women are incapable of any sin other than the sin of cooperating in their own victimization. Both males and females, as human persons, have the capacity to do evil. Historically, however, women, as well as subjugated men, have not had the same *opportunities* to do so. The monopolization of power and privilege by ruling-class males also means a monopolization of the opportunities for evil. This means not only that men have been the primary decision makers of human history but also that the very modes of relationship set up by this monopoly of power and privilege create violent and oppressive ways of pursuing the "good ends" envisioned by this male ruling class.

This does not mean that women and subjugated men are not also capable of evil, but their opportunities to do evil have been generally limited to the subsystem relationships within this overall monopoly of power and privilege by the male ruling class. Women sin by cooperating in their own subjugation, by lateral violence to other women who seek emancipation, and by oppressing groups of people such as children and domestic servants under their control. Women can be racist, classist, self-hating, manipulative toward dominant males, dominating toward children. But these forms of female evil cooperate with and help to perpetuate an overall system of distorted humanity in which ruling-class males are the apex. Thus women, or other oppressed groups, are not wrong when they claim that while we are all capable of evil we have not all been, in the same way, equally responsible for it.

A false individualizing of responsibility for sin is also a major way of trying to evade the reality and responsibility for the history of distorted humanity. White male ethics reduces sin and evil to the individual and then claims that liberation theologies are "guilt-tripping" males. This claim is itself puzzling, since Christian theology has always made central to repentance a facing up to one's guilt. To refuse to be guilty is also to refuse to be responsible, to refuse *to respond* to this reality in such a way as to liberate oneself from it and make a new humanity possible.

To sort out our appropriate responsibility we have to recognize both the difference and the interconnection between individual and social evil. Sin always has a personal as well as a systemic side. But it is never just "individual"; there is no evil that is not relational. Sin exists precisely in the distortion of relationality, including relation to oneself. Although there are sins that are committed primarily as personal self-violation or violation of another individual — abuse of one's body by intoxicants, rape, assault, or murder of another — even these very personal acts take place in a systemic, historical, and social context.

The ancient religious writers of late Judaism and early Christianity were not wrong in suggesting that there is a pervasive "atmosphere" of malevolent influences that dispose the self to choose evil more often than good. But they were wrong in scapegoating women for the advent of these forces, or in abstracting evil into demonic powers beyond humanity. Powers and principalities exist as the precondition of evil choices. But these powers and principalities are precisely the heritage of systemic social evil, which conditions our personal choices before we choose and prevents us from fully understanding our own choices and actions. Sexism is one of these powers and principalities of historical, systemic, social evil that conditions our choices as males and females from before our birth.

In this sense, no male as an individual can or is expected to carry the total burden of guilt for sexism. We have all, males and females, been shaped by a preexisting system of male privilege and female subordination. Long before we can even begin to make our own decisions, we are already thoroughly its product. Women who call for men to stop using sexist language were themselves called to stop using it by others only a short time before. We are all products of the original sin of sexism.

But this systemic and historical aspect of sexism does not mean that there is no personal responsibility. Sexism as a system was originated by human persons and perpetuated today by human persons, male and female, continuing to cooperate with it. The system is not just the sum of the individuals. Precisely as a system it becomes bigger than any of us or all of us *as individuals.* We are entrapped by our own collective, historical selves. The system transcends us as individuals in space and time. It forms an organizational structure of society and social ideology, which is itself the product of many centuries and generations.

This system is so much larger than any individual that one could easily imagine oneself totally helpless, the captive of demonic powers beyond one's control. Yet this system is the creation of humans, not of God or fallen angels. We made it. We perpetuate it by our cooperation with it. Without our many-sided cooperation with it, it could not continue to stand. Thus, in spite of the reality of systemic evil which we inherit, which has already biased us before we can choose, we have not lost our ability to choose good rather than evil, and hence our capacity for responsibility. We can unmask sexism as sin. We can disaffiliate with it. We can begin to shape at least our personal identity and then our more immediate relationships with others in a new way.

We recognize that these steps are limited. The larger system still entraps us and limits our choices. We await that massive repentance of all humanity, that great *metanoia,* in which all humans decide to disaffiliate from violence and cooperation with violence. This would deprive the whole system of power and make possible a complete redemption. This is the future that eludes us, not because it is not within our power as *humans,* but because it is not within our power as *individuals* or small groups. It demands the conversion of all, not only as individuals, but as a collective system. Although the transformation of the whole, or what theology has called the Shalom of God, eludes us, we can make a beginning. In making a beginning, we can discover that the power of sexism has already been disenchanted. It has begun to be defeated "spiritually," that is, it has lost its authority over our lives. We can begin to act differently.

CONVERSION FROM SEXISM:
FEMALE AND MALE JOURNEYS

Consciousness of sexism as evil necessarily begins with females. It is sometimes asked why feminist consciousness has emerged so recently. Why didn't women "revolt" against their subjugation long ago? The intimation behind this question is often that sexist subjugation, in fact, suits women's "nature" and so women have complied with it and supported it. There are several aspects of an answer to this question. There has always been a level of noncompliance or proto-feminist consciousness among women. Women, listening to male ideology against them, have never appreciated this ideology or fully believed it. They have expressed their noncompliance in the networks of communication among women. In every period in which some writings from women have survived, elements of this resistance to male definitions of women can be seen. What men have condemned as female gossip ("bitchiness") is precisely this network of female communication and covert resistance.

This proto-feminist consciousness could not develop into real feminist thought and practice until certain conditions were present. A new cultural ideology had to arise that supported the equal humanity of all persons and called for a new social order that expressed this view. Hierarchicalism, as the established and only possible human order, had to be thrown into question. Only then could feminism, as well as all the modern emancipation movements, begin to arise.

Consciousness is much more of a collective social product than modern individualism realizes. No one can affirm an idea against the dominant culture unless there is at least a subcultural group that gives people both the ideas and the social support for an alternative position. The dominant ideology and social order have to have become weakened and discredited enough that such countercultural groups can build up their position and survive.

Dissenting groups with alternative views on women arose in the Middle Ages and Reformation, but they were soon ruthlessly crushed by the dominant system or else they learned to retreat and accommodate to the dominant culture by suppressing their "heretical" views. Even in the French Revolution, the leading feminist, Olympe de Gouges, was guillotined and her pleas for inclusion of women in the "rights of man" were disregarded in a new Napoleonic code of laws that reinforced female subordination.[18]

The Female Journey

The woman who experiences dissenting thoughts alone, without any network of communication to support her, can hardly bring her own dissent to articulation. Without a social matrix, she will simply be terrorized into submission by the authorities that surround her or acquiesce in their judgment that she is a "witch" or a "madwoman." Only where there is a feminist movement that has been able to survive, to develop networks of communication, and to provide some alternative vision of life is feminist consciousness a real possibility.

Openness to feminist consciousness demands that the ideology and socialization into feminine "virtue" become existentially discredited. All the ways a woman has been taught to be "pleasing" and "acceptable" to men must be recognized as tools of her own seduction and false consciousness. Every woman has bought into some of these roles. We have been the pretty girl-child who is played with and praised for her cuteness; or the sexy lady who manipulates her physical attractiveness; or the good wife who wins praise by her diligent housekeeping and attentive service to male needs — all these prevent a woman from asking herself who she is as a human person.

Much of the strongest feminist consciousness arises not in teenagers or young adults but in older women who have already played out these roles and learned their hollowness. Yet if women comply too long in these traditional female roles, it becomes difficult to break the mold. They have lost so much time. They have missed the chance to develop first-rate skills for a self-defined life. It becomes too painful to face up to one's own years of betrayal. Thus it is the group of women who have already committed ten or twenty years to traditional wifehood that become prime candidates for antifeminist and anti-ERA crusades, particularly if they are supported by their husbands at an affluent economic level.

The cruel fact, which these women know in their bones but dare not articulate, is that they have no skills to support themselves at their present economic level. They are "one man away from welfare." If one does not have the "courage to see," the alternative is to become vehement supporters of female subordination as the only way to shore up one's present mode of survival. Thus the courage of feminist consciousness is always great, but it becomes more difficult or easy depending on one's sexist indoctrination, one's education and skills, and one's place in the life cycle and in class and race hierarchies.

For Christian women, particularly in more conservative traditions, one of the most difficult barriers to feminist consciousness is the identification of sin with anger and pride, and virtue with humility and self-abnegation. Although this doctrine of sin and virtue supposedly is for "all Christians," it becomes, for women, an ideology that reinforces female subjugation and lack of self-esteem. Women become "Christ-like" by having no self of their own. They become the "suffering servants" by accepting male abuse and exploitation. Women are made to feel profoundly guilty and diffident about even the smallest sense of self-affirmation. They fear the beginning steps of asking who they are and what they want to do, rather than "putting others first."[19]

In this context, conversion from sexism is truly experienced as a breakthrough, as an incursion of power and grace beyond the capacities of the present roles, an incursion of power that puts one in touch with oneself as a self. *Metanoia* for women involves a turning around in which they literally discover themselves as persons, as centers of being upon which they can stand and build their own identity. This involves a willingness to get in touch with their own anger. Anger is liberating grace precisely as the power to break the chains of sexist socialization, to disaffiliate with sexist ideologies.

Virtue for women demands a new sense of pride, not in the male sense of "lording it over others" but in the sense of basic self-esteem. Without basic self-esteem one has no self at all, as a base upon which to build an identity or to criticize past mistakes. The whole male ideology of pride and humility has to be reevaluated by women. The acceptance of liberating anger and the reclaiming of basic self-esteem allow a woman to look honestly at the situation that has shaped her life. She is able to acknowledge her own compliance with the systems that have diminished her humanity. The shackles of this system on her mind and energy begin to shatter, and she gains the courage to stand up against them.

This breakthrough experience is the basis for the development of consciousness. Women read their own history within the history of patriarchy. They become aware of the depths of the system that has entrapped them and discover a hidden community of women of the past. They reclaim their own history as witnesses to an alternative possibility and also become increasingly conscious of the complexity of the global socio-economic system that subjugates woman. The difficulty of the task of emancipation becomes clearer. It is no longer just a matter of settling accounts within interpersonal relationships.

This expanded consciousness deepens one's sense of alien-ation and anger so that one senses oneself ready to "go mad" with alienation and anger. Males take on a demonic face. One begins to doubt their basic humanity. One desires only to be with women, to distance oneself from the whole male world with its myriad games. Most women are deeply afraid of this deeper anger and alienation and stop well short of experiencing it. Their immediate ties of survival and service to men and children are too deep. Moreover, they believe that "loving everyone" and affirming everyone's humanity disallows the experiencing of this anger.

This creates a parting of the ways between feminists — those who are ready and willing to experience this deeper alienation and anger and those who draw back from it. Those who enter into deeper alienation become the "bad feminists," the sepa-ratists, lesbians, radicals. Those who take a more moderate stand are tempted to get "brownie points" for not being like those "bad feminists." Yet the depths of anger and alienation to which some women point are not inappropriate. It really has been "that bad." Unless one is willing to take the journey into that deeper anger, even to risk going a bit mad, one really will never understand the depths of the evil of sexism. The great importance of a feminist thinker like Mary Daly is precisely that she insists on taking herself further and further into that journey and insisting that others who wish to be honest follow her. She lays before our eyes the "passion drama" of female crucifixion on the cross of male sexism.[20]

The journey into that deeper anger does not mean that one needs to remain there permanently. There are, as Anne Wilson

Schaef points out in her book *Women's Reality,* "levels of truth."[21] One needs to go through a certain level of truth before one can move on to another level. Those who are afraid of anger and alienation always have a tendency to hurry women on to another stage where they become "reasonable" and "gain perspective." But one cannot do that with integrity until one has genuinely faced up to sexism as a massive historical system of victimization of women and allowed oneself to enter into one's anger and alienation. To skip over this experience is to become "reconciling" in a way that is basically timid and accommodating and not really an expression of personal freedom.

Only by experiencing one's anger and alienation can one move on, with real integrity, to another level of truth. One is able, with freedom, to refuse a reversed female chauvinism that would cause one to lose touch with the human face of males and to begin to imagine that women alone are human and males are evil and defective. As one experiences women's groups and movements, one recognizes that women too are capable of the corruptions of egoism and power. As a woman breaks the ties that bind her to a relatively powerless world, she needs to acknowledge that she too can become an oppressor of others. One gains "humility" in one's criticism of arrogant egoism in males. Humility here is no longer a tool of timidity and servitude but assumes its rightful meaning as truthful self-knowledge of one's own capacity for oppressive pride. Women must refuse the egoistic self, modeled on male individualism, and affirm instead the "grounded self" which is related to others and to mutual service.

The systems of domination, then, are "male" only in the historical and sociological sense that males have shaped and benefited from them, not in the sense that they correspond to unique, evil capacities of males that women do not share. Women have no guarantees, because of a different "nature," that they will act differently. They do have some different experiences that may help them avoid acting in the same way, but only if they can develop the grounded self that avoids both timidity and reversed egoism. The struggle to shape an alternative system is fundamentally a human struggle, and it demands psychic and social holism. We appropriate into a new, grounded self the suppressed, relational side of our psyches, and we begin to shape new social systems of relationship that allow and support this alternative. One cannot be a grounded self in a vacuum, but only in new, emergent relationships.

The Male Journey

Having seen something of the female conversion journey, one might ask whether there is a comparable male conversion journey from sexism. In principle, one must say that there must be. Sexism is not just a female problem. Indeed, it is primarily a male problem that men have imposed on women. Sexism cannot be solved by women alone. It demands a parallel male conversion. There is ultimately no "new woman" without a new humanity. But I cannot describe the male journey from inside. That has to be done by males, grounded in a male liberation movement. However, as a white that worked in the Black movement for many years, I have some ideas of what conversion is like from the side of the "oppressors." Also, as a woman who has observed males in various stages of response to women's liberation, I have some idea of how that appears to women. On this basis I can suggest some stages of the male journey.

The first stage of male response to women's criticism of sexism is trivialization and ridicule. Men really can't believe that women are an oppressed group. They are convinced of their own benevolence toward women. They individualize the issue and abstract and universalize the situation of relatively privileged wives. They claim that the women they know are "well taken care of" and ought to be happy (grateful). They are unable to see the stresses and vulnerabilities of dependency even in this situation, much less the total system of sexism across classes and history. They laugh off the silliness of "women's lib" (a trivializing diminutive used only for female and homosexual liberation movements).

The second stage of male response is co-optation. Men become aware that the historical polarization of the sexes is a real issue. They leap quickly to the thought that men too have suffered from sexism; indeed, they have suffered "equally." Whole dimensions of their being — their ability to cry, to feel, to relate, to be sensitive — have been repressed in order to shape them for male roles of domination. They too need to be liberated. They need to recover the "feminine" side of themselves. This line is frequently adopted by clergy and other males who belong to the more humanistic disciplines and who find themselves marginalized from the centers of (male-macho) power. Jungian psychology provides the intellectual base for this male "feminism."

Such male feminists often become very dogmatic about what feminism means. They soon imagine that they know more about it than women. In their identification of their own suppressed self with the "feminine," they think they have a handle on women's true "nature." They want women to cultivate this male definition of the "feminine" in order to nurture the "feminine side" of men. They purport to understand and sympathize with women and, no doubt, sincerely think they do. But they tend to become very hostile when women suggest that this definition of the "feminine" is really a male projection and not female humanity. The male ego is still the center of the universe, which "feminism" is now seduced into enhancing in a new way. Such male feminists are sometimes worse enemies of women's emancipation than outright chauvinists.

These two stances are not conversion, but ways of resisting conversion from sexism. Men who are stuck in either of these positions often don't grow out of them. Real conversion from sexism begins to happen only when a man is able to enter into real solidarity with women in the struggle for liberation, often by being involved in a relationship with a particular woman who is pursuing her own liberation. By entering into her struggle, seeing the world of sexism from her eyes, he begins to be able to understand some dimensions of sexism. He attempts to change aspects of his male lifestyle to support her ability to work or go to school. He shares housework and child care. He begins to feel that he too is recovering a more holistic self in the process.

But the vulnerabilities of this type of supportive male are real. If he goes too far in sharing domestic work, so that it interferes with the exclusive male priority of the "job," he soon finds that he loses advancement in the world of male competition. The male who takes paternity leave when his wife has a baby may discover that he is a pariah on the job. He is passed up for promotion, left out of the networks of communication. He learns not to talk about women's rights on the job, much less analyze what women's rights would mean for his own organization. He is tempted to think of his support for "his woman" as a private issue. Sexism is really her problem. He is "helping" her with it, but in a way that can't interfere too much with his own male status.

Deeper male conversion from sexism involves a willingness to enter into risks to himself. He has to recognize his own profound fear of loss of affirmation by the male group ego if he departs from male roles. This may cause him loss of male economic status and privilege as well. But the fear of being repudiated or scorned by other males as "unmanly" is usually his greatest terror. Thus, for men as well as women, conversion means a receiving of a grounded self that not only repudiates male group egoism but also overcomes the passivity that acquiesces to the group ego. Men need to overcome not only their "pride" in masculinity that oppresses women but also their fear of loss of male status by which they oppress themselves and each other. At this point, males are able to recognize, without trying to either co-opt or pander to women, that the struggle against sexism is basically a struggle to humanize the world, to humanize ourselves, to salvage the planet, to be in right relation to God/ess. At this point, men and women can really join hands in a common struggle.

Chapter 8
Ministry and Community for a People Liberated from Sexism

We have named sexism as a serious expression of human sinfulness, of alienation from authentic existence. Such a recognition of sexism as sin requires a radical redefinition of ministry and church. The grace of conversion from patriarchal domination opens up a new vision of humanity for women and men, one that invites us to recast and re-create all our relationships. Church, as the avant-garde of liberated humanity, should be the support system for this process. Conversion to a new humanity cannot take place in isolation. Psychologically, one cannot affirm a feminist identity against the historical weight of patriarchal oppression by oneself. Theologically, it is essential to understand redemption as a communal, not just an individual, experience. Just as sin implies alienation and broken community, so rebirth to authentic selfhood implies a community that assembles in the collective discovery of this new humanity and that provides the matrix of regeneration.

It is precisely when feminists discover the congruence between the Gospel and liberation from sexism that they also experience their greatest alienation from existing churches. The discovery of alternative possibilities for identity and the increasing conviction that an alternative is a more authentic understanding of the Gospel make all the more painful and insulting the reality of most historical churches. These churches continue to ratify, by their language, institutional structures, and social commitments, the opposite message. The more one

193

becomes a feminist the more difficult it becomes to go to church.

The women's movement does create its own alternative expressions of community. Women bond together in support groups and coalitions for action. They gather in many places, often outside the formal organizations of church and society, to share experiences and analysis. They begin to build their own organizations. Seldom does such feminist networking allow women to name the religious dimension of their struggle or to get in touch with healing spiritual power to support their new options. Religious feminists experience a starvation of sacramental nourishment, a famine of the Word of God/ess. The churches, the great symbol-making institutions of their traditions, operate as a countersign to their hopes.

Is the Christian Church usable as ecclesia for women and men seeking liberation from patriarchy? Will the increasing participation of women in ministry provide alternative options in the foreseeable future? Or has the recent entry of women into ministry in token numbers failed to challenge, for the most part, the patriarchal interpretation of Christianity? We need to recapitulate briefly the theologies that have excluded women from ministry and also those that have included women. This will lead us to ask what kind of ministry women (and men) can exercise in the Church today that is compatible with liberation from patriarchy.

WOMEN AND MINISTRY: THEOLOGIES OF EXCLUSION AND INCLUSION

The patriarchal theology that has prevailed throughout most of Christian history in most Christian traditions has rigidly barred women from ministry. The arguments for this exclusion are identical with the arguments of patriarchal anthropology. Women are denied leadership in the churches for the same reasons they are denied leadership in society. Contrary to some recent apologetics,[1] the Christian tradition never affirmed women's inclusion in social leadership while arguing for women's exclusion from ministry based on the special nature of ministry. The arguments for women's exclusion from ministry are applications of the general theology of male headship and female subordination. This subordination, while attributed to women's physiological role in procreation, extends to an inferiority of mind and soul as well. Women are categorized as less capable than men of moral self-control and reason. They can play only a passive role in the giving and receiving of ministry. They should keep silent.

Priestly traditions also define women's "uncleanness" in religious terms. Female bodiliness is seen as polluting and defiling the sacred. Women must be distanced from the Holy. Holiness becomes a male mystery that annuls the finitude and mortality of birth from the female. Women may be baptized, but they cannot represent this process of rebirth and nourishment in the realm of male holiness. The near hysteria that erupted in recent years in the Episcopal Church when women began visibly to use the priestly sacramental symbols reveals the pathology that underlies the exclusion of women from ministry.[2] The pathology seems to be even more violent when the issue is not just women as preachers but women as priests. This shows the extent to which the rejection of woman as maternal flesh adds another dimension beyond simply negation of woman as teacher. The most extreme repugnance against the idea of women in ministry typically is expressed in the question "Can you imagine a pregnant woman at the altar?"

Recent feminist scholarship has pointed to the existence of an alternative tradition in the Jesus movement and early Christianity.[3] This alternative Christianity could have suggested a very different construction of Christian theology: women as equal with men in the divine mandate of creation, restored to this equality in Christ; the gifts of the Spirit poured out on men and women alike; the Church as the messianic society, not over against creation but over against the systems of domination. We see hints of this vision in the New Testament.

But the Deutero-Pauline recasting of Christianity in patriarchal terms made this inclusive theology nonnormative.

Inclusive or "counter-cultural Christianity"[4] did not disappear, but it went underground. It became identified with heretical sects whose traditions are preserved only in fragments or through the polemics of the dominant religion. Moreover, the Gnostic interpretation of this inclusive Christianity in the second and third centuries creates a dualism between the eschatological realm and the world of material creation. Gnosticism thus shares with patriarchal Christianity the assumption that women are subordinate in the material or procreational order. Only as an ascetic elite do women and men share leadership power in anticipation of the heavenly realm above, in which there is no procreation and no sexual division.

The difference between this Gnostic option and the patriarchal Church lies in the Gnostic assumption that the Church and its ministry follow the eschatological, not the creational, order.[5] This concept of the Church led by an inclusive celibate elite was rediscovered in Albigensian sects that appeared in the Middle Ages[6] and in the Shakers in the early modern period. But the dominant patriarchal Church marginalized even this idea of women's public ministry as members of the celibate elite.

Prophetic charisms have also been a way of including women in ministry. The Christian churches have never denied that the gifts of the Spirit are poured out on men and women alike. But in the second and third centuries rising episcopal power struggled to suppress the autonomous power of prophets. The historical ministry of bishops, as keepers of the keys and discerners of spirits, claimed the right to judge and control the occasional ministry of prophets and prophetesses. It routinized the power of the Spirit as automatically transmitted through apostolic succession and thus illegitimized any prophecy not under episcopal control.[7]

Nevertheless, the phenomenon of independent prophets and prophetesses does not disappear from popular Christianity.

Medieval Christianity sought either to discipline such persons within religious orders or to suppress them as heretics, as is evident by the contrary fates of Franciscans[8] and Waldensians.[9] The initial power accorded Joan of Arc testifies to the medieval openness to the prophetess as long as she appeared to be winning. Her execution and subsequent exoneration by the French monarchy she helped restore to power reflects a conflict between contrary alignments of ecclesiastical and political power — the one seeking to illegitimate her victories by defining her as a witch, the other legitimating their own power by vindicating her as a true prophet-emissary from God.[10]

In the left-wing sects of the Reformation is a new appearance of groups who define the free prophetic Spirit as the true author of Christian ministry. For radical Puritan sects in the seventeenth century, the Spirit can raise up preachers of the Word who speak with authority, not from the authorized channels of feudal priest or university cleric but among the humble weavers and spinsters of the lower orders of society.[11] In movements in which the Spirit authorizes ministerial gifts directly, in which the community rather than the institutional authorities validate the authenticity of the gifts, women occasionally are found as preachers. This is the case among Baptists and Quakers in the seventeenth-century English Civil War sects and again in the nineteenth-century American Pentecostal and Holiness movements.[12] The Spirit is no discriminator among persons on the basis of gender but can empower whomever it will. Ministry is proven by its gifts, not by its credentials.

But prophecy is unstable as a means of long-term inclusion of women in ministry. Movements that accepted in the first generation women's right to preach and teach as prophetesses later become institutionalized, and the gifts of the Spirit are routinized in an ordained clergy that excludes the participation of women. Women's ministry based on charismatic gifts is both continually reborn in practice and continually marginalized from power in historical Church institutions.

Nineteenth-century America represents a new stage in the

conflict between woman's capacity for holiness and her right
to exercise ministerial roles. The disestablishment of the
churches and the privatization of religion shift the cultivation
of piety to the home. Femininity and piety become increasingly
identified.[13] This suggests to many women that they are
uniquely capable of evangelizing others. Conservative churchmen seek to control this by segregating women's evangelical
role strictly within the home, as uplifter of husband and
children, and within the private women's prayer group.[14]

But once empowered, women's evangelizing activities
constantly break out of these domestic limits. The prayer group
turns into a revival meeting with women as organizers and then
as preachers.[15] Benevolent societies turn into women's home
and foreign missionary societies with their own budgets, their
own leadership in women's hands.[16] From these roles as
evangelical preachers and organizers of benevolent societies
women begin to demand ordained ministry.[17]

Liberal feminism succeeds in opening up the ordained
ministry to women. The liberal tradition reclaims the idea of
women's equality in the *imago dei,* but it secularizes it. Women
are declared to be sharers of a common human nature, which
is the basis of social rights. Natural rights become the ideological basis for renovating the social order. The arguments
for women's ordination in the nineteenth century also draw
on prophetic and romantic themes. The text of Acts 2:17–18,
in which the gifts of the Spirit are said to be poured out on
men and women alike, was constantly evoked to justify
women's right to preach. Likewise it is said that women's
altruistic and nurturing nature and her natural spirituality
especially suit her for ministry. But these arguments carry
weight only when combined with the liberal assumption that
a just social order should grant equal rights and opportunities
to all its members.

These various traditions were brought together in the sermon
delivered by Luther Lee, an evangelical preacher who led the
ordination service for Antoinette Brown, the first woman

ordained to the Congregational ministry, in 1853.[18] Lee took his text from Galatians 3:28: "In Christ there is neither male nor female." And he combined it with Acts 2:17–18. He argued that the preaching office is the same as the prophetic office. Since the gifts of prophecy are given to women as well as men in the New Testament, there has never been any excuse for excluding women from the ordained ministry. The preaching office was given to women by Christ. Lee's argument depended on the identification of prophetic charisms and historic ministry.

Antoinette Brown's ordination was part of the first wave of liberal feminism, which is manifest in the Seneca Falls Women's Rights Convention of 1848. The leaders of this convention base their Declaration of the Rights of Women on the American Declaration of Independence and Bill of Rights. They protest against patriarchal theology, declare the equality of women and men in creation to be the authentic Biblical view, and call for the inclusion of women in theological study, teaching, and ministry. Among the "repeated injuries and usurpations on the part of man toward woman, having the direct object of establishing an absolute tyranny over her," against which they protest in this document are numerous matters having to do with male religious privilege. The document ends with a final resolution, offered by Lucretia Mott, herself a Quaker minister, which reads:

> *Resolved:* that the speedy success of our cause depends upon the zealous and untiring efforts of both men and women for the overthrow of the monopoly of the pulpit, and for the securing to women of equal participation with men in various trades, professions and commerce.[19]

Although a few Protestant groups begin to ordain women in the nineteenth century, it is not until the mid-1950s to 1970s that most major American Protestant denominations begin to ordain women. Only since 1970 have sufficient numbers of women begun to attend seminary and to become ordained for ministry that the implications for the nature of Church and ministry have begun to be raised. We begin to see that the securing of women's ordination through liberal assumptions contains the seeds of its own contradiction. Women are included in ministry through a concept of justice as equal opportunity. But this perspective neglects any critique of the public order beyond a demand for equal opportunity of all persons in it regardless of gender. The shaping of the form and symbols of ministry by patriarchal culture, to the exclusion of women, is not seen as making the historic form of ministry itself problematic. Women win inclusion in this same ministry, without asking whether ministry itself needs to be redefined.

The patriarchal symbols and the hierarchical relationship of the ministry to the laity are still taken as normative. Women are allowed in token numbers to integrate themselves into this male-defined role. They adopt the same garb, the same titles (Reverend, if not Father), the same clerical modes of functioning in a hierarchically structured church. They too stand in the phallically designed pulpit and bring down the "seminal" word upon the passive body of the laity. Women's ordained status thus remains symbolically and socially anomalous. Even winning the legal right to ordination is not secure. Later, a backlash against it may occur, as in the Swedish Lutheran Church, in which male priests and theologians dragged out all the old arguments linking maleness and priesthood, including pollution taboos, to argue for the illegitimacy of women's ordination.[20]

Women play the ministerial role by endlessly proving that they can think, feel, and act like "one of the boys." The "boys," in turn, accept them only in token numbers that do not threaten their monopoly on ecclesiastical power (anything above five percent is perceived as a threat to this monopoly). But they continually subvert women in practice, intimating that they should retain their "femininity" by exercising a different ministry from men, as assistant minister in charge of children, youth, and the aged, not as "the Minister" with full authority.

Women in ministry, like all women trying to function in public roles under male rules, find themselves in a double bind. They are allowed success only by being better than men at the games of masculinity, while at the same time they are rebuked for having lost their femininity. In such a system it is not possible for women to be equal, but only to survive in a token and marginal way at tremendous physical and psychological cost.

MINISTRY AND COMMUNITY FOR LIBERATION FROM PATRIARCHY

Church as Liberation Community

Feminist liberation theology starts with the understanding of Church as liberation community as the context for understanding questions of ministry, creed, worship, or mission. Without a community committed to liberation from sexism, all questions such as the forms of ministry or mission are meaningless. Conversion from sexism means both freeing oneself from the ideologies and roles of patriarchy and also struggling to liberate social structures from these patterns. A feminist liberation Church must see itself as engaged in both of these struggles as the center of its identity as Church. Joining the Church means entrance into a community of people who share this commitment and support one another in it.

Where can we find such a community? Can the historical churches be transformed by new leadership and theology to become vehicles for this way of being Church? A beginning of this transformation might happen in the local churches of more liberal denominations, with women pastors or women and men in team ministry who share a vision of the Gospel as liberation from patriarchy. Some of these local churches are beginning to integrate feminism into their understanding of being Church. They seek to reflect this in their language, ministerial form, and social commitments. Such churches begin not only to use inclusive language for humanity and God but also to transform liturgy to reflect the call to liberation. They take steps to overcome the monopolization of ministry by the ordained and to create shared ministry of the whole community. The Church sponsors projects, such as a battered-women's shelter or a rape hotline, that show its commitment to justice for women.

These kinds of changes are possible only in denominations of relatively free polity where local churches do not face constant intervention and coercion from hierarchical authority. But even in such churches there are many other constraints that keep the Church tied to its role as validator of patriarchy. Conservative laity use both lay voting power and financial contributions to block the efforts of ministers with feminist consciousness from changing language or social commitments. Such laity are hostile to a liberation understanding of the Church in any form. They wish to preserve the separation between private piety and the public order, which defines religion as comfort and escape from social realities while indirectly validating the status quo.

In order to transform a local church into a liberation community, feminist ministers must be free to take many more risks with the financial base of the institution than they are normally allowed by either laity or denominational authorities. They must be able to enter into a process of rending and sowing in which the preaching and teaching of a liberation understanding of the Gospel may drive some people, often the wealthiest and most influential, out of the congregation. The ministry must be able to do this in a creative and constructive way that at the same time converts to the new vision those "who have ears to hear." Ministers must be able to shape a new system of adult catechetics and participation in ministry that educates people in the theology and practice of the Church as liberation community. Other people who are hungry for such a church will join. Gradually a new community will come into being that really shares a common faith about the meaning of the Church and is ready to explore the further implications for faith and action.

What I have described is a clergy-led revolutionizing of a local church. The difficulty with such a top-down transformation is that the clergy are seldom willing to let go of their own clerical prerogatives at the appropriate moment and really begin to share power for shaping the preaching, teaching, and social action with the people. The people remain dependent for liberating theology and programs on the clergy and are not being trained to take responsibility for defining these themselves.

There are instances where a clergy-led revolution is able to transform itself into a genuine liberation Church. In the Italian Basic Christian Community of St. Paul's Outside the Walls in Rome, the revolution began with the vision of the abbot of the Benedictine community of this historic basilica, Dom Giovanni Franzoni. In the early 1960s, during the Second Vatican Council, Franzoni began inviting the laity to reflect with him on the Scriptures every Saturday night. He then preached his Sunday homily from this shared reflection. Gradually those who gathered with him came to number in the hundreds and those who came to hear him on Sunday in the thousands. Franzoni became radicalized by this shared reflection about both the nature of the Gospel and the mission of the Church. A core community of several hundred people began to reshape the liturgy in a more participatory way and also to engage in direct political action on such issues as war and unemployment.

The Roman hierarchy then moved to strip Franzoni of his office as abbot. The community, together with the abbot, decided to leave the basilica and to move into an independent location. Franzoni and other priests in the community gradually declericalized themselves and became simply members and resource persons for a community organized around shared ministry. The Roman hierarchy then stripped Franzoni of his priest's orders.[21] The price of creating a liberation community was the loss of all official institutional ties, although the group understands itself theologically and culturally as a renewal movement within Catholic Christianity.

The relationship of base communities to the institutional Church varies in contemporary Catholicism. In Latin America, base communities have been mandated by the hierarchy as sub-communities of the parishes. They are seen by the hierarchy as instruments of evangelization of the masses by lay catechists in a church that has far too few ordained persons to handle this task. In practice, however, many base communities take on their own agenda as liberation communities quite apart from hierarchical objectives. But the base communities do not confront the clerical issue directly by taking sacramental power into their own hands, and the feminist issue is seldom addressed at all. The conflict between the hierarchical and the liberation understandings of base communities is thus papered over.[22]

In Holland, base communities are not in direct confrontation with the hierarchy, as they are in Italy, or legitimated, as they are in Latin America. Often such groups begin with the marriage of a radical priest, whom the community wishes to retain as its pastor. Sometimes the bishops accept this by redefining the priest as pastoral worker. Many communities develop their own patterns of worship, ministry, and theological reflection independent of the traditional parish and often in a new location. But the liberal bishops try to maintain communication with these groups culturally, even though they are not in direct control of them. The Vatican, however, has increased pressure upon the Dutch hierarchy to discard the middle ground and to reject married priests and also women as pastoral workers.[23]

It may be possible within more congregational Protestant churches for ministers to develop a feminist liberation understanding of the Church without being evicted from the institutional base, although few ministers desire to do this or are able to take the risks of reshaping the congregation that this would entail. In Roman Catholic parishes the problems of maintaining such a revolution within the institutional framework are even more intractable. Some university communities and chaplaincies approach nonsexist commitments at least on the level of theology and language, but the male clerical system and its dependence on the hierarchy for legitimacy prevent such groups from carrying out the inclusion of women in a structural way. It seems that for most Christians the only alternative is to turn to the creation of autonomous feminist base communities as the vehicle for developing a community of liberation from sexism.

A feminist base community is an autonomous, self-gathered community that takes responsibility for reflecting on, celebrating, and acting on the understanding of redemption as liberation from patriarchy. Such a community might take on as many or as few of the functions of Church as they choose. They might range from consciousness-raising groups that primarily share experiences, to groups who engage in study and analysis as well, to groups that also worship together. From a study, teaching, and worshiping group, such a community might also choose to share means of livelihood with one another. They might further choose to make their shared spiritual and social life together the base of political action.

The formation of such feminist base communities does not necessarily imply a sectarian rejection of institutional churches. People who find their primary support in such feminist communities might also participate in various structures of institutional church life. Some might be lay members or even clergy of local churches, members of religious congregations, teachers in theological schools, or denominational employees, while drawing support for a more radical vision for social action from the base community. The transformed liturgies, theological reflection, and social action developed in base groups could then be brought to bear on the institutionalized Church. The creation of "liberated zones" in at least some sectors of institutional churches would be seen as one of the "fields of mission" of the base community.

The exodus out of the institutional Church into the feminist base community would be for the sake of creating a freer space from which to communicate new possibilities to the institutional Church. The relationship between the two becomes a creative dialectic rather than a schismatic impasse. Indeed, precisely as one takes seriously one's responsibility to transform the historical Church, it becomes essential to have a support community that really nurtures liberated ways of living together rather than remaining crabbed and frustrated by religious experiences of alienation and negation of this vision.

A dialectical relationship between base community and historical institution is also necessary if one is serious about the communication and historical transmission of the liberating options of the base community. By retaining lines of communication into the historic institution, one can also find ways to communicate these options to a much larger public than is possible from the resources of the small group. Many other groups of people can then hear the "good news." New communities can be touched by the flame and take fire. Some parts of the historical structures then become vehicles for transmitting the message of the Gospel as redemption from patriarchy. Even if the base community itself dissolves, the historic institution becomes a means of transmitting the memory of these new options to other groups and new generations. Only by this creative dialectic between renewal community and historical institution is the Church regenerated by the Spirit within history. This is the inescapable paradox of living in the liberating community within the framework of historical existence.

Ministry as Mutual Empowerment

Feminist liberation communities necessarily must dismantle clericalism, which is an understanding of leadership as rule that reduces others to subjects to be governed. Clericalism, by definition, disempowers the people and turns them into "laity" dependent on the clergy. The basic assumption of clericalism is that the people have no direct access to the divine. The clergy monopolize the instrument of mediation between God and the laity. The clergy alone have authorized theological training; they alone are authorized to preach, to teach, to administer the Church. They alone possess sacramental power.

Male laity may be allowed subordinate roles within this system of clerical power. Women often are excluded even from lay leadership roles. Women become the archetypal representatives of the passive recipients of clerical sacral power. Clericalism is built upon and presupposes patriarchy. The symbols of clerical power duplicate on the level of ecclesiastical hierarchy the symbols of patriarchal domination of men over women, fathers over children. It is impossible to liberate the Church from patriarchy and retain a clerical definition of the ministry.

Such dismantling of clericalism is implicit in the Gospel concept of ministry as *diaconia* or service. *Diaconia* is *kenotic* or self-emptying of power as domination. Ministry transforms leadership from power over others to empowerment of others. The abdication of power as domination has nothing to do with servility. The call to ministry is not a call to become the passive supporter of the public order or the toady of the powerful in the Church or society. Rather, ministry means exercising power in a new way, as a means of liberation of one another. Service to others does not deplete the person who ministers, but rather causes her (or him) to become more liberated. Ministry overcomes competitive one-up, one-down relationships and generates relations of mutual empowerment.

Ministry in the community of liberation assumes that some people have special gifts and may play particular and different roles. But this specialization of some as teachers, some as administrators, some as liturgical poets and artists, some as community organizers is for the sake of empowering the whole community. Teachers teach to overcome the gap between those who know and those who do not.[24] Their teaching gradually creates fellow teachers who can teach others. The community as a whole becomes empowered to articulate the faith and to speak the Word to each other. The sort of teaching that perpetuates the gap between teaching authority and the "ignorant" is not real teaching, but the clericalization of learning.

Ministry should draw out the unique gifts of each person in the community and give each person the confidence and skills to develop these gifts for the sake of the others. Some people gifted in poetry or artistic expression may develop new language, new symbols, new celebrations to express the growing consciousness of the community. Others may be skilled in administration and set about the practical aspects of the community's internal affairs and social commitments. Others may have the outrage against injustice that constantly pushes the community to deepen its social involvements, and others may be gifted at the social analysis and organizational forms that give these social commitments effective shape. All these gifts are essential to a liberation Church. No one person has them all. Each gift must cross-fertilize with the others to create a community that truly reflects and acts on the Gospel of liberation together.

The liberation of the Church from clericalism also means reclaiming the sacraments as expressions of the redemptive life of the Church that the people are empowered to administer collectively. The community may designate various people at different times to develop and lead liturgical expressions, but this does not mean these persons own or possess a sacramental power that the community does not have. Rather, it means these persons represent and gather into a collective experience the sacramental life processes of the people.

The Italian Basic Christian Community Movement has spoken of this process of declericalization as "reappropriation theology."[25] Clericalism has expropriated the people's collective participation in ministry, word, and sacrament. Reappropriation theology reflects on and facilitates the taking back of ministry, word, and sacrament by the people. Reappropriation of the sacraments means that not only the exercise but also the interpretation of the sacraments arises from the community's collective experience of its life in grace. The baptism of each individual involves all members of the community, who midwife each other's rebirth from alienated to authentic life. Penance means forgiving one another. It is not the disciplinary tool of any elite. Eucharist is not an objectified piece of bread or cup of wine that is magically transformed into the body and blood of Christ. Rather, it is the people, the ecclesia, who are being transformed into the body of the new humanity, infused with the blood of new life. The symbols stand in the midst of and represent that communal reality.

The residue of clericalism gives even liberal Protestants the impression that the administration of the sacraments is a function that most especially must be exercised by persons set aside in specialized ministry. But, in fact, representation of the community in rites of baptism, forgiveness, or Eucharist depends very little on specialized skills or learning. It is significant that the New Testament contains many words for special charisms and skills, but that they are not identified with special offices responsible for the sacraments of baptism or Eucharist. Even in the most clerical material in the Pastoral Epistles, the office of bishop is designated as teaching, not as administration of sacraments. Regardless of whether the two were already becoming identified, it is significant that the New Testament authors do not feel a need to mention a connection between them.[26]

Many people assume that if "just anyone" presides at the Eucharist or baptism, it will be done in a sloppy or uninformed way that will erode the seriousness of the symbol. But this is not so if the members of the community are really becoming skilled and empowered to minister. European basic communities accomplish this by dividing the larger community into smaller study groups that reflect on Scripture and study theology and tradition together. These small reflection groups then become the base for the development of preaching and Eucharist. Each week a different reflection group takes responsibility for preparing the homily out of their discussion, and the whole community then enters into dialogue. The reflection group also shapes the songs and symbolic expressions of the Eucharist to reflect the theme of the week's reflection.

There may be people with special musical or poetic skills or special knowledge in Scripture and theology who can become teachers and resource persons. Increasingly, people become empowered to make their contribution to shaping the worship life of the community. Thus leadership does not disappear but assumes its true functionality when it is liberated from clerical monopoly over ministry, word, and sacrament. Leadership is called forth from within the community rather than imposed on it in a way that deprives the community of its own self-articulation.

Ritual, Creed, and Mission

Christian tradition has developed three primary rites: the rite of initiation into redemptive life; the rite of penance from all that continues to alienate us from each other and from our true selves; and the rite that brings together teaching and reflection on redemptive life with continued nourishment and growth in it. In addition, many particular rites are related to the time of the year, such as the birth of the redemptive child at the winter solstice, and the springtime celebration of resurrection from evil and death. Rites of passage from one state of life to another — marriage, divorce, new jobs, crises of political and social life, times of special joy or sorrow — can also be the focus of community ritual.

For the feminist Church, rituals are written and shaped to express the root message of redemption as liberation from sexism. These must take the form of increasingly creative exploration of the deeper dimensions of growth to fuller personal potential and to transformed social life, as people experience themselves breaking out of the oppressive structures that have bound their lives. Although people with special liturgical gifts and knowledge might take particular responsibility for developing rituals, each member of the community needs to be involved at one time or another in shaping the symbols of newness of life that express his or her own story.

Once the community has freed itself from clerical domination, it can be open to rediscover the value of special celebration garments, artistically designated spaces set aside for worship, and special modes of communication such as ritual gestures, chant, and song that distinguish liturgy from ordinary life. This does not mean that liturgy refers to some reality other than ordinary life but that it opens up the deeper dimension of transformed life that refers us back to ordinary life with renewed energies and consciousness. If liturgy is fused into the style and setting of ordinary life, this deeper dimension is not plumbed, and transformed life is not nurtured.

Feminist churches might wish to develop creedal statements in which they express their faith in God/ess as the foundation of redemptive personhood of women and men, their judgment upon sin as broken relationality, their experience of newness of life, and their hopes for a liberated future world. Such a creed would express their basic faith in their relation to God/ess as the power of liberation from patriarchy. Such a statement would not be fixed but open to continual revision as the community expands its vision of what liberation means.

The code of a feminist Church might take the form of a regular covenanting in which commitments are spelled out. Such covenants might include commitments for a stated period of time to certain social ministries and contributions of both time and money to such projects. It can also include reflections on commitments to each other in the crises of daily life: How does the community understand its responsibility for the social ethics of its members? If a woman in a relationship is struggling to enter a new stage of life, if her husband or lover is deeply disturbed by her changed relationship to him (or her), if there are children who will be left without adequate parenting by such changed relationships, how does the community see its responsibility to each person in this situation?

The community needs to regularly talk through and come to shared understandings of the extent to which individuals or households invest their private life in the group. Basic housekeeping matters, such as how tasks and responsibilities are distributed, need to be worked out and publicly covenanted. Every community needs a rule of life, not as a set of laws fixed in stone but as a livable pattern that can be revised periodically.

A liberation community has both an internal and an external mission. It needs to balance these so that all its energies do not become expended on the internal nurturing of its members at the expense of the world outside and also so that its energies do not become so outward directed that it neglects to heal its own hurts and nurture its own strength. It needs to ask what healing and nurturance mean not only in terms of theological or liturgical expressions but also in terms of concrete commitments to each other in the stresses of daily life. Should the community, for example, develop collective child care, operated by both men and women, only for its own members, or should it develop a neighborhood child-care group that could include both its own members and others?

The community's mission to society is based on a vision of a transformed world beyond the alienating isms of exploitation and oppression. A world without militarism, a world with systems of production and consumption in harmony with nature, is as much a part of the hopes of feminism as are changed relationships between men and women. The community needs to develop and nurture people's ability to see the interconnections between various forms of liberation and to develop ways of connecting changed lifestyle within the community with projects of political action that address the larger structures of society.

The concretization of the internal and external missions of the community expresses the particularity of each group and its stage of development. Projects should be chosen both for their direct relevance to the people within the group and for their paradigmatic significance in addressing the larger realities of oppressive structures. In one case this might mean developing neighborhood alternative technology, in another anti-nuclear action.

The praxis of a community needs to be focused sufficiently to create significant and effective engagement on an issue. It needs to resist the pressures of endless fragmentation of energy that result in much talk and little action. Sorting out a meaningful union of inward spiritual growth and social praxis amid an overload of communication stimuli that could drag the group in many directions, preventing effective action, is an essential task of contemporary liberation communities.

This discussion of a feminist base community describes what it would mean to become Church if we were truly free and empowered to do so. In taking some responsibility to communicate this vision and transform some areas within historical churches, the base community does not concede that these institutions are more truly Church than they are. On the contrary, whether it be as parish or as base community, we are engaged in the same process: to become Church as community of liberation and to cease to be the sacralization of the powers and principalities. Base communities need not regard themselves as better than others; rather they should recognize that no part of the Church, no part of the world, is liberated until we are all liberated.

Whether we gather in living rooms, warehouses, or church buildings, the marks of the authentic Church are the same. The Church is where the good news of liberation from sexism is preached, where the Spirit is present to empower us to renounce patriarchy, where a community committed to the new life of mutuality is gathered together and nurtured, and where the community is spreading this vision and struggle to others.

Chapter 9
The New Earth: Socioeconomic Redemption from Sexism

Christianity has, in its New Testament foundations, traditions that would affirm the equality of woman in the image of God and the restoration of her full personhood in Christ. But even the primarily marginalized traditions that have affirmed this view through the centuries have not challenged the socioeconomic and legal subordination of women. Equality in Christ has been understood to apply to a new redeemed order beyond creation, to be realized in Heaven. Even when anticipated on earth, equality in Christ is confined to the monastery or the Church, the eschatological community. Patriarchy as order of nature or creation remains the underlying assumption of mainstream and radical Christianity alike. If woman becomes equal as virgin, prophetess, martyr, mystic, or even preacher, it is because these roles are seen as gifts of the Spirit and harbingers of a transcendent order. Only with the Enlightenment is there a shift to an egalitarian concept of "original nature" that challenges the "naturalness" of hierarchical social structures.

The claim that redemption in Christ has a social dimension has come about in modern Christianity only by an identification of its inherited messianic symbols with their secular interpretation in liberalism and socialism. But this new consciousness is still under continuous challenge by conservative Christians who seek to invalidate any theology, whether from a feminist, class, or racial minority perspective, that would make socioeconomic liberation an intrinsic part of the meaning

214

of redemption. Such Christians would claim that redemption is a purely spiritual matter and has nothing to do with socio-economic changes.

This individualizing and spiritualizing of salvation is the reverse side of the individualizing of sin. Sin is recognized only in individual acts, not structural systems. One is called to examine one's sinfulness in terms of abuses of oneself and personal unkindness to one's neighbor, but not in terms of the vast collective structures of war, racism, poverty, and, least of all, the oppression of women. In more sophisticated circles, Reinhold Niebuhr's division between "moral man" and "immoral society" is used to declare that altruism and love is possible, if at all, only on the interpersonal level. Collective groups, especially large ones, like nation-states, can only pursue an ethic of self-interest.

This "realism" is distorted by neoconservatives into an attack on any effort to create a more just society as fanatical and utopian. Liberation theology is condemned as a "heretical" effort to transcend the limits of historical existence, as though the present Western capitalist society represented the "limits" of historical existence and the "best of all possible worlds."[1] Such thinking neglects the early Niebuhr for whom such reflections on human limits are also an effort to find a solid basis for building a more just society. Niebuhr's working model of a more just society was democratic socialism. And he did not hesitate to think that even violent revolution might be ethically justified, at times, to break chains of colonial oppression and bring about the basis for such a new possibility.[2]

The working assumption of this feminist theology has been the dynamic unity of creation and redemption. The God/ess who underlies creation and redemption is One. We cannot split a spiritual, antisocial redemption from the human self as a social being, embedded in sociopolitical and ecological systems. We must recognize sin precisely in this splitting and deformation of our true relationships to creation and to our neighbor and find liberation in an authentic harmony with all that is incarnate in our social, historical being. Socioeconomic humanization is indeed the outward manifestation of redemption.

The search for the good self and the good society exists in an unbreakable dialectic. One cannot neglect either side. One cannot assume, with Marxism, that new, just social institutions automatically will produce the "new humanity." But one also cannot suppose that simply building up an aggregate of converted individuals will cause those individuals to act differently, changing society without any attention to its structures. The sensitized consciousness causes individuals to band together to seek a transformed society, and new and more just social relations cause many people to act and become different.

In this chapter I examine different traditions of feminist liberation, specifically liberal, socialist, and radical feminism. I summarize the main aspects of each perspective and also the limits that seem to appear in each. We will ask on the socioeconomic level the question that we asked at the conclusion of chapter 4, on anthropology: Can we begin to envision a more comprehensive vision that encompasses all three traditions rather than sets them up as competitors of each other?

LIBERAL FEMINISM

Liberal feminism has its roots in a feminist appropriation of the liberal traditions of equal rights, rooted in the doctrine of a common human nature of all persons. The liberal feminist agenda has been focused on the historic exclusion of women from access to and equal rights in the traditional male public sphere. It has sought to dismantle the historic structure of patriarchal law that denied women civil rights as autonomous adults. It has sought the full equality of women before the law, as citizens. This has entailed the repeal of discriminatory laws that denied property rights to married women especially, under the common-law rubric that the married woman was "civilly dead" and that her husband was her legal representative.

The apex of the campaign for autonomous civil status was suffrage, the granting of the vote to women, which also opened up all other political rights under the Constitution, such as the holding of political office. Another major emphasis of liberal feminism has been in the educational and professional spheres. Women sought full access to higher education, which historically had been denied to them. Education was seen both as an expression of women's human right to develop their intellectual potential and also as the key to all those professions of power and profit that men monopolized by denying women educational credentials and licenses, particularly law, medicine, and the ministry. Liberal feminists also sought to change marriage laws: Loss of property rights in marriage and inequitable divorce and child custody laws were areas of early and continuing concern.[3]

Twentieth-century liberal feminism has taken this quest for equal rights further: equal pay for equal work, equal access to all levels of a profession once women are admitted to it, the breaking down of formal and informal structures of power by which women in professions are excluded from top leadership roles. Caucuses within every profession spring up to examine these structures and act as advocates and networks of power and communication.

Liberal feminism has also turned to the whole underside of male control over women's bodies which nineteenth-century feminists only began to question: women's right to reproductive self-determination, sex education, birth control, and abortion. It has focused on women's right to dignity and control over their sexual persons, against sexual harassment on the job, wife battering in the home, rape in the streets (or home), and pornography, which dehumanizes the cultural imagination about women. Lesbianism also has achieved its place in the liberal feminist agenda, although not without considerable stress. Liberalism defines the lesbian as a "minority" person who should not be denied human and civil rights because of sexual preference.

The consistent pursuit of the liberal feminist agenda of equal rights continually pushes the limits of liberalism itself. Zillah Eisenstein, in *The Radical Future of Liberal Feminism,*[4] shows how the pursuit of the egalitarian claims by women continually transcends and challenges the limits of the patriarchal-capitalist system. The search for equality for women cannot be accommodated within this system, and consistent liberal feminists come increasingly to recognize the need to transform fundamentally the larger system.

In the socioeconomic sphere, liberal feminism begins to analyze the basic inequality of women in the economic hierarchy of paid labor and also the interconnections between women's work role in the home and the treatment of women on the job. Corporate capitalism treats women as a marginal labor force to be hired when needed and fired at will. In times of expanding industrialization, women were needed to work in factories and they were exploited with low pay and miserable working conditions. But more advanced industrialism, with a shrinking need for labor-intensive production, allies with "reform" measures that aim at removing women from the labor force and returning them to the home as their "true sphere."[5]

Likewise, in wartime all the ideological media of communication of society reverse their usual messages and call women to become truck drivers and workers in heavy industry, to fill the empty seats in the universities, and even the pulpits, as their "patriotic duty." But when the war is over the old messages return. Women are told to go home, to make room for the returning males who have prior rights to the jobs, and to produce babies to replace the slaughtered population.

Women in the work force are confined primarily to a female job ghetto. The kinds of work women do at home condition fundamentally the work to which they are directed in the paid labor force. Child care, nursery school and primary school teaching, food service, office maintenance — all this is women's work, although men may act as managers in more sophisticated and prestigious versions of such work. Above all, women have become the clerical workers of advanced industrialism, coping with the vast piles of paperwork and communication systems that hold this global apparatus together. They do the rote labor of the paper and electronic empire but have almost no input or control over its content. The male executive elite stands on a vast pyramid of female labor: file clerks, "charwomen," and, finally, their own wives, who free them for exclusive attention to decision making. The richer and more powerful the executive, the higher and more intricate the pyramid of class-, race-, and gender-based division of labor that supports his power and profits.

Female work in this system is typically poorly paid and has little job security. It is the least likely to be protected by unions or secure contracts. Perhaps no more than ten percent of women work in what are considered professional occupations, but even these are often segregated as female professions. Nurses, teachers, medical technicians, and librarians receive much lower remuneration than men in comparable positions demanding a similar level of specialization and education. A tiny number, about three percent, of women work in the prestigious male professions: university professor, lawyer, doctor, minister. Here, too, women are generally found to have lower rank and poorer pay.[6]

Women in the United States achieved their largest percentages in the male professions between 1900 and 1920, and their numbers declined thereafter. Only with the spectacular efforts of the feminist revival in the late 1960s to the present have their proportional numbers in these professions begun to equal what it was in 1920! Thus, despite all appearances of women crowding into law, medical, and theological schools, graduate departments of science, and so on, the economic structure of industrial capitalism is one of pervasive, structural discrimination against women.

Women's work role in the home both doubles the burden and reinforces the stereotype of women's low status on the job.

Despite recent adjustments in dual-career marriages, in which men seek to share housekeeping and childraising, the structure and culture of corporate industrialism are deeply set against allowing them to do so. Despite all goodwill, men seldom have any real understanding of the extent and complexity of the work that goes into homemaking. Women are so socialized to feel they have to do this work (and men to think they don't have to do it) that they generally find it easier to do most of it themselves rather than expend the emotional energy trying to get men (or children) to do their share. Males tend to assume that if they have picked up a child from nursery school once a week, wiped the dishes, and helped with the shopping, they have "shared" housework.

Statistical studies of women's domestic work continue to show that when women work, they still do almost all the housework. The housework is simply squeezed into the after-hours and less is done.[7] This adds to a woman's sense of harassment since she feels constantly responsible for a sector of work that she cannot accomplish adequately. This is not simply a matter of her own psychology, because the culture constantly scapegoats married working women as the cause of a variety of social problems, from homosexuality to juvenile delinquency, because they are not full-time mothers and homemakers.

This "second shift" of domestic work also fundamentally mitigates women's equality in the paid work force, in three ways. First, the psychological and cultural model of women's work in the home creates a model of women's work on the job that makes men hostile to women's equality with them in the same type of work. Second, women's time commitments to domestic work prevent them from putting in extra time after hours for travel, education, and committee work, which advance people in the meritocracy. Third, the first two factors shut women out of the networks of communication that are used to compete on the job.

The ideology of equal rights obscures as much as it aids women's real equality. Official liberalism may have won all the laws on the books that appear to grant women full equality. It is very hard to uncover the actual structures that prevent this in practice and that relegate women to low-paid and low-status sectors of the work force. Appearances justify the impression that women simply don't have the "drive" to achieve equality with men. The hidden work role of women masks the fact that women have to work at least half again as hard as men in order to be "equal" in this system.

Zillah Eisenstein argues that these contradictions between the liberal ideology of equality and the structures of job hierarchy and the double work shift that prevent equality give rise to the radicalization of liberal feminism. The more women analyze these contradictions, the more they realize their inability to achieve this equality within the structures of capitalism. A fundamental transformation of the work structures both in the home and in the paid labor force is necessary. Only socialist feminism provides tools for analyzing these contradictions and envisions a new system that might solve them. Liberal feminism and socialist feminism are not in irreconcilable conflict, however. The logical and social contradictions of liberal feminism lead to its transformation into socialist feminism.

One should not assume that those operating within a liberal feminist perspective will automatically be led in this direction. The traditional complaint of socialist feminists against liberal feminism was that its ideology and practice is encapsulated within the class interests of the bourgeois. Liberal feminists sought political rights and educational and professional roles within the same framework as male roles of their own class. But they seldom realized the very different concerns of working-class women, racial minority women, and poor women, who were shut out of exercising class-based "rights." This bias came out clearly in the later phases of the suffrage struggle in the late nineteenth century when a sizable part of the movement switched from arguing for the vote on the basis of equal rights to arguing for it on the basis of "expediency."

It was said that middle-class Anglo-Saxon women had the education and culture to exercise the vote "properly." To give it to them would double the vote of the "responsible citizens" (WASP middle class). This drift took place at a time when blacks and immigrants were being disenfranchised by Jim Crow and literacy laws.[8]

Women always occupy two interlocking kinds of social status. As a gender, all women are marginalized and subjugated relative to males. But as members of class and race hierarchies, women occupy class levels comparable to, although as secondary members of, their class and race. Any strategy of women's liberation must recognize the interface and contradictions between these two ways of determining women's social status. Marginalization as women can lead to a sense of cross-class and cross-race solidarity of women along lines of common gender discrimination. But women's membership in class and race hierarchies can draw women into a primary identification with the males of their class and race, against women and men of other classes and races.

White middle-class women are tempted to compensate for gender discrimination by using women of the lower class to do their "women's" work, thereby freeing themselves to compete as equals with men of their group. The dual-career family at upper executive levels is made possible by the affluence that can hire the housekeeper and the private secretary. This is then touted as the fulfillment of the promise of liberal feminism, although actually the economic position of the white upper middle class is being reinforced against women and men of lower classes and races. Such equality at affluent levels remains token. Its visibility and acclaim only serves to disaffect poor women, working-class women, minority women, and women as housewives from feminism. The glitter of feminist "equality," as displayed in *Cosmopolitan* and *Ms.*, both eludes and insults the majority of women who recognize that its "promise" is not for them.

SOCIALIST FEMINISM

Is socialist feminism, then, the answer to the insufficiencies and limits of liberal feminism? Does one not have to lead liberal feminism explicitly to an analysis of the class contradictions of women under capitalism, rather than waiting for liberal feminism to "automatically" produce this radicalization? I believe this is the case. Yet socialist feminism also produces its own contradictions, some of them analogous to those of liberal feminism.

The tradition of socialist feminism goes back to the classic study by Friedrich Engels, *The Origin and History of the Family, Private Property and the State* (1884). Engels recognized that the ideology of woman as weak, timid, and incompetent was fundamentally a class myth of bourgeois society shaped to sanctify the family patterns of middle-class men who did not need their wives' labor in the work force. But working-class women had to go into the factories to provide income for the survival of their families, in a system of exploitative wages for working-class men and women. The woman who dragged coal carts in the mines or labored for ten hours a day at machines could not cultivate the pretenses of "feminine" delicacy, nor was she given the deference and protection of the "lady." This same woman returned from long hours at work only to take on a second work role in the family. In so doing, she exposed and contradicted the class-based myths of female weakness by her very ability to cope with these exhausting conditions.

The key to Marxist feminism, as developed by Engels and his successors, was the restoration of women to economic autonomy, under socialist conditions in which the exploitation of the proletariat had been abolished. Modern industrialization was in fact beginning this liberation of women by forcing working-class women into wage labor. But it was doing so under oppressive capitalist conditions. Under socialism, the means of production would be owned and managed by the workers themselves. Then women, along with men, as workers, would have an equal share in the fruits of their productive labor. Under these conditions, women as independent wage earners would be able to relate to men as equal partners, both on the job and within marriage. Economic independence, not simply civil rights, was seen as the key to women's liberation. Without economic independence under equal working conditions, the civil rights that liberal feminism would win — the rights to vote, to be educated, and to own property — remained class privileges.

Socialist and Communist governments, in practice, have carried through the basic outlines of this tradition of socialist feminism. On gaining power, such governments have legislated civil equality for women. They have dismantled the patriarchal laws that discriminated against women in marriage and divorce and that denied women political rights and access to education and employment. They have done this with the assumption that these rights are effective only within a socialist society in which women have full and equal employment with men. So the main socialist agenda has been to integrate women into the work force.[9]

Moreover, socialist societies have recognized that women cannot compete with men as equals as long as they are handicapped by the second shift of domestic work. They have tried to alleviate this handicap by socializing certain aspects of women's work. Most typically, this means state-supported daycare centers and nursery schools, which allow mothers to return to work within a year of childbearing. Maternity leave and guaranteed reentry to jobs further compensate for women's work in reproduction. Some socialist societies have also experimented with collective laundries and kitchens. Low-cost or free contraceptives and abortions encourage planned childbearing.

All this represents a significant advantage for women in socialist societies in contrast to capitalist societies, which have resisted such efforts to alleviate women's domestic role by various appeals to the sanctity of the (patriarchal) family. The result is that the contradictions between women's work and domestic role is exacerbated and rendered chaotic, with a worsening of the very conditions of stress on the family that bourgeois patriarchy claims to deplore by blaming them on "working mothers."

Although socialism has ameliorated the handicap of women in industrial society, it has not fundamentally altered it. An analysis of women's work in socialist or communist societies shows that the same contradictions between unpaid domestic and low-paid wage labor continue. Despite the efforts of government to integrate women equally into the work force, women are still found at the lower levels of every job hierarchy, from politics to business to factory work. They receive lower pay and fewer benefits than men at the same level. The stereotype of women's inferiority persists, and men object to having a woman in a superior position.

Why is this? It has been concluded in various studies that the primary cause of this continuing inequality of women in communist societies is the double work burden of unpaid domestic labor. Women work approximately four hours a day more than men in order to provide domestic services. This second job sends women scurrying to shops (to stand in long lines), to nurseries, and to kitchens after work. By contrast, their male "peers" use this time to volunteer for political offices, to sit on factory committees, to take refresher courses, or to go to the gyms or bars where they win points in the meritocracy and forge the vital links with their male colleagues that advance them up the job ladder.

Women's second job has the same effects in socialist societies as in capitalist countries: preserving the stereotype of women as low-level workers under men, leaving women exhausted and unable to compete with men, and eliminating women from the after-hours roles by which men advance in the meritocracy. It would seem that patriarchy plus industrialism is the cause of this pattern. Socialism rationalizes, but does not fundamentally solve these contradictions.[10]

The answer of socialist feminism has been to analyze women's domestic work role as a major source of gender-based "class structure." As long as women continue to carry a double work role, they cannot compete as equal with men in the paid labor force. But it is not clear that socialist feminism has an answer to this, except to extend further the socialization of women's domestic role. This means collective kitchens, collective laundries, collective housecleaning — indeed, the collectivization of housing altogether in dormitories that would abolish the home as a private space. Perhaps some socialists would even go further and imagine some technology that would alleviate women's role as childbearers with test-tube fertilizations and mechanical wombs.[11] Presumably, such technology would provide jobs well paid and shared by men and women alike.

But one must ask whether such a vision is the ultimate liberation or the ultimate enslavement? If collectivism means state control, then an abolition of the home would be the total alienation of one's life to institutions external to one's own control and governed by a managerial elite. In the name of the liberation of women, we would hand over the remnants of that self-employed and autonomous sphere of life where we own and control our own means of production — our reproductive organs, our kitchens, and so on.

Socialism, like liberalism, operates under an unstated androcentric bias. It assumes that the male work role is the normative human activity. Women are to be liberated by being incorporated into the male realm. Liberalism would extend to women the legal right to do so, while socialism would provide women with the economic capacity to take advantage of such rights. Both assume that women are liberated insofar as they are enabled to function like men in the public realm.

One must ask whether the dominant socialist traditions (democratic socialism and Marxism-Leninism) have not fundamentally misconstrued the socialist agenda of restoring ownership of the means of production to the people. In terms of factories and workplaces, this should mean giving ownership and management into the hands of local committees of workers, rather than making the workers employees of a state bureaucracy. Socialist ideology seems to contain a fundamental contradiction: It has seen itself as restoring ownership of the means of production to the people, while at the same time it continues the process of industrialization, that is, collectivization of work outside the home. It has identified ownership by the people with ownership by the state and management by the party bureaucracy. The result has been a deepening of the alienation of people from their labor and the creation of a new ruling class, the party bureaucracy.

When the question of collectivization of work is applied to the remaining roles of women in the home, this issue becomes radicalized. Do we want to continue this process of further alienation of our life processes? Is it not necessary to imagine an entirely different model for socialization — namely, taking back to communalized households work functions that have been taken over by capitalist or state party managers? In this light, the work functions of women in the home appear as the remnants of a preindustrial world of home-based economy. In contrast to state socialism, communitarian or utopian socialism has understood socialism as the communalization of work on the base of a communal family. The split between home and work, women's work and men's work, is overcome by reintegrating them in a community that both raises its children collectively and owns and manages its own means of production. It is not accidental that feminists who have tried to imagine a reconstructed, nonsexist society have instinctively gravitated toward some form of the utopian socialist model rather than to state socialism.

Thus the feminist issue, when pursued within socialism, also seems to explode the limits of the dominant socialist traditions and to suggest that the feminist question cannot be solved within the limits of its system. Instead, we are forced to ask, in a much more fundamental way, the difference between

women's role as childbearer and nurturer and the male
economic and political role that has been defined over against
it. Feminism needs to ask whether, instead of making the male
sphere the human norm and attempting to assimilate women
into it, it is not necessary to move in the opposite direction.
Should we not take the creation and sustaining of human life
as the center and reintegrate alienated maleness into it? This
leads to the third tradition of feminism — radical feminism
— which takes the gender division as primary and insists that
women's liberation is first and foremost liberation from male
domination.

RADICAL FEMINISM

For radical feminism the core issue is women's control over
their own persons, their own bodies as vehicles of autonomous
sexual experience, and their own reproduction. Patriarchy
means, above all, the subordination of women's bodies,
sexuality, and reproduction to male ownership and control.
Rape, wife beating, sexual harassment, pornography, the
ideologies, culture, and fashions that socialize women to
becoming objects of male sexual control, the denial of birth
control and abortion, and, ultimately, the denial of female
initiation and control over sexual relations — all are ramifica-
tions of the fundamental nature of patriarchy, the expro-
priation of woman *as body* by man. Any theory of women's
liberation that stops short of liberating women from male control over their bodies has not reached the root of patriarchy.

For many, the logic of this position leads to lesbian
separatism. Women can't be liberated from patriarchy until
they are liberated from men. Women need to see the community of women as their primary base. Women bonding
together both in love relationships and for primary support,
together with their (female?) children, is women's base and
identity. It is on this base that feminism needs to build an
alternative women's world. Women must question not only

the ideologies of sexism but of heterosexism, that is, the basic assumption that men and women are naturally attracted to each other sexually and that male-female couples are necessary for human families.

In feminist utopian novels, ranging from Charlotte Perkins Gilman's *Herland* (1915)[12] to Sally Gearhart's *Wanderground,*[13] we have visions of a world of women liberated from men. Men are seen in these novels as alien to women, as creatures in some fundamental way inhuman. They are characterized by aggressive sexuality and domineering attitudes toward women and nature. Theirs is literally a "rape culture." In the feminist utopia, a select community of women have escaped from male control. Key to this is a recovery of love between women and, with it, the ability to reproduce independent of men. (This, in fact, is not biologically implausible. The male sperm acts to stimulate the female egg to start to divide and grow. It has been postulated that this could be done by another agent, such as another female egg, in which case all the offspring would be female.)[14]

The female utopia cultivates a women's culture. High values are placed on intuitive and poetic forms of communication and on mutuality and care for the earth. Eden is restored. One might say that, with the ejection of men, evil is eliminated from human (female) relationships. But men still roam like beasts of prey outside the magic circle of women's world. Women must be constantly on guard against letting men into their good land of peace and plenty.

Various radical feminist writers have developed aspects of this separatist vision. Mary Daly concentrates on a passionate exposé of the inhumanity of males and their culture of rape, genocide, and war. The history of women becomes a trail of crucifixions, with males as the evil archons of an anticosmos where women are entrapped. For Daly, liberation for women is primarily spiritual. They discover an alternative land within their inner selves, then learn to communicate with a new language that breaks apart and transforms the dominant language.

They escape together through the holes rent in the fabric of patriarchal ideology into a separate and higher realm of female interiority.[15] Daly's vision moves to a remarkable duplication of ancient Gnostic patterns, but now built on the dualism of a transcendent spirit world of femaleness over against the deceitful anticosmos of masculinity.[16]

Goddess religion represents a somewhat different movement, which may or may not be lesbian separatist. But in either case the dominant divine symbol is the Great Mother, linking Womanhood and Nature. Authentic humanity and the good earth reign under the sign of the Mother. Eden can be restored only by subordinating the male to the female. The horned God or male consort of the Goddess is not her equal, much less her "father," but her son-lover. Men, if they are accepted, must recognize their subordinate place in the female-centered world.[17] The male characteristics of linear thinking and objectification can be deprived of their evil-making tendencies only when assimilated into and under the female properties of love, mutual service, and intuitive knowledge. The suppressed powers of the human self are released to become the basis of a new culture and mode of relating and communicating.[18]

Other radical feminists concentrate more on the alternative social base for a women's world. They seek to build women's work collectives in which women are no longer dependent on male ownership and male hierarchical methods of organization of work. Such work collectives can be developed in urban settings in a variety of professions: women's health centers, law collectives, media collectives, and the like. The ultimate separatist vision moves toward the country collective, where women create an alternative, communitarian society. Here the women's community — as female bonding, family, culture, spirituality, and participatory, nonhierarchical ways of organizing — can flourish in an organic community.

Is this direction of radical feminism the ultimate vision of feminism? Do feminists who wish to be radical (to get to the root of patriarchy) and consistent necessarily have to break their ties with men and move into this separatist perspective? I believe that this stance, although attractive in many ways, is delusive. Women's affirmation of their own humanity as more fundamental than their sexist conditioning demands a like affirmation of the humanity of males. Separatism reverses male hierarchicalism, making women normative humanity and males "defective" members of the human species. This enemy-making of males projects onto males all the human capacities for competitive relations and ego-power drives and hence denies that women too possess these capacities as part of their humanity.

Such enemy-making of men would ultimately subvert the whole dream of a women's culture based on mutuality and altruism. The very process of projecting the negative part of their own psychic potential onto males, and failing to own these themselves, would tend to make such women's groups fanatical caricatures of that which they hate. The dehumanization of the other ultimately dehumanizes oneself. One duplicates evil-making in the very effort to escape from it once and for all, by projecting it on the "alien" group.

This does not mean that women's communes and collectives and lesbian families cannot exist as good human relationships, as well as experimental bases for an alternative humanity. One could indeed look to such communities as harbingers of an alternative culture of nonhierarchical relationships. But they can function in this way only when they do not wall themselves into a separatist ideology that identifies femaleness with goodness and maleness with evil and when they take responsibility for the ambiguity of their own humanity. On that basis we can then see the development of women's culture and modes of organization as experiments on behalf of humanity, male and female. We draw on capacities for mutuality that men possess as well as women. We criticize tendencies toward egoism that women possess as well as men. It is true that women, because of their relative powerlessness within history, have cultivated values and modes of relationships that are less dehumanized than male culture. But the effort to imagine symbols and systems of life that draw on these must do so for the sake of liberating these capacities in men as well, on behalf of the whole of humanity.

IS THERE AN INTEGRATIVE
FEMINIST VISION OF SOCIETY?

The search for an integrative vision starts with the assumption that feminism must include the liberal, socialist, and radical traditions. Each of these traditions shows its limitations precisely at the point where it tries to become final and to encapsulate itself within its own system. It remains insightful and authentic to the extent that it also remains open-ended. We have seen how the insufficiencies of each perspective suggest the need for the others. Liberal feminism opens into the questions of the economic hierarchies of work explored by socialist feminism. Radical feminism moves into an increasingly isolated, separatist utopianism that largely fails to address the real possibilities of most women and men, and so calls for its reintegration back into questions of social reorganization of mainstream society. Each of these perspectives can provide a part of a larger whole to the extent that we refuse the temptation to set up any one in a mutually exclusive relationship to the others.

What is the society we seek? We seek a society that affirms the values of democratic participation, of the equal value of all persons as the basis for their civil equality and their equal access to the educational and work opportunities of the society. But more, we seek a democratic socialist society that dismantles sexist and class hierarchies, that restores ownership and management of work to the base communities of workers themselves, who then create networks of economic and political relationships. Still more, we seek a society built on organic community, in which the processes of childraising, of education, of work, of culture have been integrated to allow both men and women to share child nurturing and homemaking and also creative activity and decision making in the larger society. Still more, we seek an ecological society in which human and nonhuman ecological systems have been integrated into harmonious and mutually supportive, rather than antagonistic, relations.

There are two ways to imagine going about building this new society. One is to build an alternative, communitarian system by a small voluntary group with a high intentionality and consciousness. Such a group would seek to put together all aspects of this feminist, socialist, communitarian, and ecological vision in a small experiment conducted on a separate social and economic base from the larger society. Such communal experiments have been carried out within history. They can be reasonably successful in fusing all aspects of the vision. Their limitation lies precisely in their inability to move beyond the small voluntary group and create a base for the larger society.

A second method is to work on pieces of the vision separately: a communal child-care unit within an educational institution or workplace; an alternative energy system for an apartment building; solar greenhouses for a neighborhood; a women's collective that produces alternative culture for the society. We might develop within a self-managed institution less hierarchical forms of organization, more equal remuneration for all workers, men and women, regardless of their jobs. We might plan communities that allow more humanized relationships between the various aspects of people's lives. We might encourage a plurality of household patterns, homosexual as well as heterosexual, voluntary as well as blood- and marriage-related, where groups can share income and homemaking. We can think of these separate pieces of a mosaic that we are putting in place, gradually replacing the present picture with a new vision.

But the alternative nonsexist, nonclassist and nonexploitative world eludes us as a global system. This is not so much because of our inability to imagine it correctly as because of the insufficient collective power of those already converted to an alternative vision. The powers and principalities are still very much in control of most of the world. The nucleus of the alternative world remains, like the Church (theologically, *as* the Church), harbingers and experimenters with new human possibilities within the womb of the old.

Chapter 10
Eschatology and Feminism

DOES FEMINISM HAVE A STAKE
IN IMMORTALITY?

To ask whether feminist consciousness has a stake in the idea of immortality may seem odd. If there is any place where men and women are equal, it is in their basic finitude. Death levels all socially constructed differences between the genders, races, and classes. The question is not whether men and women share the same mortality; it is whether women have the same stake in denying their mortality through doctrines of life after death, or whether this is not the apogee of male individualism and egoism. Anne Wilson Schaef, a psychotherapist, in her book *Women's Reality,* strongly suggests the latter conclusion:

> Since White Male-System persons so firmly believe that it is possible for one to become God, they are understandably concerned with the issue of immortality. Female-System persons, on the other hand, realize that immortality is not a genuine possibility and spend little or no time worrying about it.[1]

Schaef goes on to say that she has seldom found a male in therapy who was not concerned about his own immortality on some level, while very few of the women she has worked with in therapy have been concerned about it. If women think about it at all, it is primarily in the context of relationship — they would like to be able to see loved ones who have died — while males are primarily concerned about their own self-perpetuation.

In 1923 feminist economist and philosopher Charlotte Perkins Gilman published a book called *His Religion and Hers* in which she outlines two fundamentally different orientations to life based on the crises of male and female experience. For man, historically as hunter and warrior, the pivotal experience is death, both as killer of animals and other humans and as one threatened by violent death himself. Male religion thus becomes centered on the "blood mystery" of death and how to escape it. For woman, on the other hand, the pivotal experience is birth and her basic concern is how to nurture ongoing life here on earth. In Gilman's words:

> To the death-based religion, the main question is, "What is going to happen to me after I am dead?" — a posthumous egoism.
> To the birth-based religion, the main question is, "What is to be done for the child who is born?" — an immediate altruism.
> ...The death-based religions have led to a limitless individualism, a demand for the eternal extension of personality...The birth-based religion is necessarily and essentially altruistic, a forgetting of oneself for the good of the child, and tends to develop naturally into love and labor for the widening range of family, state and world.[2]

Perkins believes that religion needs to be transformed by focusing on the female birth experience rather than on the male death experience. While avoiding an outright denial of the truth of immortality, Gilman argues that the primary human responsibility is to preserve and promote a human life for future generations yet to be born rather than to be narcissistically concerned about one's individual survival of death. The latter, she believes, leads to a neglect of ongoing life on the planet. Although Gilman's anthropology may be a bit simplistic, her book raises an issue similar to Schaef's. Is the idea of immortality the expression of a male individualism and abstractionism from real-life processes that feminist consciousness should reject? To approach an answer to this question we need to explore more deeply why the desire for immortality has

arisen in human religion and to look at the various kinds of
eschatology in Biblical as well as non-Biblical religions.

THREE PATTERNS OF HOPE

All humans know they are mortal. They exist for a finite term
of years. Why is this finite span regarded as insufficient for
the boundaries of human life? The reason has something to
do with the ability of the human to stand out against the environment and to imagine a better alternative. Human consciousness is not bounded by the "facts" of existing reality
but imagines ideal possibilities set against the present. This
allows humans to set about changing interpersonal relationships, changing relations to the environment, modifying tools,
altering social systems in search of this better alternative. The
alternative is an ideal against which present reality is measured
and found wanting.

Human ideas of their relationship to this ideal have differed.
Most traditional human societies have thought of this projected
ideal as a sacred ambience surrounding ordinary human life
that one imitates in ritual activity, thereby blessing and pro-
tecting the life processes. Hebrew tradition is unique in projecting this ideal as a future, redeemed era of life on earth.
Only in modern times has this Hebraic concept of a redeemed
future been imagined as something achievable through secular
processes of historical change.

Regardless of how one relates to the ideal, there remains
a gap between the ideal and actual life. This gap becomes a
crisis of meaning only if one aspires to realize this ideal in the
future rather than simply allowing it to sacramentalize daily
life. This drive to realize the ideal in a future era of redemption
does not at first raise the question of immortality in Hebrew
thought because Hebrew religion focuses on the collective,
tribal self, not the fate of the individual. The collective, tribal
self, in its continuing history with God, would one day experience redemption. Only in the Hellenistic period, when a greater

238 Sexism and God-Talk

sense of individualism develops, does this answer seem inadequate, and so the concept of the resurrection of the dead is developed. Resurrection allows individual righteous persons of past periods of history to rise and join the future community of Israel in the vindication of God's ideal on earth.

Even with this idea of the resurrection of the dead, Hebrew thought does not fully develop a concept of personal immortality. The basic concept of the human being as mortal, bound by a certain limit of years, remains. Moreover, this limited term of life is regarded as natural and good. What is evil is not that humans die as the terminus of old age, but that they die untimely deaths, that they are cut off by war and disease and fail to live out their full potential. Society is riddled by injustice in which the evil prosper and the good are oppressed. Thus, for much of Hebrew apocalyptic thought, the future redeemed era is not seen as a time of endless or deathless life that will heal the affront of human mortality. Rather it is thought of as a time, itself bounded by a limit of years (a millennium), in which injustice is redressed. The evil ones who have prospered will be punished. The good ones who have suffered rejoice and will be at ease. In the words of the prophet Isaiah:

> For behold I create new Heavens and a new earth,
> and the former things shall not be remembered or come to mind...

> No more shall there be in it an infant that lives but a few days,
> or an old man who does not fill out his days,
> for the child shall die a hundred years old,...

> They shall build houses and inhabit them;
> they shall plant vineyards and eat their fruit.
> They shall not build and another inhabit;
> they shall not plant and another eat...

> They shall not labor in vain or bear children for calamity;
> for they shall be the offspring of the blessed of the Lord
> (Isa. 65:17, 20-21, 23)

Here no immortality is envisioned, but rather a new age when the evils that prevent the enjoyment of human life within its full temporal life span are overcome. The blessed will work and enjoy their harvests for the "ideal" life span of a hundred years, without the calamities of disease or warfare that sweep away the fruits of one's life and toil. Even in some of the more developed apocalyptic texts — in which the dead are envisioned as arising in their bodies, the good and evil judged, the evil consigned to punishment and the good to the enjoyment of a blessed life — this is still seen as going on within a limited temporal span of years. In the first book of Enoch V, 9 it is said that the risen ones

> shall not transgress again, nor shall they sin all the days of their life, but they shall complete the number of the days of their life, and their lives shall be increased in peace.[3]

Not immortality but a blessed longevity is the ideal realized in the resurrection.

When the Greek idea of immortality of the soul begins to make its impact on Jewish thought, there is at first an effort to accommodate it within an extended and immortalized concept of the messianic age. But gradually the two ideas are distinguished. Apocalyptic thought, in its fullest development, moves toward a "double scenario." A historical millennium fulfills the demands of justice and a realized natural life, followed by the end of the world and the creation of a new immortal world where the righteous can live an everlasting life. Even here the remnants of a basically historical way of thinking persists. The eternal world is still seen as historically future to the present one, to be created by a new act of God at the historical completion of this present creation. The notion of immortality as a rejection of the naturalness of finite life itself remained somewhat foreign to Hebraic thought. It was oddly inserted into the framework of this worldly historical hope.

Greek philosophical thought contains a rejection of mortal life as inadequate for the good life even under "ideal" conditions. Instead, the ideal is split from the real as a transcendent realm juxtaposed above and beyond this present finite world. The ideal world above is the realm of eternal life. There, Being is perfect and fulfilled, without change or corruptibility. Below is the lower realm of change and becoming, of finite life that comes into existence and passes away again. The human is split between the two realms. The body belongs to the lower world of change and corruptibility, and the soul, especially its higher rational part, to the realm of immutable Being.

This dualism devalues life in the body. Bodily life becomes a kind of living death, trapped in the mortal flesh. The very existence of the soul in this dying flesh has come about through an accident or some sin that caused the soul to fall from its original higher state of blessedness in the heavens. Salvation consists of "mortification" or the practice of dying. The soul must control and repress the effects of the mortal body and its passions upon its higher state of being. It must seek to gradually separate the soul from the flesh and thus anticipate its final separation in death, when the soul will return to a blessed life in the heavens and will leave behind the corruptible hulk of flesh in which it was temporarily incarcerated.[4]

Within ancient Mediterranean and Near Eastern thought we can distinguish three very different views of the relationship between ideal and actual existence. I call these nature religion, historical religion, and eschatological religion. The tendency of modern theology to label all these relations "eschatological" is confusing. I prefer to reserve *eschatological* for a view that believes in the possibility of human transcendence of mortality.

Nature Religion

In Babylonian thought there is an idea of a shadowy underworld or kingdom of the dead, but it is hardly a blessed or ideal existence. It is the realm where the dead are held in a tenuous existence by the commemoration of their living descendants. The dead hold on to this shadowy life through the veneration offered them by their families. The festal libations renew their spirits. Such ideas form a substratum of thought about the dead found throughout the Mediterranean world, in Hebraic as well as Greek religion.

The basic thought of Babylonian religion, however, is that human beings are fundamentally mortal. Death is their portion. It is precisely mortality that separates humans from the Gods and Goddesses. The divine ones are immortal; humans are mortal. The great Babylonian epic of Gilgamesh explores the theme of man's (the male's?) vain search for immortality. The hero, Gilgamesh, is brought face to face with the specter of his own mortality through the death of his friend, Enkidu. "When I die, shall I not be like Enkidu?" weeps Gilgamesh. He undertakes a search for his ancestor, Utnapishtim, a Noah figure from the time before the Flood, who has learned the secret of escape from death. Significantly, it is a woman, the alewife, who warns Gilgamesh of the futility of this quest for immortality:

> Gilgamesh, whither rovest thou?
> The life thou pursuest thou shall not find.
> When the gods created mankind
> Death for mankind they set aside.
> Life in their own hands retaining.[5]

She advises Gilgamesh to eat, drink, and be merry, marry and enjoy the fruits of relationship with wife and child, and give up the futile search for life beyond death. The epic confirms this advice in an ironic way. Gilgamesh discovers his ancestor and then learns from his wife of the existence of a wonderful plant that cures advancing age and makes one eternally young. But, having brought up this plant from the bottom of the sea, he is negligent of it for a moment and it is eaten by a snake. Thus, the snake who sloughs off its skin attains continuous renewal of its life, while the human is doomed to death. There are no prospects except dismal Shoel beyond this temporal span.

But the denial of the possibility of human immortality does not mean a denial of religious hope within the limits of finite life. Ancient Near Eastern culture sees the cycles of renewal of nature as the key to the constant hope for renewed life, resurrected from drought and death. The Gods and Goddesses were not outside but within this struggle for life against death. The New Year's festival annually celebrated this victory of life over death, cosmos over chaos. In this victory the communities of the ancient Near East expressed their hope not only for renewed rains and fertility of the land, bountiful crops, and healthy offspring for human and animal but also for peace, social order, and justice, security against outside enemies, and good rulers who would protect the poor and liberate the captive. Among the hopes generated by the New Year celebration, according to one Babylonian kingship psalm, are

> ...a gracious reign, orderly days, years of righteousness, abundant rains, copious inundations, acceptable prices...old men dance, young men sing, matrons, maidens are gay with laughter, men take wives, they bring about births, they bring sons and daughters to birth, reproduction is prosperous.
>
> To him whose sin condemned him to death, the King-Lord has given new life; those who have been imprisoned many years, thou settest free; those who have been sick many years regain life; the hungry are satisfied; the lean grow fat; the destitute are supplied with clothing.
>
> Ahad let loose his showers; Ea opened his fountains; the corn grew five ells high in its ear; the spike became five-sixths of an ell; the harvest was good; there was fullness of Nisba; the giraru tree was ever-bearing; the fruit trees brought fruit to luxuriant issue; the cattle were fertile in giving birth; in my reign exuberance superabounds; in my reign abundance is heaped up.
>
> The evil were held in check who planned insubordination within city and house. A man did not take away with force what belonged to the neighbor; within the area of the whole land, no one caused an injury; only the one who passed on his way in peace, entered upon the long journey; there was no plunderer shedding blood; nor was there an outrage perpetuated; the lands were inhabited as a peaceful dwelling place.[6]

Historical Religion

Hebrew religious hope for the coming of God's Kingdom is built on the Canaanite-Babylonian pattern. Hebraic hope transforms this pattern of the annual New Year from a sacramental to a historical framework. Now the defeat of natural and social chaos and the advent of renewed life, peace, and justice is not simply a sacred canopy that arches over and blesses ordinary events; it has become a historical struggle. One discerns in the signs of the times military defeats or unexpected restorations, the hand of God working in history. The people's apostasy or fidelity to God is the fulcrum that turns the course of history from divine wrath to divine blessing.

Historical hope locates the ultimate achievement of the ideal in a final era of world history. After the ups and downs of human infidelity and divine punishment, there comes a time when the people turn wholeheartedly to God. The Messiah appears and defeats the enemies of God, both human and demonic. An age of blessedness reigns for the righteous. But this pattern of hope, like modern revolutionary hope, which is its secular expression, has no immediate answer to the untimely sufferings and deaths of present and past generations. At best, meaning can be given to their deaths because they died in hope for the revolution and those around them feel that their sufferings contributed to the coming of the better future.

The Hebraic idea of the resurrection of the dead was intended to bridge this gap between present unjust sufferings and the future era of vindication. But modern revolutionary hope cannot promise resurrection of the dead; it can promise only that someday our descendents will see a better day. For the peasant whose child has died of malnutrition, the promise of the coming revolution must seem more remote and "eschatological" than the promise of Heaven into which the innocent soul can enter immediately.

Eschatological Religion

By the later Persian and Hellenistic periods, Jewish thought begins to incorporate ideas of an immediate judgment of the soul after death and of a foretaste of punishment or blessings. But the ultimate vindication is reserved for the end of time, either within a historical millennium or beyond it, in eternal heaven and earth. Christian eschatology fuses the apocalyptic eschatology of post-Biblical Judaism with the Platonic eschatology of the soul that separates itself from its bodily encumbrance through mortification and returns to its true home in Heaven.

The book of Revelation in the New Testament exhibits the eschatological pattern of late Jewish apocalyptic. First, there is a millennium in which the righteous Christians arise and reign with Christ. When this thousand years is ended, there is a final skirmish with the Devil, who is defeated and thrown into an everlasting pit of fire. Then there is a general resurrection and judgment of all. The evil are thrown into the eternal lake of fire, and a new eternal heaven and earth descend from above. The ancient promises are finally fulfilled. The dwelling place of God is established on an immortalized earth "where every tear is wiped from their eyes and death shall be no more" (Rev. 21:4).

This kind of apocalyptic eschatology becomes increasingly distasteful to a Hellenistic Christianity of the late-second to fourth centuries. It resembled too much the Jewish hopes for a divine overthrow of the Roman Empire. Only by a compromise between the Greek and Latin churches was the book of Revelation in the canon of the New Testament at all. But by the Constantinian era the millennial hopes that are still found in earlier theologians, such as Justin Martyr and Irenaeus, have been marginalized. Mainstream Christianity focuses on the drama of the personal soul, reborn to eschatological life in Christ. This rebirth of the soul to eternal life through baptism is continued through a moral struggle against carnality in this life. The soul enters its final glorification as it separates from the body at death and ascends to Heaven.

Eschatology has been severed from historical hope. The drama of the resurrection from the dead, the final judgment, and the eternal Kingdom of Heaven beyond the end of history are still retained as orthodox theory. But Christian hope focuses on the personal eschatology of the soul, which passes on to places of punishment, purgation, or glory immediately after death in a realm transcendent to this present finite world. The eschatology of space has triumphed over the eschatology of time. Millennial hope does not vanish from Christianity, but it becomes the preserve of heretical sects and is revived, in secular, anticlerical form, in modern revolutionary hope.

THE AMBIGUITY OF
CHRISTIAN ESCHATOLOGY TOWARD WOMEN

The eschatological thought that developed in classical Christianity is characterized by extreme ambiguity toward women and what they represent (for males). Female sexuality and giving birth are seen as the antithesis of the escape from mortal life that the reborn virginal Christian seeks. Femaleness is both symbol and expression of the corruptible bodiliness that one must flee in order to purify the soul for eternal life. Female life processes — pregnancy, birth, suckling, indeed, female flesh as such — become vile and impure and carry with them the taint of decay and death. In the late second-century pseudo-Clementine letters "to Virgins," the male ascetic is instructed to shun places inhabited by women, including female virgins. If he has to lodge with them, he should not touch anything they have touched or sit in any place where they have been seated. He should allow only an aged female virgin to escort him to his chamber. A similar phobia toward women characterizes the sayings of the Desert Fathers, the paragons of asceticism for fourth-century Christians. Thus, in one saying we read:

> A certain brother was going on a journey, and he had his mother with him, and she was old. They came to a certain river, and the old woman could not cross it. And her son took off his cloak and wrapped it around his hands, lest he should in any wise touch the body of his mother, and so carrying her, he set her on the other side of the stream. Then said his mother to him, "Why dids't thou so cover thy hands, my son." He answered, "Because the body of a woman is fire. And even from my touching thee, came the memory of other women into my soul."[7]

But the other side of his phobia toward carnal femaleness, as we have seen in chapter 6, on Mariology, is the sublimation of the "feminine" as the substratum of spiritual rebirth and transcendence of material existence. Christian virgins, and particularly Mary, represent the spiritual insemination of the soul by Christ. As virginal mother, the Church and Christian virgins become spiritually fecund and bear much fruit in virtue. The Christian is like a new babe in the faith who is reborn in the womb of mother Church in baptism and fed on milk from the breasts of Christ. All the imagery of female life-giving processes can be taken over by the male celibate Church and referred to that higher birth into transcendent life that negates carnal birth from women.

Mary represents the virginal body of the eschatological Church. Her Assumption into Heaven prefigures the glorious resurrection and sublimation of the flesh as it rejoins the soul in the new age to come. Thus, maternity and the female body are negated in their physical form and yet appropriated in spiritualized form to provide the substratum for the "spiritual body" of the Church. In the resurrection, paradoxically, the very carnality of the flesh is overcome. The flesh is no longer finite and corruptible, but joined to the eternal life of the soul. Thus, Christian eschatology recognizes that the soul cannot finally exist apart from the body, so it seeks to reclaim the body in a "spiritual" form that will be freed from finite limitations.

This peculiar idea of the spiritual body is first developed in Paul (1 Cor. 15:42–44). In Gregory of Nyssa, the idea of the spiritual body of the resurrection is spelled out so we should have no doubt about its meaning.

> Just as if a man, who, clad in a ragged tunic, has divested himself of the garb, feels no more its disgrace upon him, so we too, when we have cast off that dead, unsightly tunic made from the skins of brutes and put upon us (for I take the "coats of skins" to mean that conformation belonging to a brute nature with which we were clothed when we became familiar with passionate indulgence) shall, along with the casting off of that tunic, fling from us all the belongings that were round us of that skin of a brute; and such accretions are sexual intercourse, conception, parturition, impurities, suckling, feeding, evacuation, gradual growth to full size, prime of life, old age, disease and death. If that skin is no longer round us, how can its resulting consequences be left behind within us?...
>
> The Divine power, in the superabundance of Omnipotence, does not only restore you that body once dissolved, but makes great and splendid additions to it, . . . the human being deposits in death all those peculiar surroundings which it has acquired from passionate propensities; dishonor, I mean, and corruption and weakness and characteristics of age; and yet the human being does not lose itself. It changes. . . into incorruption, that is, and glory and honor and power and absolute perfection; into a condition in which its life is no longer carried on in the ways peculiar to mere nature, but has passed into a spiritual and passionless existence.[8]

To understand this eschatology of the "spiritual body" in Gregory Nyssa, one must also refer to his doctrine of creation. For Gregory and others in the Greek Platonic tradition, the soul was originally created with a spiritual body. This means that the bodily substratum of the soul, as created, was transparent and glorious and without all the "propensities" — birth, growth, eating, sleeping, evacuation, old age, and death — of the present finite body. Only in the Fall did the sinful creatures take on those "coats of skin" to hide their original purity ("nakedness," Gen. 3:7).[9] The hides of animals with which Adam and Eve clothed themselves (following the Septuagint version of Genesis) represent for Gregory the devolution of the original spiritual body into a carnal body subject to decay and death. Only then does sexual intercourse and birth become necessary in order to reproduce what now has become a mortal creature.

Mortality is fundamentally unnatural to Gregory. It was not a part of the original nature of creation, and hence neither were sexual intercourse and reproduction. One might also ask, as Thomas Aquinas was to do in the Middle Ages,[10] whether the very existence of woman would have been necessary in the original creation, since woman's only function was reproduction, which would have been originally unnecessary. Indeed, the Greek Fathers, following Philo, suggest that gender division and the existence of woman are a kind of divine afterthought created with a view to the Fall and not a part of the original perfection of the spiritual nature.[11] It follows then that in redemption these accretions of the carnal body will be thrown off and humanity will return to its original spiritual and incorruptible body in the resurrection.

This raises the question for the Church Fathers of whether women will exist in the resurrection of the dead. Both Gnostic and orthodox Christian thought in the Patristic period equate becoming virgin with becoming male. Maleness expresses the spiritual nature and femaleness the carnal nature. It follows then that female virgins are regularly referred to as having become "virile and manly." Thus Leander of Seville, in his treatise to nuns, speaks of the virginal woman as

> forgetful of her natural feminine weakness, she lives in manly vigor and has used virtue to give strength to her weak sex, nor has she become a slave to her body, which by natural law should be subservient to a man.[12]

Such ideas suggest that in the resurrection of the dead the female body will be transformed into that of a male.

Augustine and Jerome reject these speculations and affirm that humanity will rise male and female, even as it has been created by God male and female. But Greek speculations of the original and eschatological "spiritual body" also are reflected in their thought. Augustine, in the *City of God,* says that in the original creation there would have been not only male and female but also sexual intercourse and reproduction. There would have been no sexual libido, however. The male would have sown his seed in the woman in a rational and passionless manner "just as a farmer sows his seed in a field." Moreover, the original bodies of humans, while corruptible, would have been held in a state of incorruption by the adherence of the soul to God. Only after the Fall did death appear, as the soul lost its adherence to God and so the body revealed its natural corruptibility.

Augustine assumes, however, that reproduction would have been a part of the original divine plan, in order to fill up the number of the human race. Women then are a part of the original nature of things because they are necessary for reproduction, an opinion to be repeated by Aquinas. It follows then that in the resurrection of the dead, humans will rise in male and female bodies. The sexual organs of women will be transformed in some mysterious way, however, so they will no longer excite lust or be fitted to childbearing. The differentiation into male and female is appropriate to the resurrection also because it represents the union of Christ and the Church.

Thus the female is allowed into the Christian Heaven only by having the specifically female parts of her body "transformed" from their old "uses" in sex and childbearing to "a new beauty, which, so far from exciting lust, now extinct, shall excite praise to the wisdom and clemency of God."[13] As such, she can then represent that spiritual feminine of the resurrected body. The female, as sublimated cosmos or Church, united to Christ, as divine power, then symbolizes the final consummation of God with creation.

A FEMINIST CRITIQUE OF ESCHATOLOGY

Beginning in the sixteenth-century Renaissance in Europe there has been a progressive criticism of an eschatological orientation that devalues life in this world. Science reclaimed the material world as a realm of immanent reason and divine law. History came to be seen as an arena in which progress is possible, rather than simply a devolution from past ideals ending in catastrophe and final judgment. Modern science and psychology contributed to a sense of the conscious self or soul as the interiority of the body itself rather than its antithesis. In recent years, feminism, the ecological movement, and a revival of the world view of native peoples have all challenged the eschatologies of both an ultimate future at or beyond the end of history and the escape of the soul from the body to Heaven.

Vine Deloria, in his book *God Is Red,* offers a criticism of both of these kinds of eschatologies from the perspective of Native American religion.[14] In Deloria's view the idea of a universal linear project of salvation through history, leading from creation and the saving acts of God in Israel and Christ through the Church to the end of the world, translates into a universal imperialism. Christians alone are the privileged line of history. Other peoples are denied the right to exist. They are either to be absorbed into the Christian world or eliminated from the stage of history.

The Christian view of historical "man" also translates into ecocide, in Deloria's view. The human is set above the non-human in a way that allows the human infinite rights to manipulate, use up, or destroy the nonhuman. For the Christian, God is a power related primarily to humans. Humans alone bear the "image of God." Indians, by contrast, have a sense of the human and the nonhuman as one family of life. God/ess is the great Spirit that animates all things. Each tribe or nation, with its community of human and nonhuman beings, constitutes one family, one living ecosystem. The human is not outside, but within, the great web of life.

This view of the whole cosmos as a community of life conditions the way the Indian views death. For Deloria, the white man's religion (Christianity) promises immortality but creates a fear and obsession with death. The Indian is fearless toward death because the Indian lives on, not as an isolated individual but in the collective soul of the tribe. The ancestors survive not in a distant heaven unrelated to ongoing life but within the earth, in communion with present members of the tribe. This sense of collective immortality in the tribe is rooted in the tribe's covenantal relationship with its natural matrix. The bones of the ancestors are planted in the earth as the seedbed from which the new generation of the tribe arises.

The Indian accepts personal finitude and can receive death as the proper culmination of life. Since Indians do not live individualistically, death is not the end but only a point of transformation to another state of life. Earth and people are one. One generation arises from the womb of the earth as the previous generation returns into the earth. To root up ancestral graves and transport the contents to museums, as white people do to Indian burial places, is nothing less than a destruction of the ongoing being of tribal life itself as living process, under the guise of preserving historical knowledge of Indian life as something past and dead. The white race remains a spiritual stranger to the land it has stolen. White people do not know its sacred places. They have no sense of their own ancestors' bones in the soil as the roots of their own ongoing existence. In 1854 Chief Seattle, on signing the treaty of Medicine Creek, gave a speech in which he summarized this difference between Indian and white views of land and people, life and death:

> To us the ashes of our ancestors are sacred and their resting place hallowed ground. You wander far from the graves of your ancestors and seemingly without regret...
>
> Your dead cease to love you and the land of their nativity as soon as they pass the portals of the tomb and wander way

beyond the stars. They are soon forgotten and never return. Our
dead never forget the beautiful world that gave them being...

Every part of this soil is sacred in the estimation of my people.
Every hillside, every valley, every plain and grove, has been
hallowed by some sad or happy event in days long vanished.
The very dust upon which you now stand responds more lovingly
to their footsteps than to yours, because it is rich with the blood
of our ancestors and our bare feet are conscious of the
sympathetic touch. Even the little children who lived here and
rejoiced here for a brief season will love these somber solitudes
and at eventide they greet shadowy returning spirits. And when
the last Red Man shall have perished and the memory of my
tribe shall have become a myth among the White Man, these
shores will swarm with the invisible dead of my tribe...The
White Man will never be alone.

Let him be just and deal kindly with my people, for the dead
are not powerless. Dead, did I say? There is no death, only a
change of worlds.[15]

In my feminist analysis of eschatology, I wish to expand on
two aspects of Deloria's criticism of Christian patterns of
eschatology: historical eschatology and personal immortality.

Historical Eschatology

Not only Biblical religion, but also modern revolutionary
movements, has been based on a linear view of history as a
single universal project leading to a final salvific end point.
This is thought of as a final era of millennium in which all
the contradictions and evils of history have been overcome and
goodness reigns. In liberal thought, this is imagined to happen
in an evolutionary manner. Through science and education,
social reform gradually will eliminate want, disease, and injustice and bring about the good life. This good life is seen
as endlessly advancing "from glory to glory." Marxist ideologies take more seriously the evil character of present social
arrangements and so assert that a revolutionary overthrow and
reconstruction of social and economic relations is necessary

before this evolution from "the kingdom of necessity to the kingdom of freedom" can take place.

Both of these visions of the final end point of history, as infinitely expanding technological prosperity, are increasingly revealed as antiecological. They disregard finite limits and relationships between humanity and the nonhuman environment. The projection of human hope on one final era or system of redemptive relationships, to be sought (or given by God) through a single linear process, contradicts the possibilities of historical existence. Such a myth of the millennium creates its own denouement. There are two possibilities: Either the end point occurs outside of history altogether and so fails to provide a point of reference for historical hope. Historical becomes eschatological hope, and history itself is reduced to "one damn thing after another" leading nowhere. Or this final era of salvation is identified with a particular social revolution. The revolution thereby becomes absolutized, and its social organizers take on the aura of infallible and divinely privileged bearers of final truth and goodness. All defects of their achievements are projected upon enemies within and without. Critics of the system become subversive evildoers. The system gradually turns repressive and totalitarian. It is unable to imagine or countenance any options outside of or beyond its own system.

Christian critics of Marxist millennialism have generally reaffirmed the idea of eschatology as a transcendent end point beyond history. This end point is not seen as something that can actually be achieved or can ever "happen" on earth. Rather, it is regarded as a useful myth for keeping history itself open. Since whatever we do on earth is always incomplete from the standpoint of this transcendent end point, our achievements remain relative. We are able to relativize them, criticize them, and constantly imagine further alternatives, rather than absolutizing a particular revolutionary construct.

This desire to keep history open and able to constantly transcend itself is an important concern, but it is still based on a model of endlessly stretching forward into the future. God, the ideal humanity and ideal world, exists only in the unrealized future. It has no roots in an ontology of creation and in God/ess as ground of creation. There are no clues to the good in that which is natural. This endless flight into the future idolizes change and fails to respect the relational patterns of our bodies as ground of holy being.

Instead of endless flight into an unrealized future, I suggest a different model of hope and change based on conversion or *metanoia*. Conversion suggests that, while there is no one utopian state of humanity lying back in an original paradise of the "beginning," there are basic ingredients of a just and livable society. These ingredients have roots in nature and involve acceptance of finitude, human scale, and balanced relationships between persons and between human and non-human beings. These ingredients can be expressed in many variants and cultures, adapted to different environments. They include a human scale of habitats and communities, an ability of people to participate in the decisions that govern their lives, work in which everyone can integrate intelligence and creativity with physical participation, a just sharing of profits and benefits of production, an interpenetration of work and celebration, a balance of rural and urban environments. All these ingredients contribute to what we spontaneously recognize to be a livable, as distinct from an unlivable, environment.

Hebrew thought was based on a combination of linear and cyclical patterns. There was a sense of the trajectory of history, but also a point of reference in the past as well as the future for the good world as God intended it. In the Jubilee tradition, this is thought of not as one "great cycle" defining history from beginning to end but as a series of revolutionary transformations that continually return to certain starting points. The Jubilee tradition of Leviticus 25:8–12 teaches that there are certain basic elements that make up life as God intended it. Each family has its own land, its own vine and fig tree. No one is enslaved to another. The land and animals are not overworked.

But human sinfulness creates a drift away from this intended state of peace and justice. Some people's land is expropriated by others. Some people are sold into bondage. Nature is over-worked and polluted. So, on a periodic basis (every fifty years), there must be a revolutionary conversion. Unjust debts that have piled up are liquidated. Those who have been sold into slavery are released. The land that has been expropriated is returned. Land and animals are allowed to rest and recover their strength. Humanity and nature recover their just balance.

This revolutionary transformation cannot be done once and for all. A humane acceptance of our historicity demands that we liberate ourselves from "once-and-for-all" thinking. To be human is to be in a state of process, to change and to die. Both change and death are good. They belong to the natural limits of life. We need to seek the life intended by God/ess for us within these limits. This return to harmony within the covenant of creation is not a cyclical return to what existed in the past, however. Each new achievement of livable, humane balances will be different, based on new technologies and cultures, belonging to a new moment in time and place. It is a historical project that has to be undertaken again and again in changing circumstances.

Each great social movement, such as the labor movement or the women's movement, leaves undone some needed changes and generates other contradictions over time. It is left to the new generation to undertake the project of a just and viable life for its time. But it is the responsibility of the present generation to create and preserve the base of a livable world that makes such a project possible for its descendents. The sins of the parents that set the children's teeth on edge are the inheritance of intractable evils that cannot be undone by the next generation. In Charlotte Perkins Gilman's thought, we must adopt the maternal perspective that lives not just for ourselves but for our children and children's children. We must do this, not just individually or as "nuclear families," but collectively, as a global people.

This concept of social change as conversion to the center,

conversion to the earth and to each other, rather than flight into the unrealizable future, is a model of change more in keeping with the realities of temporal existence. To subject ourselves to the tyranny of impossible expectations of final perfection means to neglect to do what can and must be done for our times. Jesus' own vision of the Kingdom of God as release of captives, remissions of debts, and provision of daily bread may have had more to do with the Jubilee pattern than with the apocalyptic doctrine of the end point of history later incorporated into the Gospels. In the words of an old Shaker hymn:

'Tis a gift to be simple; 'Tis a gift to be free;
'Tis a gift to come down where you ought to be;
And when we find ourselves in the place just right,
'Twill be in the valley of love and delight
When true simplicity is gained, to bow and to bend we shall
    not be ashamed.

To turn, turn will be our delight,
Till by turning, turning, we come round right.

By "turning around" we discover the blessedness and holy being within the mortal limits of covenantal existence. This is the Shalom of God that remains the real connecting point of all our existence, even when we forget and violate it. Redemptive hope is the constant recovery of that Shalom of God/ess that holds us all together, as the operative principle of our collective lives. It is the nexus of authentic creational life that has to be reincarnated in social relationships again and again in new ways and new contexts by each generation.

Personal Eschatology

It is this shaping of the beloved community on earth, for our time and generation to bequeath to our children, that is our primary responsibility as human beings. But what of the sad insufficiencies of human finitude and the consequences of social evils that take the lives of little children and cut off adults in the prime of life before they can make their contribution? What of the vast toiling masses of human beings who have had so little chance to fulfill themselves? What of the whole tragic drama of human history, where so few have been able to snatch moments of happiness and fulfillment in the midst of toil and misery? What even of those worthies who have made good contributions and lived a full life? Do their achievements live on only in our fading memories, or is there some larger realm where the meaning of their lives is preserved?

The appropriate response to these questions is an agnosticism. We should not pretend to know what we do not know or to have had "revealed" to us what is the projection of our wishes. Moreover, whatever we wish is not thereby proved to be probably true or something upon which we should "wager" our lives. There needs to be a compatibility between our wishes and what we know of our finite nature and primary responsibilities. What we know is that death is the cessation of the life process that holds our organism together. Consciousness ceases and the organism itself gradually disintegrates. This consciousness is the interiority of that life process that holds the organism together. There is no reason to think of the two as separable, in the sense that one can exist without the other.

What then has happened to "me"? In effect, our existence ceases as individuated ego/organism and dissolves back into the cosmic matrix of matter/energy, from which new centers of the individuation arise. It is this matrix, rather than our individuated centers of being, that is "everlasting," that subsists underneath the coming to be and passing away of individuated beings and even planetary worlds. Acceptance of death, then, is acceptance of the finitude of our individuated centers of being, but also our identification with the larger matrix as our total self that contains us all. In this sense, the problem of personal immortality is created by an effort to absolutize personal or individual ego as itself everlasting, over against the total community of being. To the extent to which we have transcended egoism for relation to community, we can also accept death as the final relinquishment of individuated ego into the great matrix of being.

All the component parts of matter/energy that coalesced to make up our individuated self are not lost. Rather, they change their form and become food for new beings to arise from our bones. To bury ourselves in steel coffins, so that we cannot disintegrate into the earth, is to refuse to accept this process of entering back into the matrix of renewed life. Such a manner of burial represents a fundamental refusal to accept earth as our home and the plants and animals of earth as our kindred. In this way we also fail to recognize the redemptive nature of our own disintegration-reintegration back into the soil.

But what of the meaning of our lives; what of the good to be remembered and the evil redressed? Is this merely the disintegration of centers of personality into an "impersonal" matrix of the all? If the interiority of our organism is a personal center, how much more so is the great organism of the universe itself? That great matrix that supports the energy-matter of our individuated beings is itself the ground of all personhood as well. That great collective personhood is the Holy Being in which our achievements and failures are gathered up, assimilated into the fabric of being, and carried forward into new possibilities.

We do not know what this means. It is beyond our power and our imagination. It is not then our direct responsibility. We can do nothing about the "immortal" dimension of our lives. It is not our calling to be concerned about the eternal meaning of our lives, and religion should not make this the focus of its message. Our responsibility is to use our temporal life span to create a just and good community for our generation and for our children. It is in the hands of Holy Wisdom to forge out of our finite struggle truth and being for everlasting life. Our agnosticism about what this means is then the expression of our faith, our trust that Holy Wisdom will give transcendent meaning to our work, which is bounded by space and time.

Postscript
Woman/Body/Nature:
The Icon of the Divine

In these chapters we have explored the links between woman/body/nature; the links forged between woman as dominated body and woman as exploited labor; woman as icon of body and nature. We have seen something of the history of use and misuse of woman as body, as mediator of embodied nature; the denouement to which this use of woman and nature has led us; the human crisis we all now face within ourselves, with each other, with our environment. We have also explored the possibilities, the intimations of new relationships that might have existed, might still exist, if we come to know ourselves more truthfully and to deal with each other more justly.

Layer by layer we must strip off the false consciousness that alienates us from our bodies, from our roots in the earth, sky, and water. Layer by layer we expose the twisted consciousness that has distorted our relationships and turned them to their opposite. But in so doing we discover that the Big Lie has limited power. Earth is not mocked. She brings her judgment, and this judgment can no longer be confined to the ghettos and the reservations of the poor.

The stench of it, the floating poison, the underground rumblings begin to reach out to the suburbs of affluence, signaling the beginning of the end of a way of life, a question mark over a social system. But also the possibility of asking the question, the question of new relations: simpler, more harmonious, more just, more beautiful patterns of life. Woman/body/nature, no longer as the icon of carnality, sin, and death, but as the icon of the divine, the divine *Shekinah,* the Wisdom of God manifest, alive in our midst as the true center that holds us all together.

THE FIRST LEVEL: CONTROL OVER THE WOMB

The first subjugation of woman is the subjugation of her womb, the subjugation of access to her body, so that she should not choose her own beloved or explore the pleasures of her own body but that her body and its fruits should belong first to her father, who would sell or trade her to her husband. She must be delivered as undamaged goods, duly inspected, any signs of previous use punished by death. Only the male to whom she has been legally handed over may put his seed in her body, so that he can be sure that the children that emerge from her body belong to him, pass on his name, inherit his property. Boy children are preferred. Too many girl children bring shame, perhaps expulsion, for the errant mother.

Philosophers minimize her contribution to the acts of conception and birth. Aristotle proclaims through two thousand years of teachers that woman is a misbegotten male, that the male seed alone provides the form of the child, the woman is only the passive receptacle for man's active power.

Moses teaches that the male is the original human model. The woman was created second, out of man's rib, to be his helpmate. Man gives birth to woman, she is his offspring and creature, formed from his side to serve him in lowliness. In these ways the power of her motherhood is stolen from her, and she is reduced to an instrument of his virility.

The Christian Church teaches that birth is shameful, that from the sexual libido the corruption of the human race is passed on from generation to generation. Only through the second birth of baptism, administered by the male clergy, is the filth of mother's birth remedied and the offspring of the woman's womb made fit to be a child of God. Woman is taught that the worst of sins, the worst of crimes, is to deflect the male seed from its intended course in her womb. This is more sinful than rape, for the rape of a woman does not interfere with the purposes of the seed, while contraception wastes the precious seed and defeats its high purposes. Anatomy is destiny, the psychologists teach. Woman must subject herself to necessity, for this is the divine will. She must obediently accept the effects of these holy male acts upon her body, must not seek to control their effects, must not become a conscious decision maker about the destiny of her own body.

THE SECOND LEVEL: EXPLOITED LABOR

The control of woman's womb means the subjugation of her person. From person she becomes property to be bought and sold, passed from father to husband for the price of two good plow oxen. To violate her is to offend the property rights of her husband. If she does not resist to the death, she can be divorced, perhaps even killed by her outraged male relatives. Girl children are expendable; perhaps they are exposed on hillsides at birth or sold into slavery.

Her labor belongs to him. To labor from before dawn to after dusk in his household is her purpose for existence. She has no need to read and write, no need to learn, to travel, to dream. Her sphere is defined, confined; she must not stray from it. Each generation of daughters must have its wings clipped early to be fed back into the treadmill. For him she sets her maidservants spinning and weaving before dawn. She considers a field and buys it, plants it with her own hands, harvests it, sells its produce. Her lamp does not go out at night. Her labor frees him for the momentous tasks of war and politics. He is known at the gates. She is not to be known in public. She is to remain invisible. When he returns in the evening, his food shall be ready, his clothes in order, his couch prepared. In this way her history is stolen from her. It is said that she did nothing. It is his achievements that we read about in books; his laws, his wars, his power, his mayhem. He is the achiever, carried about on the backs of the laborers. The laborers who carry him have done nothing; they are invisible, silent. No scrolls testify to their experience. No monuments mark the places of their sufferings and deaths. Their laboring hands and backs hold him up to the light of history, and they sink down into the dark earth again.

Woman, the nonachiever, becomes woman the nonworker, the ornament of conspicuous consumption, the object of pride of ownership and economic prowess. Her furs testify to her husband's success. She adorns his household, displaying dainty feet that cannot walk, polished nails that cannot work. The pinnacle of his success is to no longer need her work, to possess her only as a toy and a plaything. Black women, brown women, immigrant women toil silently in the background, supporting the display, polishing the cage of the songbird. The wife herself must conceal the signs of her own toil, ease the lines of suffering from her face, the marks of labor from her hands, keep up appearances. Women are set at enmity with each other while collaborating in his service.

Early in the morning the army of chars, waitresses, secretaries, nurses, librarians, and teachers march from their houses. The morning chores are rushed, the children pressed through breakfast and off to school so that women can get to work at the same time as men whose women do these chores for them. On the job the women service male work: clean the offices, prepare the food, type the letters, answer the phones, research the studies. Upon this pyramid of female labor the executive arises, seemingly imbued with superhuman wisdom and magnified power drawn from the combined force of a vast, invisible reservoir; he stands upon it commanding, pronouncing, deciding...

At five o'clock the army of women scatter to markets, nurseries, and kitchens to prepare the home, so that, when the men return, the children are already fetched, the food bought and cooked, the house cleaned. The men linger to consolidate the networks that advance them on the ladder. Women, it is said, just can't compete; they lack what it takes, the drive, the ambition...

THE THIRD LEVEL:
THE RAPE OF THE EARTH AND ITS PEOPLES

The labor of dominated bodies, dominated peoples — women, peasants, workers — mediate for those who rule the fruits of the earth. The toil of laboring bodies provides the tools through which the earth is despoiled and left desolate. Through the raped bodies the earth is raped. Those who enjoy the goods distance themselves from the destruction.

The gold wrested from the mines of Mexico and Peru is carried across the oceans in Spanish galleons, stolen by fast ships of Dutch and English merchants, and ends up in banks in Amsterdam and London. The Indians who mined it die of starvation. The pineapple and banana plantations ship their succulent fruits to adorn the tables of Yankees whose own soil is stony, whose climate is cold and damp. But those who are blessed with warm suns and rich soil cannot afford to taste their own fruits. The strip mines of Appalachia do not despoil the golf courses and parks of the mine owners. No, they despoil the rocky hillsides of the dirt farmers. The detergents flow through the streams where Indians live. The fish upon whom the Indian depends for food floats belly up in the soapy water.

It is said that these people are lazy, backward, that they are poor because they have few resources and no energy...that we have gained a head start because of our hard work. If we help them, maybe they can catch up. So we ship down armies of technologists and allow the poor to mortgage their future on loans for development.

The development displaces the poor from the countryside and gives the land to the plantation owners. The industries of the nation are bought by the multinationals. The peasants who come to the city for work shine shoes and sell chewing gum. They multiply like festering sores around the glittering steel and glass monuments to development. The mood grows ugly. We send their governments population-control experts and counter-insurgency police. We finance the hardware of repression, and we call it the Alliance for Progress. Armies of teenage girls in border towns assemble electronic systems by day for a few dollars, return home at night to cook beans in shanty kitchens. The electronic assemblies are shipped back across the border to add to the fame and fortune of Yankee ingenuity.

On the backs, through the hands of vast toiling masses in Asia, Africa, Latin America, the affluent colonizers arise, congratulate themselves on their progress, and wonder at the poverty and ingratitude of those whose bananas, gold, oil they have consumed. A bomb crashes through the plate-glass window, blowing a hole in the dream of progress.

THE FOURTH LEVEL: THE BIG LIE

Those who rule pay their professors to proliferate lies, to generate a mental universe that turns everything upside down. The Big Lie makes those who toil appear to be idle, while those who speak into dictaphones appear to be the hard workers. It makes women appear the offspring of males, and males the primary creators of babies. It makes matter the final devolution of the mind, and mind the original source of all being. It regards the body as an alien tomb of the soul, and the soul as growing stronger the more it weakens the body. It abstracts the human from the earth and God from the cosmos, and says that that which is abstracted is the original, and the first, and can exist alone and independent.

The Big Lie tells us that we are strangers and sojourners on this planet, that our flesh, our blood, our instincts for survival are our enemies. Originally we lived as disincarnate orbs of light in the heavenly heights. We have fallen to this earth and into this clay through accident or sin. We must spend our lives suppressing our hungers and thirsts and shunning our fellow beings, so that we can dematerialize and fly away again to our stars.

It is said that mothers particularly are the enemy, responsible for our mortal flesh. To become eternal and everlasting we must flee the body, the woman, and the world. She is the icon of the corruptible nature, seduced by the serpent in the beginning. Through her, death entered the world. Even now she collaborates with devils to hold men in fast fetters to the ground. A million women twisted on the rack, smoldered in burning fagots to pay homage to this Lie.

It is said that enlightened man must drive the devils and witches from the world, restore order, put himself in charge, reduce nature to his control. With numbers and formulas he can search out her innermost secrets, learn all the laws of her ways, become her lord and master. The cosmos is reduced to elements, molecules, atoms, positive and negative charges, infinitely manipulatable, having no nature of her own, given to him to do with what he will. He will mount upon her with wings, fly away to the moon, blow her up in the flash of atomic energy, live forever in a space capsule, entombed in plastic, dining on chemicals.

THE COLLAPSE OF THE HOUSE OF CARDS: THE DISCLOSURE OF DIVINE WISDOM

The facade starts to crumble. We discover buried histories. "We Shall Overcome." "Sisterhood Is Powerful." "Viva la Huelga." "Bury My Heart at Wounded Knee." We begin to understand the hidden costs. "Hello, carbon dioxide; the air, the air is everywhere." Carcinogens in our health food, strontium 90 in mother's milk. Atomic fallout in our swimming pool. Threats to generations yet unborn. We are held hostage by the colonized, blackmailed by the poor rich in raw materials. The Petroleum Age starts to run out of gas.

Through the fissures of the system we glimpse the forgotten world of our homeland. We learn to walk again; to watch sunsets; to examine leaves; to plant seeds in soil. Turn off the TV; talk to each other to ease the frenetic pace; get in touch with our circulatory system, with the rhythms of our menstrual cycle that link us to the pull of the moon and tides of the sea.

The scales begin to fall from our eyes, and all around us we see miracles. Babies grow in wombs without help from computers. The sun rises every day. Con Ed sends no bill for sunshine. The harmony is still there, persisting, supporting, forgiving, preserving us in spite of ourselves. Divine Grace keeps faith with us when we have broken faith with her. Through the years of alien madness, she did not abandon us; she kept the planets turning, the seasons recurring, even struggled to put the upside down right side up, to cleanse the channels of the garbage, to blow the smog out to sea.

To return Home: to learn the harmony, the peace, the justice of body, bodies in right relation to each other. The whence we have come and whither we go, not from alien skies but here, in the community of earth. Holy One, Thy Kingdom come, Thy will done on earth. All shall sit under their own vines and fig trees and none shall be afraid. The lion will lay down with the lamb and the little child will lead them. A new thing is revealed; the woman will encompass the warrior. Thou shalt not hurt, thou shalt not kill in all my holy mountain.

The Shalom of the Holy; the disclosure of the gracious *Shekinah;* Divine Wisdom; the empowering Matrix; She, in whom we live and move and have our being — She comes; She is here.

Notes

1: Feminist Theology: Methodology, Sources, and Norms
(pages 1-46)

1. See Judith Plaskow, *Sex, Sin and Grace: Women's Experience and the Theologies of Reinhold Niebuhr and Paul Tillich* (Washington, D.C.: University Press of America, 1980), pp. 29-50.

2. Sallie McFague, *Metaphorical Theology: Models of God in Religious Language* (Philadelphia: Fortress, 1982), chap. 5.

3. Robert L. Wilken, *The Myth of Christian Beginnings: History's Impact on Belief* (Garden City, N.Y.: Doubleday, 1971).

4. For the classic texts of Marxist critique of religion, see *Marx and Engels on Religion,* introd. Reinhold Niebuhr (New York: Schocken, 1964).

5. See Rosemary Ruether, *Disputed Questions: On Being a Christian* (Nashville: Abingdon Press, 1981), pp. 43-74.

6. Zechariah 14:16-19.

7. Elisabeth Schüssler Fiorenza, "Word, Spirit and Power: Women in Early Christian Communities," in *Women of Spirit: Female Leadership in the Jewish and Christian Traditions,* ed. R. Ruether and E. McLaughlin (New York: Simon and Schuster, 1979), p. 31. See also Fiorenza's *In Memory of Her: A Feminist Theological Reconstruction of Christian Origins* (New York: Crossroads, 1983).

8. Fiorenza, "Women, Spirit and Power," pp. 39-44.

9. Elaine Pagels, *The Gnostic Gospels* (New York: Random House, 1979), pp. 48-70.

10. The Gospel of Mary, in *The Nag Hammadi Library in English,* ed. James M. Robinson (New York: Harper & Row, 1977), pp. 471-474.

11. Fiorenza, "Women, Spirit and Power," pp. 44–51.

12. Stevan Davies, *The Revolt of the Widows: The Social World of the Apocryphal Acts* (Carbondale: Southern Illinois University Press, 1980).

13. E. Thomas, "Women and the Civil War Sects," *Past and Present,* 13 (1958): 42–62. Also see Joyce Irwin, *Womanhood in Radical Protestantism, 1525–1675* (New York: Mellen Press, 1979), pp. 200–237.

14. Margaret Fell, *Women's Speaking Justified, Proved and Allowed of by the Scriptures* (London: n.p. 1667), pp. 200–202, 283–290.

15. Isabel Ross, *Margaret Fell: Mother of Quakerism* (London: Longman and Green, 1949), pp. 283–302.

16. R. Ruether and R. Keller, "Women in Utopian Movements," in *Women and Religion in America: The Nineteenth Century: A Documentary History* (San Francisco: Harper & Row, 1981), pp. 46–100.

17. The major spokespersons for Goddess spirituality and some of their works are as follows: Carol Christ, "Why Women Need the Goddess: Phenomenological, Psychological and Political Reflections," in *Womanspirit Rising: A Feminist Reader in Religion,* ed. Carol Christ and Judith Plaskow (San Francisco: Harper & Row, 1979), pp. 273–287; Naomi Goldenberg, *Changing of the Gods* (Boston: Beacon Press, 1979); Starhawk, *The Spiral Dance: The Rebirth of the Ancient Religion of the Goddess* (New York: Harper & Row, 1979); Z. Budapest, *The Holy Book of Women's Mysteries,* parts 1 and 2 (Los Angeles: Susan B. Anthony Coven, No. 1, 1979, 1980). The positions of Christ, Goldenberg, Starhawk, and Budapest are not exactly alike. There are important nuances of difference between them in style and viewpoint, but they generally concur in regarding Goddess religion as rooted in an ancient (neolithic) religion that was positive for women and in regarding the Biblical tradition as irredeemably sexist.

18. Important sources for romantic, countercultural feminism are Robert Graves, *The White Goddess: A Historical Grammar of Poetic Myth* (New York: Octagon, 1972); J. J. Bachofen, *Myth,*

Religion and Mother Right (1861; Princeton: Princeton University Press, 1967); and Margaret Murray, *God of the Witches,* 2nd ed. (London: Oxford University Press, 1952), and *The Witch Cult in Western Europe* (London: Oxford University Press, 1921).

19. Mary Wakeman, "Response to Judith Ochshorn" (unpublished paper, Religious Studies Department, University of North Carolina, Greensboro, AAR, 1981), p. 6.

20. For information about the appropriation of romanticism by fascism, see particularly George Mosse, *The Crisis of the German Ideology: The Intellectual Origins of the Third Reich* (New York: Grosset and Dunlap, 1964).

2: **Sexism and God-Language: Male and Female Images of the Divine** *(pages 47-71)*

1. E. O. James, *The Cult of the Mother Goddess: An Anthropological and Documentary Study* (New York: Barnes and Noble, 1959), p. 24.

2. Ibid., pp. 23-46.

3. Mary Wakeman, "Ancient Sumer and the Woman's Movement" (unpublished paper, Religious Studies Department, University of North Carolina, Greensboro), pp. 9, 24.

4. Isaac Mendelsohn, ed., *Religions of the Ancient Near East: Sumero-Akkadian Religious Texts and Ugaritic Epics* (New York: Liberal Arts Press, 1955), p. 34, ll. 93-104; p. 35, ll. 135-141.

5. Charlene Spretnak's *Lost Goddesses of Early Greece* (Boston: Beacon Press, 1978) is an example of Jungian-feminist assumptions that the Goddess represented a matriarchal world rooted in nature fertility. W. A. Visser t'Hooft's *The Fatherhood of God in an Age of Emancipation* (Geneva: World Council of Churches, 1982), pp. 130-132, makes the same assumption as a way of rejecting any symbol of God as female.

6. See particularly Judith Ochshorn, *The Female Experience and the Nature of the Divine* (Bloomington: Indiana University Press, 1980).

7. M. Kay Martin and Barbara Voorheis, *The Female of the Species* (New York: Columbia University Press, 1975).

8. E. O. James, *The Worship of the Sky God: A Comparative Study of Semitic and Indo-European Religion* (London: Athlone Press, 1963).

9. Phyllis Bird, "Women in the Old Testament," in *Religion and Sexism: Images of Women in the Jewish and Christian Traditions,* ed. R. Ruether (New York: Simon and Schuster, 1974), pp. 48–57.

10. Raphael Patai, *The Hebrew Goddess* (Philadelphia: Ktav, 1967), pp. 36–45, 49–50 (236 out of 370 years).

11. Ibid., pp. 99–100.

12. Phyllis Trible, *God and the Rhetoric of Sexuality* (Philadelphia: Fortress Press, 1978), p. 48.

13. Patai, *The Hebrew Goddess,* pp. 137–156.

14. Leonard Swidler, *Biblical Affirmations of Women* (Philadelphia: Westminster Press, 1979), pp. 57–73. Edgar Hennecke and Wilhelm Schmeemelcher, eds., *New Testament Apocrypha,* The Gospel of Hebrews, vol. 1 (Philadelphia: Westminster Press, 1963), p. 164.

15. Ibid., Acts of Thomas, vol. 2, p. 471.

16. The Gospel of Philip, in *The Nag Hammadi Library,* p. 134.

17. Swidler, *Biblical Affirmations,* p. 60.

18. The Trimorphic Protenoia, in *The Nag Hammadi Library,* pp. 461–471.

19. Fourteenth-century fresco in Catholic Church in the Village of Urshalling, near Prien am Chiemsee, reproduced on jacket of Swidler, *Biblical Affirmations.*

20. Jacob Boehme, *Mysterium Magnum: An Exposition of the First Book of Moses Called Genesis,* vol. 1, trans. John R. Sparrow (London: John M. Watkins, 1924), pp. 121–133. See R. Ruether and R. Keller, *Women and Religion in America: The Nineteenth Century: A Documentary History* (San Francisco: Harper & Row, 1981), pp. 46–48, 60–65.

21. Norman K. Gottwald, *The Tribes of Yahweh: A Sociology of the Religion of Liberated Israel, 1250–1050 B.C.* (Maryknoll, N.Y.: Orbis Press, 1979), pp. 210–219, 489–587, 692–709.

22. See, for example, Matt. 15:21–28; Mark 5:25–33; Luke 7:11–17, 7:36–50, 10:38–42, 13:10–17.

23. Robert Hamerton-Kelly, *God the Father: Theology and Patriarchy in the Teachings of Jesus* (Philadelphia: Fortress, 1979), pp. 21–28.

24. Ibid., pp. 70–81.

25. The revolt of women against the patriarchal authority of fathers, husbands, or fiancés, as well as political authority, is found continuously in Christian popular literature of the second and third centuries, particularly in martyrologies and apocryphal Acts. See Stevan Davies, *The Revolt of the Widows: The Social World of the Apocryphal Acts* (Carbondale: Southern Illinois University Press, 1980), pp. 50–69. This theme is continued in medieval lives of female saints. See Eleanor McLaughlin, "Women, Power and the Pursuit of Holiness in Medieval Christianity," in *Women of Spirit: Female Leadership in the Jewish and Christian Traditions,* ed. R. Ruether and E. McLaughlin (New York: Simon and Schuster, 1979), pp. 108–111. The theme is also typical in conversion stories of nineteenth-century Evangelical women. A dramatic example is found in the diary of the black Shaker Rebecca Jackson. See Jean McMahon Humez, *Gifts of Power: The Writings of Rebecca Jackson* (Amherst: University of Massachusetts Press, 1981), pp. 18–23 and passim.

3: Woman, Body, and Nature: Sexism and the Theology of Creation *(pages 72–92)*

1. Sherry B. Ortner, "Is Female to Male as Nature Is to Culture?" in *Woman, Culture and Society,* ed. M. Z. Rosaldo and L. Lamphere (Stanford: Stanford University Press, 1974), pp. 67–87.

2. Yolanda Murphy and Robert F. Murphy, *Woman of the Forest* (New York: Columbia University Press, 1974), pp. 78–110.

3. Ibid., pp. 92–95, 107.

4. Plato *Timaeus* 28–50.

5. Ibid., 42; also Plato *Phaedrus* 246–249.

6. Aristotle, *Politics* bk. 1, ch. 5.

7. Plato, *Timaeus* 42; see also 91.

8. The Hypostasis of the Archons, *The Nag Hammadi Library in English,* ed. James M. Robinson (New York: Harper & Row, 1977), pp. 152–160. See also Hans Jonas, *The Gnostic Religion: The Message of the Alien God and the Beginnings of Christianity* (Boston: Beacon Press, 1958), pp. 174–194.

9. Katherine Rogers, *The Troublesome Helpmate: A History of Misogyny in Literature* (Seattle: University of Washington Press, 1966), p. 70.

10. Eleanor McLaughlin, "Women, Power and the Pursuit of Holiness in Medieval Christianity," in *Women of Spirit: Female Leadership in the Jewish and Christian Traditions,* ed. R. Ruether and E. McLaughlin (New York: Simon and Schuster, 1979), p. 254.

11. Carolyn Merchant, *The Death of Nature: Women, Ecology and the Scientific Revolution* (San Francisco: Harper & Row, 1980).

12. Pierre Teilhard de Chardin, *The Phenomenon of Man* (New York: Harper, 1959), pp. 53–74.

13. Ibid., pp. 209–210.

14. Sally P. Springer and Georg Deutsch, *Left Brain, Right Brain* (San Francisco, Freeman, 1981), pp. 121–130.

4: Anthropology: Humanity as Male and Female
(pages 93–115)

1. See Phyllis Bird's careful exegesis of Genesis 1:27b: "Male and Female, He Created Them: Gen 1:27b in the Context of the Priestly Account of Creation," *Harvard Theological Review* 74, no. 2 (1981):129–159. Bird makes clear that the original account does not refer to the bisexuality of God, nor does it assign either subordinate or complementary roles to women *vis à vis* men. Adam as a species, and thus all members of Adam, male and

female, possess the image of God. This possession of the image is understood by the priestly writer primarily in terms of dominion over the earth, "like God." Maleness and femaleness constitute a second, separate clause that is not intended to modify the image of God or project back on the relation of deity or the relation of the sexes to each other. It simply defines Adam as bisexual as a creature, like other creatures, and thus as having been given the blessing of fertility and the mandate to propagate and "fill the earth."

2. Thomas Aquinas, *Summa Theological* pt. 1, q. 92, art. 1. See also Kari Bǿrresen, *Subordination and Equivalence: The Nature and Role of Women in Augustine and Thomas Aquinas* (Washington, D.C.: University Press of America, 1981) (original in French, 1968).

3. Martin Luther, *Lectures on Genesis,* Gen. 2:18, in *Luther's Works,* vol. 1, ed. Jaroslav Pelikan (St. Louis: Concordia Publishing House, 1958), p. 115.

4. Ibid., Gen. 3:16, pp. 202–203.

5. Karl Barth, *Church Dogmatics,* vol. 3, sec. 4 (Edinburgh: Clark, 1975), pp. 158–172.

6. Margaret Fell (Fox), *Women's Speaking Justified* (London: n.p., 1667).

7. "Condorcet's Pleas for the Citizenship of Women," *Journal de la Société de 1789,* 3 July 1790. English trans.: *The Fortnightly Review* 13:42 (June 1870), pp. 719–720.

8. See Sally M. Gearhart, *Wanderground: Stories of the Hill Women* (Watertown, Mass.: Persephone, 1979), or the feminist utopia of an earlier generation, Charlotte Perkins Gilman *Herland* (New York: Pantheon, 1979).

9. This way of defining androgyny is typical of Jungianism; it makes Jungianism seductive for women who fail to perceive its fundamentally androcentric and antifeminist bias. See C. G. Jung, *Aion: Research into the Phenomenology of the Self,* in *Collected Works,* vol. 9, pt. 2 (New York: Pantheon, 1959).

10. The experimental evidence for more lateralized brain development in males and more integrated brain development in

females is controversial. See the article by Jeannette McGlone and the accompanying discussion in *The Behavioral and Brain Sciences* 3 (1980), pp. 215–263. It is important to note that the evidence for gender difference in brain lateralization cannot be construed as invariable. At most, one can say there is evidence of a statistical tendency for women to integrate the functions of the brain across left and right hemispheres and males to separate brain functions between the hemispheres and to create left-brain dominance. But there is greater difference between females and between males on brain lateralization than between males and females. Moreover, there has been insufficient cross-cultural research to determine whether this tendency is more pronounced among white Western Europeans, while cultures that encourage males to develop intuitive and artistic capacities might differ. At most, we can say that the human brain has a capacity to develop either in more balanced and integrated modes of functioning between the two hemispheres or more lateralized modes and that, among white Westerners, there is some evidence that females tend more toward the first type of brain development and males more toward the second.

11. See Lynda M. Glennon, *Women and Dualism: A Sociology of Knowledge Analysis* (New York: Longman and Green, 1979), pp. 97–115.

12. Sallie McFague, *Metaphorical Theology: Models of God in Religious Language* (Philadelphia: Fortress, 1982). See chapter 4 on models in theology.

5:   Christology: Can a Male Savior Save Women? *(pages 116–138)*

1. Sigmund Mowinchel, *He That Cometh* (New York: Blackwell and Abingdon, 1955), pp. 96–154.

2. Albert Nolan, *Jesus Before Christianity: The Gospel of Liberation* (Capetown: David Philip, 1976).

3. Joachim Jeremias, *The Parables of Jesus* (New York: Scribner's, 1955), pp. 70–74. See also Constance Parvey, "Women in the New Testament," in *Religion and Sexism: Images of Women in the Jewish and Christian Traditions,* ed. R. Ruether (New York: Simon and Schuster, 1974), pp. 138–142.

4. Walter Bauer, *Orthodoxy and Heresy in Earliest Christianity* (Philadelphia: Fortress, 1971), particularly develops the evidence for Gnostic and prophetic forms of Christianity preceding orthodoxy (characterized by episcopal succession) in major centers of Eastern Christianity.

5. Hans Conzelmann, *The Theology of Luke,* trans. Geoffrëy Buswell (London: Faber and Faber, 1960), shows the roots in Lucan theology of the idea of Christ as the midpoint of history. The original title of Conzelmann's book was *Die Mitte der Zeit.*

6. Eusebius of Caesarea, *Ecclesiastical History* X. 1. 4.

7. Eusebius of Caesarea, *Oration on Constantine* 10. 7.

8. Thomas Aquinas, *Summa Theologica,* pt. 1, q. 92, art. 1, 2; q. 99, art. 2; pt. 3, supp. q. 39.1.

9. John Saward, *Christ and His Bride* (London: Church Literature Association, 1977), presents the conservative Anglican position. The Roman Catholic version of this argument is found in the "Declaration on the Question of Admission of Women to the Ministerial Priesthood," Vatican City, 15 October 1976.

10. "Declaration on the Question," sec. 27.

11. Julian of Norwich, *The Revelation of Divine Love,* trans. James Walsh (New York: Harper, 1961).

12. Horace Bushnell, *Women's Suffrage: The Reform Against Nature* (New York: Scribner's, 1869).

13. Herbert Musurillo, *The Acts of the Christian Martyrs* (Oxford: Clarendon, 1972), p. 75.

14. Epiphanius, *Panarion,* in *A New Eusebius,* ed. James Stevenson (New York, Macmillan, 1957), p. 113.

15. Marjorie Reeves, *The Influence of Prophecy in the Later Middle Ages: A Study in Joachimism* (Oxford: Clarendon Press, 1969).

16. Marjorie Reeves, *Joachim of Fiore and the Prophetic Future* (New York: Harper & Row, 1976), pp. 50-51.

17. *Testimony of Christ's Second Appearing* (n.p.: United Society [Shakers], 1856), pp. 506, 514-518.

18. See Richard Pankhurst, *The Saint Simonians, Mill and Carlyle* (Atlantic Highlands, N.J.: Humanities Press, 1957), chap. 8.

19. Mary Baker Eddy, *Science and Health, with Key to the Scriptures,* 68th ed. (Boston: E. J. Foster Eddy, 1894), p. 510.

20. See the sermons by Frances Willard, to the Women's Christian Temperance Union, and by Anna Howard Shaw, preached at the International Council of Women (1888), in *Women and Religion in America: The Nineteenth Century,* ed. R. Ruether and R. Keller (San Francisco: Harper & Row, 1981), pp. 325–332.

21. Elizabeth Gould Davis, *The First Sex* (Baltimore: Penguin, 1972), pp. 337–339.

6:   Mariology as Symbolic Ecclesiology: Repression or Liberation?
(pages 139–158)

1. *Song of Songs,* in *Anchor Bible,* introd. and comm. Marvin H. Pope (New York: Doubleday, 1977), p. 25.

2. Phyllis Trible, *God and the Rhetoric of Sexuality* (Philadelphia: Fortress, 1978), pp. 45ff.

3. H. H. Rowley, "The Interpretation of the Song of Songs," *Journal of Theological Studies* 38 (1937): 337–363.

4. Tosefta *Sanhedrin* 12. 10.

5. Mark 4:20; Cyprian *De Habitu. Virg.* 21; Anthanasius *Ep.* 48. 2; Tertullian *De Exhort. Cast.* 1; *Adv. Marcion* 5. 15; Jerome *Eps.* 22. 15; 48. 3; 66. 2; 120. 1. 9; *Adv. Jov.* 1. 3; Augustine *De Sancta Virg.* 45; Ambrose *De Virg.* 1. 60.

6. Jerome, *Ep.* 107. 13, to Laeta.

7. John Rist, *Eros and Psyche: Studies in Plato, Plotinus and Origen* (Toronto: University of Toronto Press, 1964).

8. Richard A. Baer, *Philo's Use of the Categories Male and Female* (Leiden: Brill, 1970), pp. 42–44, 55–61, n. 2.

9. Origen, *Commentary on the Song of Songs,* trans. R. P. Lawson (Westminster, Md.: Newman Press, 1957), p. 22 (*Ancient Christian Writers,* no. 26).

10. Bernard of Clairvaux, *Sermons on the Canticle of Canticles,* I, 3.

11. (Boston: Kneeland, 1719). See Margaret W. Masson, "The Typology of the Female as a Model for the Regenerate: Puritan Preaching, 1690–1730," *Signs* 2:2 (Winter 1976): 304–315.

12. Ibid., 309–310.

13. Ibid., 310.

14. Carol Karlsen, *The Devil in the Shape of a Woman* (Ph.D. diss., Yale University, 1980), p. 191.

15. Luke chapters 1–2; Justin Martyr *Dial. Trypho* 100. 3; Irenaeus *Adv. Haer.* 5. 19. 1.

16. Mark 6:6; Matt. 13:44; Luke 4:22; Mark 3:31–35; Matt. 12:46–50; John 7:33. See R. Ruether, "The Collision of History and Doctrine: The Brothers of Jesus and the Virginity of Mary," *Continuum* (Spring 1969), pp. 93–105.

17. The idea of the perpetual virginity of Mary first appears in the *Proevangelium of James,* whose tradition goes back to c. 200 A.D. It is Jerome who argues this doctrine for Western orthodoxy in the fourth century: *Against Hevidius on the Perpetual Virginity of Mary Library of Nicene and Post-Nicene Fathers,* 2nd ser., vol. 6 (New York: Christian Literature Co., 1893), pp. 334–345.

18. Giovanni Miegge, *The Virgin Mary* (London: Butterworth, 1955), pp. 83–132.

19. Otto Semmelroth, *Mary, the Archetype of the Church* (New York: Sheed and Ward, 1963), pp. 166–168.

20. Compare Luke 1:26–37 with Matthew 1:18–24. See R. Ruether, *Mary, the Feminine Face of the Church* (Philadelphia: Westminster, 1977), p. 32.

21. See also Matt. 12:46–50; Luke 8:19–21.

7: The Consciousness of Evil: The Journeys of Conversion *(pages 159–192)*

1. The tribal name as generic name for human is found in many tribal languages, such as the African and Amerindian languages.

2. The male generic is found in languages all over the world that have an unmarked or generic pronoun. See Ann Bodine, "Androcentrism in Prescriptive Grammar: Singular 'They,' Sex-Indefinite 'He,' and 'He or She,' " *Language and Society* 4:2 (August 1975): 129–146.

3. P. Masani, "Humanization as De-Alienation," *Alternatives* 7 (1981): 265–290.

4. Hesiod, *Work and Days* ll. 47–105.

5. *Testimony of Reuben,* chap. 5–6. See Bernard P. Prusak, "Woman, Seductive Siren and Source of Sin?" in *Religion and Sexism: Images of Women in the Jewish and Christian Traditions,* ed. R. Ruether (New York: Simon and Schuster, 1974), pp. 89–107.

6. 1 Timothy 2:14. Christian theology interpreted this passage as largely exonerating Adam from base motives in accepting the apple from Eve. Unlike Eve, who acted from ignorance, vanity, and greed, Adam merely "went along" out of affection for Eve and unwillingness to be parted from her and again be alone. For this interpretation, see Milton, *Paradise Lost,* bk. 9, ll. 901–960.

7. Isa. 34:14: Rashi to B. Sanhedrin 109b. See Raphael Patai, *The Hebrew Goddess* (Philadelphia: Ktav, 1967), pp. 209–210.

8. Philo, *Commentary on Genesis* 46, 53.

9. J. Sprenger and H. Kramer, *Malleus Maleficarum,* trans. Montague Summers, pt. 1, q. 6 (London: Pushkin Press, 1948).

10. Carol Karlsen, *The Devil in the Shape of a Woman: The Witch in Seventeenth Century Massachusetts* (Ph.D. diss., Yale University, 1980).

11. G. G. Coulton, "Woman's Life," in *Medieval Panorama* (Cambridge, 1939), p. 615.

12. Susan Brownmiller, *Against Our Will: Men, Women and Rape* (New York: Simon and Schuster, 1975), pp. 212–216.

13. Yolanda Murphy and Robert F. Murphy, *Women of the Forest* (New York: Columbia University Press, 1974), p. 107.

14. Brownmiller, *Against Our Will,* pp. 23–118.

15. Eleanor Flexner, *Century of Struggle: The Woman's Rights Movement in the United States* (New York: Atheneum, 1972), pp. 83–84.

16. Dorothy Dinnerstein, *The Mermaid and the Minotaur: Sexual Arrangements and Human Malaise* (New York: Harper & Row, 1976), pp. 229–277.

17. Daniel Maguire, "The Feminization of God and Ethics," *Christianity and Crisis,* 42:4 (15 March 1982): 63–64.

18. Olympe de Gouges, "Declaration of the Rights of Women and Citizens" (1791), in *Princesses, Ladies and Republicaines of the Terror,* ed. Therese Louis Latour (New York: Knopf, 1930), pp. 175ff.

19. Judith Plaskow, *Sex, Sin and Grace: Woman's Experience and the Theologies of Reinhold Niebuhr and Paul Tillich* (Washington, D.C.: University Press of America, 1980), pp. 9–50.

20. Mary Daly, *Gyn/Ecology: The Metaethics of Radical Feminism* (Boston: Beacon Press, 1978), pp. 107–312. The concept of Daly's narrative of female victimization as a female "passion drama" is drawn from an unpublished article on Daly's book by Mary Jo Weaver, Religious Studies Department, University of Indiana at Bloomington.

21. Anne Wilson Schaef, *Women's Reality: An Emerging Female System in the White Male Society* (Minneapolis: Winston Press, 1981), pp. 152–159.

8: Ministry and Community for a People Liberated From Sexism
(pages 193–213)

1. "Declaration on the Question of Admission of Women to the Ministerial Priesthood," Vatican City, October 15, 1976, sec. 1–5. See also R. Ruether, *Women Priests. A Catholic Commentary on the Vatican Declaration,* ed. Leonard Swidler and Arlene Swidler (New York: Paulist, 1977), pp. 234–238.

2. See Carter Heyward, *A Priest Forever: The Formation of a Woman and a Priest* (New York: Harper & Row, 1976), pp. 107 passim.

3. See Elisabeth Fiorenza, *In Memory of Her: A Feminist Theological Reconstruction of Christian Origins* (New York: Crossroads, 1983).

4. Elisabeth Fiorenza, "Word, Spirit and Power: Women in Early Christian Communities," in R. Ruether and E. McLaughlin, *Women of Spirit: Female Leadership in the Jewish and Christian Traditions* (New York: Simon & Schuster, 1979), p. 31.

5. Both Marcionites and Valentinian gnostics are reported to have given women ministerial roles. Marcion is said to have ordained women to all ministerial offices and Marcus, a Valentinian, ordained women as prophets and co-celebrated the Eucharist with women. See Fiorenza, pp. 44–51.

6. Steven Runciman, *The Medieval Manichee: A Study of the Christian Dualist Heresy* (New York: Viking, 1961), pp. 131, 159–161. Albigensianism was enthusiastically supported by the women of the great nobility of Southern France. The sect admitted women on a basis of equality into the highest order of the Perfect, and the princess Esclarmonde of Foix was a preacher who engaged in debates with Catholic theologians. The high status given to women in the Provincial courts of love seem to have been a reflection of the underground influence of Albigensianism whose asceticism also allowed its reversal in libertinism.

7. Prophets and prophetesses in early Christianity were understood to hold the power of the keys to forgive sin. They also were regarded in many circles as the appropriate persons to call down the power of the Spirit over the Eucharistic gifts. See the *Didache* (a second-century church order), secs. 10–13. The writings and treatises of Cyprian of Carthage in the third century A.D. represent the struggle of episcopal authority against this autonomous prophetic tradition.

8. Although the Franciscan order was accepted by the papacy, its prophetic left wing, the Spiritual Franciscans, fell into conflict with the hierarchy over clericalism and poverty. See Marjorie Reeves, *Joachim of Fiore and the Prophetic Future* (San Francisco: Harper & Row, 1976), pp. 57, 74–79.

9. Waldensians have teachings very similar to those of Franciscans, but they were unlucky with the hierarchy and became persecuted

as "heretics." See Jeffrey Burton Russell, *A History of Medieval Christianity: Prophecy and Order* (New York: Crowell, 1968), pp. 145–146.

10. Marina Warner, *Joan of Arc: The Image of Female Heroism* (New York, Knopf, 1981), pp. 77–95.

11. Female Baptist preachers in the Civil War period are denounced in the treatises *A Discoverie of Six Women Preachers in Middlesex, Kent, Cambridgeshire and Salisbury* (London: n.p., 1641) and Thomas Edwards, *Gangraena,* 2nd ed. (London: n.p., 1646), in Joyce L. Irwin, *Womanhood in Radical Protestantism 1525–1675* (New York: Mellon Press, 1979), pp. 210–222.

12. See Elaine Huber, "A Woman Must Not Speak: Quaker Women in the English Left Wing," and Nancy Hardesty, Lucille Sider Dayton, and Donald W. Dayton, "Women in the Holiness Movement: Feminism in the Evangelical Tradition," in Ruether and McLaughlin, *Women of Spirit,* pp. 153–181, 225–253.

13. See Barbara Welter, "The Cult of True Womanhood, 1800–1860" and "The Feminization of American Religion, 1800–1860," in *Dimity Convictions: The American Woman in the Nineteenth Century* (Athens, Ohio: Ohio University Press, 1976), pp. 21–41, 83–102.

14. See Martha Blauvelt, "Women and Revivalism," in *Women and Religion in America: The Nineteenth Century: A Documentary History,* ed. R. Ruether and R. Keller (San Francisco: Harper & Row, 1981), pp. 1–9.

15. See Margaret Van Cott, *The Harvest and the Reaper: Reminiscences of Revival Work of Mrs. Maggie Van Cott* (New York: N. Tibbals and Sons, 1976). Also see Blauvelt, "Women and Revivalism," pp. 39–45.

16. See Rosemary Skinner Keller, "Lay Women in the Protestant Tradition," in Ruether and Keller, *Women and Religion in America,* pp. 242–253.

17. See Barbara Zikmund, "The Struggle for the Right to Preach," in Ruether and Keller, *Women and Religion in America,* pp. 193–205.

18. Rev. Luther Lee, "Woman's Right to Preach the Gospel, A

Sermon Preached at the Ordination of the Rev. Miss Antoinette L. Brown, at South Butler, Wayne County, New York, Sept. 15, 1853" (Syracuse, N.Y.: n.p., 1853).

19. "Declaration of Sentiments and Resolutions: Seneca Falls, July 19, 1848," in *Feminism, the Essential Historical Writings,* ed. M. Schneir (New York: Vintage, 1972), pp. 76–82.

20. The Swedish Lutheran Church began to ordain women in 1968, owing in part to the egalitarian policies of the socialist Swedish government, but the theologians and priests of the Church have become increasingly active in their hostility to women in ministry. Information on this crisis was derived from discussion with Swedish pastors Gorel Byström Janarv, Kerstin Lingqvist, Kerstin Billinger, Lena Olsson, and Ulla Bardh in summer 1980. See their book *Halva Himlen är Var* (Stockholm: Gummessons, 1979).

21. Edward J. Grace, "The Christian Grassroots Community of St. Paul's Outside the Walls in Rome: A Case Study," in *NICM Journal* vol. 5, no. 3 (1980), pp. 7–34.

22. See R. Ruether, "Basic Communities: Renewal at the Roots," and Philip Berryman, "Latin America: Iglesia que nace del pueblo," *Christianity and Crisis,* 21 September 1981, pp. 234–242.

23. "The Netherlands: Manifesto of a Movement," *Christianity and Crisis,* 21 September 1981, pp. 246–250.

24. This concept of education as critical consciousness was developed particularly by Paulo Freire, working with literacy campaigns in Brazil. See his *Pedagogy of the Oppressed* (New York: Herder and Herder, 1970).

25. This concept of reappropriation theology was set forth by Giovanni Franzoni in a seminar in Christian-Marxist dialogue, held at the Waldensian Seminary, Rome, Italy, March 1980. See Giovanni Franzoni, *Le comunità di base. Per la riappropiazione della parola di Dio, dei gesti sacramentali, dei ministeri, dell'autonomia politica dei credenti* (Genoa: Lanterna, 1975).

26. 1 Timothy, chapter 3. See John Knox, "The Ministry in the Primitive Church," in *The Ministry in Historical Perspective,*

ed. H. R. Niebuhr and Daniel D. Williams (New York: Harper, 1956).

9: **The New Earth: Socioeconomic Redemption from Sexism**
(pages 214–234)

1. Peter L. Berger, *Pyramids of Sacrifice: Political Ethics and Social Change* (New York: Basic Books, 1974). See also Dennis P. McCann, *Christian Realism and Liberation Theology* (Maryknoll, N.Y.: Orbis, 1981).

2. Reinhold Niebuhr, *Moral Man and Immoral Society: A Study in Ethics and Politics* (New York: Scribner's, 1932).

3. Eleanor Flexner, *Century of Struggle: The Woman's Rights Movement in the United States* (New York: Atheneum, 1972).

4. Zillah R. Eisenstein, *The Radical Future of Liberal Feminism* (New York: Longman, 1981).

5. Walter Rauschenbusch, *Christianizing the Social Order* (New York: Macmillan, 1912), pp. 413–414.

6. Eleanor Leacock, "History, Development and the Division of Labor by Sex: Implications for Organization," *Signs* 7:2 (Winter 1981): 474–491.

7. Heidi Hartmann, "The Family as the Locus of Gender, Class and Political Struggle: The Example of Housework," *Signs* 6:3 (Spring 1981): 366–394.

8. Eileen Kraditor, *The Ideas of the Woman's Suffrage Movement, 1880–1920* (New York: Norton, 1980).

9. Sheila Rowbotham, *Women, Resistance and Revolution: A History of Women and Revolution in the Modern World* (New York: Random House, 1974), pp. 140–141, 185–186.

10. Hilda Scott, *Does Socialism Liberate Women? Experiences from Eastern Europe* (Boston: Beacon Press, 1974), pp. 191–208.

11. Shulamith Firestone, *Dialectic of Sex* (New York: Bantam, 1971), p. 11.

12. Charlotte Perkins Gilman, *Herland: A Lost Feminist Utopian Novel* (New York: Pantheon, 1979).

13. Sally Gearhart, *Wanderground: Stories of the Hill Women* (Watertown, Mass.: Persephone, 1979).

14. For discussion of uniparental female reproduction see D. G. Whittingham, "Parthenogenesis in Mammals," in *Oxford Review of Reproductive Biology,* ed. C. A. Finn (Oxford: Oxford University Press, 1980), pp. 205–231. Also see P. C. Hoppe and K. Illmensee, "Microsurgically Produced Homozygons–Diploid, Uniparental Mice," *Proceedings of the National Academy of Science, U.S. A.* vol. 74, no. 12 (December 1977): 5657–5661.

15. Mary Daly, *Beyond God the Father: Toward a Philosophy of Women's Liberation* (Boston: Beacon Press, 1973).

16. The pattern of Daly's thought moves increasingly toward a concept of the male as generically evil and thus necessarily generating evil structures. The atmosphere of Daly's thought is a kind of other-worldly incantation by which one demystifies and escapes out of the existing demonic male world. See *Gyn/Ecology: The Metaethics of Radical Feminism* (Boston: Beacon Press, 1979). This is strikingly similar to the mood and world view of ancient Gnosticism. See Hans Jonas, *The Gnostic Religion: The Message of the Alien God and the Beginnings of Christianity* (Boston: Beacon Press, 1958), pp. 48–96.

17. Z. Budapest, *The Holy Book of Women's Mysteries,* parts 1 and 2 (Los Angeles: Susan B. Anthony Coven, No. 1, 1979, 1980). Naomi Goldenberg, *Changing of the Gods* (Boston: Beacon Press, 1979). Starhawk, *The Spiral Dance: The Rebirth of the Ancient Religion of the Goddess* (New York: Harper & Row, 1979).

18. Starhawk, *The Spiral Dance,* pp. 21–22, 129–137.

10:   Eschatology and Feminism *(pages 235–258)*

1. Anne Wilson Schaef, *Women's Reality: An Emerging Female System in the White Male Society* (Minneapolis: Winston Press, 1981), p. 142.

2. Charlotte Perkins Gilman, *His Religion and Hers* (New York: Century, 1923), pp. 46–47.

3. R. H. Charles, ed., *The Pseudepigrapha of the Old Testament* (Oxford: Clarendon, 1913), p. 190.

4. Plato, *Timaeus* 42; *Phaedrus* 249–250.

5. *The Epic of Gilgamesh,* Tablet X, 3, in Isaac Mendelsohn, *Religions of the Ancient Near East: Sumero-Akkadian Religious Texts and Ugaritic Epics* (New York: Liberal Arts Press, 1955), p. 92.

6. Ivan Engnell, *Studies in Divine Kingship in the Ancient Near East* (Oxford: Blackwell, 1967), pp. 43–45.

7. Helen Waddell, *The Desert Fathers* (Ann Arbor: University of Michigan Press, 1957), p. 74.

8. Gregory Nyssa, "On the Soul and the Resurrection," in *Nicene and Post-Nicene Fathers,* 2nd ser. vol. 5 (New York: Parker, 1893), pp. 464–465.

9. This is a common interpretation of the term "coats of skin" (Gen. 3:21) in the Greek Church Fathers. It is found in Gregory Nazianzus as well and goes back to Origenist exegesis. See Rosemary Ruether, *Gregory of Nazianzus: Rhetor and Philosopher* (Oxford: Clarendon Press, 1969), p. 135.

10. Thomas Aquinas, *Summa Theologica,* p. 1, q. 99, art. 2, "Whether in the Primitive State, Women Would Have Been Born."

11. Gregory Nyssa, "On the Soul and the Resurrection," p. 466.

12. Leander of Seville, *De Instit. Virg.,* preface, in *Fathers of the Church,* vol. 62 (Washington, D.C.: Catholic University of America Press, 1969), p. 192.

13. Augustine *City of God* 22. 17. See also Jerome *Epistle* 108. 23.

14. Vine Deloria, *God is Red* (New York: Grosset and Dunlap, 1973), pp. 169–187.

15. Ibid., pp. 176–177.

Index

286

Rosemary Radford Ruether is Georgia
Harkness Professor of Applied Theology
at the Garrett-Evangelical Theological
Seminary in Evanston, Illinois, and a
faculty member in the joint doctoral pro-
gram with Northwestern University. A
contributing editor to *Christianity and
Crisis* magazine, she is also the author of
*Mary: The Feminine Face of the Church,
Religion and Sexism,* and *New Woman/
New Earth.*